SONNIE-BOY'S PEOPLE

I0617625

JAMES B. CONNOLLY

1st WORLD
LIBRARY
Literary Society

Sonnie-Boy's People

James B. Connolly

© 1st World Library, 2009
PO Box 2211
Fairfield, IA 52556
www.1stworldlibrary.com
First Edition

LCCN: 2009923405

Softcover ISBN: 978-1-4218-8854-5
Hardcover ISBN: 978-1-4218-8953-5
eBook ISBN: 978-1-4218-8755-5

Purchase *"Sonnie-Boy's People"*
as a traditional bound book at:
www.1stWorldLibrary.com/purchase.asp?ISBN=978-1-4218-8854-5

1st World Library is a literary, educational organization
dedicated to:

- Creating a free internet library of downloadable ebooks

- Hosting writing competitions and offering book publishing
scholarships.

1st World Library Literary Society

Giving Back to the World

"If you want to work on the core problem, it's early school literacy."

- James Barksdale, former CEO of Netscape

"No skill is more crucial to the future of a child, or to a democratic and prosperous society, than literacy."

- Los Angeles Times

"Literacy... means far more than learning how to read and write... The aim is to transmit... knowledge and promote social participation."

- UNESCO

"Literacy is not a luxury, it is a right and a responsibility. If our world is to meet the challenges of the twenty-first century we must harness the energy and creativity of all our citizens."

- President Bill Clinton

"Parents should be encouraged to read to their children, and teachers should be equipped with all available techniques for teaching literacy, so the varying needs and capacities of individual kids can be taken into account."

- Hugh Mackay

CONTENTS

SONNIE-BOY'S PEOPLE

The man with the gold-headed cane had been headed for the cottage, but espying the boy at the water's edge, he changed his course. He crept to within a few paces of the lad before he hailed: "Halloo, little boy! I'll bet I know who your papa is."

The boy looked casually around. Seeing that it was a stranger, he faced about and stood respectfully erect.

"Mr. Welkie's little boy, aren't you?"

"Yes, sir. But I'm 'most six."

"Oh-h, I see—a big boy now. But what have you got there?"

The boy held up the toy steamer with which he had been playing.

"Oh-h, I see now. What are you going to do with it?"

The boy looked sidewise out to where in the bay a fleet of battle-ships were lying to anchor.

"Load it with sugar and pineapples, and ship 'em to the States, are you?"

"But it's a gun-ship. See—where the turrets 'n' the fighting-tops will be when papa makes them."

"Oh! and so you want to be a great merchant?"

"I want to be a fighter"—articulating slowly and distinctly—"on a big gun-ship."

"Well, if ever you do, little man, I'll bet you'll be a game one, too. Is your papa home?"

"No, sir, but Aunt Marie is."

"And is Aunt Marie busy, do you think?"

"I don't know, sir, but she's making a battle-flag for my gun-ship."

"That so? I think I will call on Aunt Marie, then."

Swinging his cane and advancing leisurely, the stranger headed for the screened veranda door.

Marie Welkie, because of having to keep an eye on her nephew from the veranda, could not avoid noticing the stranger. The clothing, the jewelry, the air of assurance, had disturbed and half amused her; but the kindly tone with the boy, the parting pat of his head, were more pleasing. She answered his knock herself.

"Good evening—Miss Welkie?" That Southern "good evening" in the middle of the afternoon likewise pleased her.

"Miss Welkie, yes."

"I'm Mr. Necker." From a gold-mounted case he drew out a

James B. Connolly

card. "I'm looking for your brother."

"He won't be home for some time yet. But won't you step in, Mr. Necker, from out of the sun?"

"Thank you. It is warm, isn't it? Warmer than ordinary?"

"No, I shouldn't say so. It's usually hot here."

"Then it must be hot here when it is hot. It wasn't so bad out in the Gulf. I just got in—from Key West. Not many passengers come here, Miss Welkie?"

"Only somebody especially interested in the works—usually from Washington. Do you mind if I go ahead with this ensign for my nephew, Mr. Necker?" She held up a partly finished American ensign. Above the top of it the visitor could see part of the very white forehead and a front of dark straight hair. "I promised to have it ready for my nephew surely by morning, and after my brother gets home there probably won't be much spare time. But were you the only passenger for here, Mr. Necker?"

"There was one other. He got off at the new fortification landing. Twenty-nine or thirty perhaps he was—a well-made, easy-moving kind." His voice was casual, but his gaze was keen enough. It never left her face. "A tall man came running down to meet him," he resumed. "They seemed terribly glad to see each other."

"That must have been my brother to meet—Mr. Balfe, was it?—your fellow-passenger."

He hesitated a moment. "Mr. Balfe—yes, that was it. The captain—or was it the captain?—said that there was a Mr. Balfe who went on special missions for the government, but whether this was the Mr. Balfe or not he could not say."

She sewed serenely on. "I've heard that that steamer captain is developing into a great gossip. Our Mr. Balfe is my brother's dearest friend and godfather to my brother's boy— the boy you were speaking to on the beach—and if he ever found himself in this part of the world without calling on us, I don't know what my brother would think."

This time Miss Welkie looked up, and Necker smiled with her. Also he peered smilingly through the veranda vine. "So that is your brother's boy out there? Well, well! And a fine boy, too! A beautifully shaped head. Bright, I'll bet?"

"Naturally"—with a tender smile—"we think so."

"I'll bet he is. And of course your brother is laying great plans to assure his future?"

"I'm afraid you are not well acquainted with my brother, Mr. Necker."

"Not personally, Miss Welkie, but surely he won't neglect his own child's future?"

"I'm afraid that would not be his way of looking at it."

"And his way is a fine way, no doubt, Miss Welkie—if a man had only himself to think of. But can, or should, his family—" he paused.

"His family? Young Greg and I are his family, Mr. Necker, and I'm sure we're not worrying about the future." Her head bent lower to her sewing, but not too low for Necker to see the little smile, half of humor, half of something else, hovering on her lips.

"Because you're too young—and too unselfish."

This time her head came up and the smile developed into a soft laugh. "No, no, nothing quite so fine as that, nor quite so awfully young. At twenty-three—"

Necker tried to meet her eyes; but the eyes were not for him, nor for the boy on the beach this time, nor for the brave warships at anchor. Her eyes were for something farther away. Necker, twisting in his chair, could distinguish through the haze the fortification walls on the other side of the little bay.

There was another little smile hovering. Necker waited hopefully. She, catching his eye, flushed and returned to her sewing. "We're all very happy here," she added after a moment, and, still flushing, resumed her needle.

Presently he pointed his cane at the boy on the beach. "A great deal of your brother in him, isn't there?"

"Very much. Our older friends back home say that it is like Greg—that is, my brother—being born all over."

"A fine boy, yes, Miss Welkie, and ought to be a great man some day. But I'll be running along now, Miss Welkie."

"You won't wait for him? He will be glad to see you, I know."

"Thank you; but after a man's been out there under that sun all day is no time for a friend to bother him. And I am a friend of your brother's, believe me, Miss Welkie. It is because I am a friend and an admirer of his that I'm here."

"But you will return later?"

"I will, thank you—after he's had time to clean up and eat and smoke, and a chat with his friend, I'll drop in for a little talk, and in that little talk, Miss Welkie, I hope you won't be against me, for I mean it for his best. So until eight o'clock to-night, Miss Welkie—*adios*." Necker, swishing his gold-headed cane, strolled leisurely away.

"I wonder what he wants of Greg," murmured Marie Welkie. And until his pea-green suit was lost to sight she speculated on his probable errand.

By and by her eyes, now less speculative, detected the smudge against the concrete walls. She took down a pair of glasses from the wall. It was the towboat leaving the wharf. The glasses took the place of her sewing, and they were still to her eyes when a sharp "Auntie!" came to her ears. "Tention, auntie! Colors!" warned the voice. Lowering the glasses, Marie came obediently to attention.

The sun was cutting the edge of the sea. The last level light lay on the long, slow, swelling waters like a rolling, flaming carpet, and in that flaming path the gray war-ships bobbed to anchor; and on the quarter-deck of every ship a red-coated band was drawn up, and from the jack-staff of every ship an American ensign was slowly dropping down. The boy stood with his back to her, but Marie knew how his heart was thumping, and she knew the light that would be on his face.

"O say! can you see—" came the swelling notes over the gently heaving bay. Marie could feel that young Greg was ready to burst; but she could not detect a move, not a quiver, out of him until the last note of the last bugle had ceased to re-echo. Then he saluted reverently, executed an about-face, and called out excitedly: "Auntie, auntie, there's papa now! Look!"

James B. Connolly

Marie pretended to see for the first time the towboat which, a hundred yards or so down the beach, was making a landing. "Sure enough, Greg!"

"And somebody else!"

"No; is there?"

"Why, don't you see—godfather, auntie! O papa! God-father!" He was off.

When he returned he was clinging on the one hand to a tall, brown, lean-cheeked, and rather slender man of thirty four or five, in dusty corduroy coat and trousers, mud-caked shoes and leggings, khaki shirt, and a hard-looking, low-blocked Panama hat; and on the other hand to a man also sun-tanned, but less tall and not so lean—a muscular, active man who may have lived the thirty years which Necker ascribed to him, but who surely did not look it now. At sight of Marie Welkie stepping down from the screened veranda he bounded like sixteen years across the beach. "Marie Welkie—at last!"

"Andie Balfe!" She took his hands within hers and drew them up in front of her bosom. The smile which Necker had so wanted to see again was there now, and now not to vanish in a moment. Balfe brushed her finger tips with his lips.

"How far this time, Andie?"

"From half the world around, Marie."

"And are you glad?"

"And I would come it twice again to see your dear eyes smile."

"Could eyes be made so dull as not to light to your poetic touch, Andie?" And then, in a low voice, "Wait for the sunset." She stood upon her toes for her brother's kiss. "Another hard, hot day, Greg?"

"No, no, a fine day, Marie. Pedro"—he motioned to the negro at their rear—"put Mr. Balfe's suit-case in the corner of the veranda there. That'll be all to-night, except to see that Mr. Balfe's trunks come up from the towboat."

He paused on the veranda steps to get a view of the bay. As he stood there in silence, the lively notes of a dozen buglers came sharply to them. He still held the boy's hand.

"Mess call, papa?"

"Getting so you know them all, aren't you, Sonnie-Boy? One minute from now ten thousand husky lads out there will be doing awful things to the commissary grub. But look there! Andie, did any of your kings or presidents ever offer you sights more gorgeous than that to view from their palace walls?"

It was the afterglow of the sunset, a red-and-orange glory fading into the blue-black velvet of a Caribbean twilight.

"It's by way of greeting to the far traveller. This may be the last place on earth here, Andie, but we warrant our sunsets to be the best on the market. But let's go inside and make ready to eat. What do you say, Sonnie-Boy?"

"But, papa, you said that when godfather came you would have the Little Men sing you a song for the steam-engine he sent me from Japan!"

"That's right, I did. But where is it?"

James B. Connolly

"Right here, papa." From the veranda corner he picked up a toy locomotive. "Look! *Lightning*, I've named it."

"A fine name for it, too. Well, let me see. How was it? Oh, yes! Lunch-time to-day it was, and your papa was smoking his cigar and looking out to sea all by himself. It was very quiet, with all the donkey-engines stopped and the men eating inside the walls. On the bluff beyond the fort I was sitting, with my feet hanging over the edge, and the mango-tree I've told you so often about was shading me from the sun. The wind was blowing just a wee mite, and every time the wind would blow and the tree would wave, a mango would drop into the bay. Plump! it would go into the ocean below, and every time a mango dropped down a Little Man in a green coat popped up."

"All wet, papa?"

"Shiny wet, Sonnie-Boy, and blowing their cheeks out like so many blub-blubs."

"What's blub-blubs, papa?"

"A blub-blub is a fat little fish who takes big long gulps deep down in the ocean and then comes to the top o' the water, and, when he sees anybody watching him, puffs out his cheeks and goes—blub-blub! like that."

"Like men sometimes, papa?"

"Just like. Well, by 'n' by there were twelve o' the Little Men in green coats, and they sat under the mango-tree all in a row and looked at me, and the one at the head o' the row puts up one finger, with his head to one side and his little round eye rolling out at me, and he says: 'Did Sonnie-Boy's godfather send him that steam-engine from Japan yet, what you told us about? 'Cause if he did, we have a fine pome about it.'

"'Yes, he did send him a fine steam-engine from Japan,' I said, 'and you go on and let me hear your pome, and if it's a good pome I'll give you all a fine ripe mango to eat.' And so they all puffs out their fat little cheeks and they begins:

> "'Godfather bought him an engine, red and black,
> It wabbles slightly and the wheels don't track—'"

"But it don't, papa, 'n' the wheels do track."

"But that's what they said."

> "'But Sonnie-Boy felt prouder than England's queen
> When it puffed real smoke and sure-enough steam.'"

"But it's a king in England, papa."

"I know, but that's the way the Little Green Men told me. Some things they don't know yet, they're so little."

> "'He named it Lightning 'cause of its speed,
> And the 'casional spills he did not heed.
> All big roads had accidents, people knew—
> There was danger sure when the whistle blew.'"

"It's true, 'bout th' accidents, isn't it, papa?"

"Nothing truer. Now, let me see. What else? Oh, yes:

> "'The Lightning Express is coming back,
> Clear the way there, people, off the track!
> Or Sonnie-Boy's engine, red and black,
> Will knock you down and hit you whack!'"

"How's that?"

"That's great, papa. And did they have a band with them?"

"No. No band, but one little six-toed fellow—I 'most forgot him—was playing on a hook-a-zoo. That's a sausage-shaped thing, with things like rabbit's ears on it. The music comes out the ears."

"And what kind of music, papa?"

"Oh, like a jew's-harp something, only being bigger 'twas louder. Zoo-zoo, zoo-zoo-zoo it went."

"I like those Little Green Men, papa, but where was the Little Blue Men to-day, did they say?"

"Oh, they'd gone to a wedding, the hook-a-zoo player said."

"They know everything, don't they, papa?"

"M-m-most everything."

"And will the Little Men tell me things when I'm a big man, papa?"

"If they don't, I won't let 'em have any more mangoes."

"An' what the bugle men play 'n' what the flags say when they hoists them up in the air on the big gun-ships, papa?"

"If you're a good boy, they will. And now what d'y' say if we go in and you tell Diana your papa wants some hot water out of the kettle. And while you're doing that and auntie and godfather are talking things over to themselves, I'll be laying out my razor and my soap 'n' things all ready to shave. There you are, there's the boy!"

* * * * *

It was after dinner on Welkie's veranda. The two friends had been smoking for some time in silence. Young Greg had just left with his aunt to go to bed. Balfe was thinking what a pity it was the boy's mother had not lived to see him now. He turned in his chair. "What would you do without him, Greg?"

Welkie understood what his friend had in mind. "It would be like the days having no sunrise. I'd be groping in the dark, and almost no reason for me to keep on groping. Splashed in concrete and slaked in lime, from head to toe, steaming under that eternal sun, five hundred spiggities and not half enough foremen to keep 'em jumping, I find myself saying to myself, 'What in God's name is the use?' and then I'll see a picture of his shining face running to meet me on the beach, and, Andie, it's like the trade-wind setting in afresh. The men look around to see what I'm whistling about. But"—Welkie sniffed and stood up—"get it?"

Balfe caught a faint breath, the faintest tang borne upon the wings of the gentlest of breezes.

Welkie went inside. Presently he returned with bottles and glasses. "When a little breeze stirs, as it sometimes does of a hot night here, and there's beer in the ice-box and the ice not all melted, life's 'most worth living. Try some, Andie—from God's country. And one of these Porto Ric' cigars. Everybody'll be smoking 'em soon, and then we poor chaps'll have to be paying New York prices for 'em, which means we'll have to make a new discovery somewhere."

"Wait, Greg—I almost forgot." Balfe stepped to his suitcase, took out a box of cigars, and handed it to Welkie.

James B. Connolly

"From Key West. Hernando Cabada. When I told him I was going to see you, he sat down and rolled out that boxful, which took him three hours, and gave them to me for you. 'For my friend, Mis-ter Wel-keey-ay,' he said."

"Good old Hernando!" Welkie opened the box. Balfe took one, Welkie took one; they lit up.

"Ah-h—" Welkie woofed a great gob of smoke toward the veranda roof. "Andie, you won't have to make any chemical analysis of the ashes of these cigars to prove they're good. There is an artist—Hernando—and more! I used to drop in to see him after a hot day. He would let me roll out a cigar for myself in one of his precious moulds, and we'd sit and talk of a heap of things. 'Some day, Hernando,' I'd say, 'along will come some people and offer you such a price for your name that I reckon you won't be able to resist.' 'No, no, my friend,' he would say. 'For my nam' there shall be only my cigar. I shall mak' the good, fine cigar—until I shall die. And for the sam'—one pr-r-ice.' How'd you come to run into him, Andie?"

"I'd heard about him and you. I suspected, too, that he could verify a few things about the Construction Company."

"And did he?"

"He did. And so they have been after you again?"

Welkie nodded.

"And offering more money than ever?"

Welkie nodded.

They smoked on. Again Balfe half turned in his chair. "I

haven't seen you, Greg, since the President sent for you from Washington that time. How did you find him?"

"Fine. And I tell you, Andie, it heartened me to think that a man with all he's got to tend to would stop to spend an hour with an obscure engineer."

"You're not too obscure, Greg. What did he have to say?"

"Oh-h—said he wanted me to do a piece of special work, and he wanted me because several people, in whose judgment he had confidence, said I was the man for the job. You were one of 'em, Andie, he told me, and I'm thanking you for it."

"I'm not sure that you ought to thank me, Greg. With that big company you would be wealthy in a few years, but the trouble is, Greg, when I'm on the job I'm as bad as you, only in a different and more selfish way. I know only one road then, and once I set out I'd brush aside anything for the one thing, Greg."

"Of course, when it's for the flag."

"Would you?"

"Could I do anything else?"

"The boy, too?"

"Where would he come into it, Andie?"

"You don't think that your feeling for the lad and your work could ever clash?"

"How could they ever clash, Andie?"

James B. Connolly

"I don't know, Greg. I hope not." He relit his neglected cigar. "But what else did the President have to say?"

"He said it was a bit of emergency work he wanted me for, that only the remnant of a small appropriation was available for it, and that if I took it I would be pitiably paid; but that he wished me to do it, because some day, and that not too far away, it might have to stand the test not of friends, but of enemies. Also he said—let me see—"

"That for foreign policy's sake it would have to be done quietly, without advertising, as a bit of departmental work?"

"That's it."

"And that you would get no great reputation out of it, that your very report would remain a supplementary paper buried in departmental files?"

"That was it."

"Did it strike you that the conditions were hard, Greg?"

"Not after he explained things. And so when the Construction people said to me later: 'You're crazy, man! Look the two propositions in the eye!' I said: 'I've looked one of 'em at least in the eye and I'm passing the other up—and the other is yours.'"

"Lord, Greg! whether you're the best or the worst concrete man in the world is a small matter—you're a great man. And if some day—" Balfe let his front chair-legs come down bang and bounded to his feet.

"Greg"—it was Marie who had returned—"I don't know how I ever forgot, but I never thought till a moment ago—there was a Mr. Necker here to see you this evening."

"Well, you don't often forget, Marie. Must be the sight of those battle-ships. Necker? I don't know any Necker. You know him, Andie?"

"I was trying to guess coming over on the boat. I was still guessing when he got off. I could guess, Greg, who he is, but it would be only a guess."

"He didn't leave any message, Marie?"

"None, except to say that he would call again at eight. He seemed to know something of you and to be friendly."

"He must be a friendly soul to come to this place to see anybody. Well, when he comes we'll know. How'd you leave Sonnie-Boy?"

"He's waiting for you to say good night."

"I'll go up to him." He went inside.

Marie picked up her ensign. Balfe placed a chair for her at the little work-table, and himself took the chair on the other side of the table.

"A great joy for you, also—young Greg, Marie?"

"If you could hold him and feel his little heart against yours when he's saying 'Good night, auntie,' after he's said his prayers! His prayers and the 'Star-Spangled Banner' are his great set pieces."

"And between you and Greg it's safe to say he's got both letter-perfect."

"And spirit-perfect, we're hoping. But I must get on with this ensign for him."

"Pretty good size, isn't it, for a toy ship?"

"But it's a battle-flag. He'll have none but battle-flags. There, I'm up to the stars."

"You're never far from them. Let me make a stretching-frame of my fingers and square this end."

"Do. Not quite so tight. And now—those new States come in so fast!—how many now?"

"Forty-six."

"M-m—four eights and two sevens?"

"Four eights and two sevens."

She sewed rapidly, and without looking up, until she had completed the first row. "There—there's one of the eights. Now you can breathe again, Andie."

Balfe sat back. "What did you make of Mr. Necker, Marie?"

She, too, sat back. "I wonder what I did make of him. He was very curious about you."

"That's interesting."

"Yes. He asked questions and I couldn't quite fib to him, and yet I couldn't see why he should expect me to tell him all about you. And so"—she paused and the little half-smile was hovering around again.

"And so?"

"And so I did not attempt to check his imagination." She repeated the conversation of the afternoon. "I meant to speak of it at dinner, Andie, to you and Greg, but I forgot."

"Here's a far traveller—" He paused. She looked up, and quickly looked down.

"—who gives thanks that you forgot, Marie, in that first glad hour, Mr. Necker and his—well, his possible mission."

"You know something of him, then, Andie?"

"I'm still guessing. But I'm wondering now if you said to yourself when he had gone: 'After all, what will Greg get out of this government work? Is it fair to himself to refuse those great offers and stick down here? And what will it mean to young Greg?'"

Marie Welkie let the ensign drop onto the table. "My very thoughts in words, Andie. And while we're speaking of it, will Greg ever get the recognition due him, Andie?"

"Surely—some day."

"Dear me, that some day! After he is dead, I suppose. You men are the idealists! But being only a woman, Andie Balfe, I don't want to wait that long to see my brother rewarded."

"And being only a man, Marie Welkie, I also want to see my friend rewarded before he's laid away."

"But will he ever?"

"Who could answer that? But I stopped off in Washington on

my way, Marie, and had a long talk with a man who is fine enough to appreciate the dreams of idealists and yet sufficiently human to allow for most human weaknesses. We discussed Greg and his work. The Construction people were mentioned. He asked me if I thought Greg would go with them. 'And if he does, Mr. President, can be he blamed?' was my answer."

"And how did he take it?"

"He leaned back in his chair and looked through his glasses with his eyebrows drawn together, in that way you'd think he was scowling if you didn't know him. After a moment he said: 'I should be sorry, but if he does, no professional or legal—no, nor moral—obligations can hold him.'"

"There! Greg does not even get credit for—"

"Wait. 'But will he?' he continued. I said that I did not think so. 'What makes you think he won't?' 'Because I know him, sir. But,' I went on, 'don't you think, Mr. President, that by this time he should have a word of encouragement or appreciation?' And that led to quite a talk."

"About Greg, Andie?"

"Greg and his work, Marie."

She leaned her elbows on the table and from between her palms smiled across at him. "When you use that tone, Andie, I know that all women should stay silent. But could—couldn't a little sister to the man in the case be given just a little hint?"

"To the little sister—Oh, much! To her I can say that I have reason to think that something is on its way to her brother which will be very pleasing to her and to him."

"For which, my lord, thy servant thanks thee."

Eight bells echoed from the fleet. "Eight o'clock, and some-body walking the beach! It couldn't be, Andie—it couldn't be that Mr. Necker—"

Balfe gravely shook his head.

"But, Andie," she whispered, "there was the most friendly expression in his eye!"

"If there's a living man, Marie"—he bent over also to whisper—"who could hold speech with you for ten seconds without a friendly gleam—" A knock on the veranda door interrupted.

It was Necker. "How do you do again, Miss Welkie?" To her his bow was appreciative, deferential. To Balfe he nodded in a not unfriendly fashion.

"I'm glad to see you again, Mr. Necker. Come in, please. I will call my brother." She pressed a button on the veranda wall. "That will bring him right down, Mr. Necker. And now I'm leaving you with Mr. Balfe. Diana, our cook's little boy has a fever—"

"Fever, Marie?"

"Oh, don't worry, Andie, if you're thinking of danger. It's only malaria. And it's only a step or two, and you must stay with Mr. Necker."

Balfe held the door open for her. She paused in the doorway. "I'll be back in half an hour."

"Half an hour! Time is no bounding youth, Marie Welkie."

"Come for me, then—Oh, when you please," she whispered, and passed swiftly out.

* * * * *

Necker was examining the shelf of books above the work-table. "Keats? Keats? Oh-h, poetry! Montaigne. Montaigne? Oh, yes!" He took it down. "H-m, in French!" and put it back. One after the other he read the titles. "Elizabethan Verse. E-u-r-i-p-i-d-e-s. Dante. H-m."

Balfe by now had turned from the screen door. Necker pointed to the shelf. "Not a book for a practical man in the whole lot, and"—he held up the ensign—"this! Isn't that the dreamer through and through?"

"But you and I, not being dreamers, consider how thankful we should be."

Necker stared in surprise, and then he smiled. "Now, now, I'm meaning no harm to your friend. I guess you don't know what I'm after, though I'll bet I can guess what you're after."

Balfe, fairly meeting Necker's eye, had to smile; and when Necker saw Balfe smile he winked. "You don't s'pose you could come down here to this God-forsaken hole, do you, without somebody getting curious?"

"I suppose it was too much to expect. Have a smoke?"

"Thanks." Necker's tone was polite, but it was a most negligent glance that he gave the box of cigars. There was no name on the box. Balfe, with unsmiling mien, pointed out two small letters on the cover. "$1.$2. Mr. Necker."

"$1.$2."

"Hernando Cabada, Key West."

"O-ho! How'd you ever manage to get hold of a box of them?"

"They're Welkie's."

"How can he afford 'em? I offered old Cabada a dollar, a dollar and a half, and finally two dollars apiece for a thousand of 'em, coming through Key West the other day— and couldn't get 'em. Nor could all the pull I had in the place get 'em for me. He wasn't going to make any more that week, he said. He's a queer one. He's got all those Socialist chaps going the other way. For why should he work four, five, six hours a day, he said, when he could make all he wanted in one or two? Sells cigars to people he likes for fifteen dollars a hundred, but wouldn't sell to me at any price. I had to take my hat off to him—he stuck. Now, how do you dope a chap like that?"

"How do you?"

"Don't know the real values in life. Maybe a bit soft up top, besides." He lit up and drew several deep inhalations. "M-m—this is a smoke for a man!" He picked up the box gently. "If I thought Welkie'd take it, I'd offer more than a good price for the rest of that box. But"—suspicion was growing in his eyes—"how does it happen—d'y' s'pose somebody's been here ahead of me after all?"

"He's coming down-stairs now—ask him," smiled Balfe.

Welkie stepped into the veranda. "I was in my workroom when the buzzer told me you had come in, Mr. Necker, but

James B. Connolly

on the way down I couldn't help looking in on young Greg. I'm glad to see you."

"I'm glad to meet you, Mr. Welkie. And to get right down to business, I'm the new president of the Gulf Construction Company, and I want to talk a few things over with you."

"Surely."

"Greg"—Balfe had opened the door—"how far up the beach to your cook's shack?"

"Oh, for Marie? A hundred yards that side."

"I'll look in there. Good night, Mr. Necker."

"Don't hurry away on my account, Mr. Balfe. I'd like you, or any friend of Mr. Welkie and his family, to hear what I have to say. It's a straight open-and-shut proposition I've got."

"Then we'll try to be back to hear some of it. Good-by for a while, then." The door closed behind him.

"Let's sit down, Mr. Necker."

"Thanks. And how did you leave that boy of yours?"

"In his little bed, with his pillow jammed up close to his window-screen, singing the 'Star-Spangled Banner' to himself and looking out on the lights of the fleet. He's afraid they'll steam away before he's seen his fill of them, and to-night he's not going to sleep till he hears taps, he says."

"It must be a great thing to have a boy like him, and to plan for his future and to look forward to what he'll be when he's grown up."

Welkie looked his interrogation.

"Surely, Welkie. A boy of brains he'll be. I don't have to look at a man or a boy twice. Brains and will power. You could make a great career for him, Welkie—a great engineer, say, if he was started right. But, of course, you'll be in a position by and by to see that he gets the start."

"Started right? What does he want when he has health and brains and a heart?"

"All fine, but he'll need more than that these days."

"Are these days so different?"

"Different, man! Why, the older a country is, the more civilized it is, the more education means, the more social position counts, the more money counts."

"How much more?"

"A heap more. Listen. Your father on twenty-five hundred a year, say, could put his children through college, couldn't he? On twenty-five hundred a year to-day a man with a family has to battle to keep out of the tenement districts. A dozen years from now, if you're getting no more money than you're getting now, you'll be wondering if you won't have to take that boy out of school and put him to work. Isn't that so?"

Welkie made no answer.

"All right. But before I go any farther, let me say that I want you, Mr. Welkie, for our new job."

"What's wrong with the man you've got?"

"He won't do. You're the one man we want, and if there's money enough in our strong box, we're going to get you. And now that I've got that off, let me show you where it is for your higher—I say your higher, not alone your moneyed—interests to come with us, Mr. Welkie. There's that boy of yours—you'd surely like to see him a great man?"

"I surely wouldn't dislike it."

"Good. Then give him a chance. Get rid first of the notion that a poor boy has as good a chance as another. He hasn't. I know that all our old school-books told us different—along with some other queer things. No wonder. Nine times out of ten they were got up by men born poor and intended for children born poor. It is a fine old myth in this country that only the poor boy ever gets anywhere. As a matter of fact, the poor boys outnumber the comfortably born boys ten to one, yet run behind in actual success. Even history'll tell you that. Alexander—son of a king. Caesar? Frederick the Great? Oh, loads of 'em! You don't seem to think much of that?"

"Not a great deal," smiled Welkie. "If you're going to call the long roll of history, it looks to me like it's a mistake to name only three, or twenty-three, or thirty-three men. You cast your eye along that little book-shelf there and—"

"Oh, I've been looking them over—Dante and Michael Angelo and Homer and Shakespeare and that knight-errant Spaniard and the rest of 'em. But I'm not talking of poets and philosophers and the like. I'm talking of the men who bossed the job when they were alive."

"But how about those who bossed it after they were dead?"

"But, damn it, Welkie, I'm talking of men of action."

"Men of action or—ditch-diggers?"

"What!"

"That's what I call most of 'em, Necker—ditch-diggers. If your man of action hasn't himself thought out what he's doing, that's what he looks like to me—a ditch-digger, or at best a foreman of ditch-diggers. And a ditch-digger, a good ditch-digger, ought to be respected—until he thinks he's the whole works. Those kings of yours may have bossed the world, Necker, but, so long's we're arguing it, who bossed them?"

"You mean that the man who bosses the world for thirty or forty years isn't quite a man?"

"Surely he's quite a man; but the man who bosses men's minds a thousand years after he's dead—he's the real one. And that kind of a man, so far's I know things, Necker, never lived too comfortably on earth. He can't. I tell you, Necker, you can't be born into a fat life without being born into a fat soul, too."

"You're not stinting yourself in the expectation of running things after you're dead, Welkie?"

Welkie noted the half-ironical smile, but he answered simply, evenly: "It's not in me; but I'd live even a sparer life than I do, if I thought anybody after me had a chance."

"You're a hard man to argue with, Welkie, and I'm not going to argue with you—not on things dead and gone. You're too well posted for me. But suppose it was that way once, is it that way to-day? I'll bring it right home to you. Here's the overpowering figure in public life, Roosevelt, a man you think a lot of probably—was he born in poverty?"

James B. Connolly

"No, but I notice he cut away from his comfortable quarters about as soon as his upbringing'd let him."

"Wait. In finance who? Morgan? All right. Son of a millionaire financier, wasn't he?"

"But if you're going to bring in money—"

"I know. What of the Carnegies and the Rockefellers? you're going to say. There's where you think you've got me, but you haven't; for I've always said that being born in poverty fits a man to make money above all things, because he's brought up to value it out of all proportion to everything else. But where are they after they get it? America's full of millionaires who came up out of nothing, but who had to work so hard getting started that they'd nothing left in 'em or didn't know anything but money when they got to where they could stop to look around. If they had any genius to start with, it was dried out of 'em trying to get going. Hitch any two-mile trotter to an ice-wagon and where will he finish? You overweight your boy going off and he will be handicapped out of the race, too. But can I have another one of those cigars?"

"Help yourself."

"Thanks. I wish I had your pull with old Cabada. Now, Welkie, I'm only trying to show you where you ought to cast aside certain outworn traditions and face actual present-day truths. Now listen. You probably don't believe I'm a villain, Welkie, and you know I represent a powerful corporation— reputable even if powerful. Yes. Well, this work of ours is good, useful work—don't you think we can fairly claim that?"

"Beautiful work—beautiful."

"Good. Then wouldn't you like to see that work growing under your hand—ten thousand men driving night and day, and that concrete structure reaching out, as you've planned it, in long white stretches to the sea?"

"It's certainly a fine prospect."

"Then why not do it? What's the use, Welkie? You're the best man in the country for us and we're the best concern for you. We offer you the biggest job in sight. What d'y' say? You've been turning us down, but think it over now."

Welkie shook his head.

"Why not?"

"Because—but they are coming back."

Necker could see the hands of Balfe and Miss Welkie unclasping in the half-darkness as they entered. He touched Welkie on the arm. "Why not tell Miss Welkie and Mr. Balfe what it is I'm after?"

"But I'm doing work here that I've got to finish, and they know that."

"I know you are, but consider this. What does the government pay you here, Welkie? I probably know, but no matter."

"Two hundred a month and this house."

"And I'm offering you two thousand! And—listen to this, please, Miss Welkie. In place of a mosquito-infested shoe-box of a shack in a God-forsaken hole, we'll give you and your brother a fine concrete house on a breezy hill in God's

James B. Connolly

own country—a real home, Miss Welkie, with great halls and wide verandas and sun-lighted rooms through which the sea breezes will blow at night so you can sleep in peace. A mansion, Miss Welkie, with reception and music rooms, where you can receive your friends in the style a lady should, or a man of your brother's ability should. A place to be proud of, Miss Welkie—palm-studded, clean-clipped lawn rolling down to the sea. And a sea—I'll bet you know it, Mr. Balfe—a blue-and-green sea rolling down over to coral reefs as white as dogs' teeth, a shore-front that needs only building up to be as pretty as anything in your swell Mediterranean places. What d'y' say, Welkie? And here's the contract now, all ready for you, and pay begins to-day."

"It's alluring, it surely is. But I must finish here."

"But you'll soon be done here. A few weeks more, they told me in Washington. What are you going to do then?"

"I hadn't thought."

"Well, why not think of it now? Consider your boy, what it will mean to him some day. Why not ask Miss Welkie?"

Welkie turned gravely to his sister. "What do you say to that fine house with the grand dining-room, and the music-room, and a jasmine-twined pergola to sit out under of a night—and watch the moon roll up from the shining sea? I know the house—it's all that Mr. Necker says it is."

"And mahogany, and all kinds of beautiful linen for the table, Miss Welkie. Imagine that, with cut glass and silver and the electric candles gleaming over it of a night."

"I would dearly love to preside at the head of that table, Mr. Necker, but Mr. Balfe was speaking of something that perhaps my brother should hear about first."

"What's that, Andie?"

"Let it wait, Greg."

"Better now. What is it?"

"You may not like it."

"Maybe not, but we may as well have it now, Andie."

"I was to tell you that after this work is done there's another job waiting you on the west coast, just as important, just as needful of your supervision, and no more reward to it than this."

"Whee-eu!" whistled Necker. "The steamer captain had him right."

"Then I'm afraid"—Welkie turned to Necker—"it's off between us."

"Don't say that yet. Wait till you hear. What are you working for? Leaving the money end out of it, which I know you don't care for and never will care for, what are you getting? You want recognition? And prestige? Do you get them? Not a bit. Who really knows of this work? A few engineers who keep tabs on everything, yes. Who else? Nobody. The government, for good reasons of their own, don't want it mentioned in the press. Why, it's hardly mentioned in the engineering journals."

"Even so. It will go down in the records that I did it."

"Will it? Look here. I've been waiting for that." From his

inside coat-pocket Necker drew out several typewritten sheets. "Mind you, I didn't want to produce this, but I'm forced to. My first interests are my company's. There is a copy of the last official report on this work. Read what that says. The credit is given, you see, to who? To you? No, no. Not a mention of you except as a civilian engineer who assisted."

"But how did you get hold of this?" Welkie held the papers, but without showing any inclination to read them.

"Does how I got hold of it matter?"

"That's right, it doesn't matter."

Welkie offered the papers to Balfe.

Balfe waved them back. "I saw the original of that report in Washington. What Mr. Necker says is so."

"There!" Necker brought his fist down on the table. "The man of all others to bear me out." He stepped close to Balfe. "I couldn't place you for a while. Thanks for that."

"Don't hurry your credit slip," snapped Balfe, with his eyes on Welkie.

Welkie silently passed the papers back to Necker.

"You believe me now, Mr. Welkie?"

"I don't know's I doubted you, Mr. Necker. It caught me just a mite below the belt, and I had to spar for wind."

"But it wasn't I who hit you below the belt, remember. Neither did I want to destroy your illusions, but I did want to show you the facts—the truth, not the glittering romance, of life. Now they're offering you another job. Will you, or somebody else, get the credit for that? You? No, sir! You'll get neither money nor reputation out of it. With us you'd get both."

"Probably that's so." Welkie spoke slowly. "But people in general will credit me with loyalty at least."

"Will they? Even where they know of your work, will they? When a man turns down an offer like ours, people in general will give him credit for little besides simple innocence. I'm telling you they'll be more likely to think you are controlled by some queer primitive instinct which will not allow you to properly value things. I'll leave it to your friend. What do you say to that, Mr. Balfe?"

"I think you're a good deal right."

"There! Your own friend agrees with me!" exclaimed Necker.

"You don't think that, Andie?" Welkie, puzzled, stared at Balfe.

"What I mean, Greg, and what Mr. Necker very well understands me to mean, is that surely there are hordes of people who never will believe that any man did anything without a selfish motive."

"That don't seem right, Andie."

"No, it doesn't, but it's so, Greg. But"—he set his jaw at Necker—"what if they do think so? Let them. Let them ride hogback through the mud if they will. Oceans of other people, oceans, will still be looking up to men like Greg

Welkie here." He rested his hand on his friend's shoulder. "You stick to your aeroplaning in the high air, Greg."

"And chance a fall?" suggested Necker.

"And chance a fall!" snapped Balfe. "But there are no falls if the machine is built right and the aviator forgets the applause."

Marie Welkie's hand reached out and pressed one of Balfe's. He held it. "It's all right—he's a rock," he whispered.

"I must say, Welkie"—Necker fixed his eyes on the floor and spoke slowly—"that the government in this case seems to be represented by a man of picturesque speech, a man with imagination. I can only handle facts, and in a matter-of-fact way. I ask you to consider this: you have a boy, and there is Miss Welkie, a lovely, cultured woman, and"—he jerked his head suddenly up—"but what's the use? Here's a contract, needing only your signature, and here's a check, needing only my signature. I said two thousand a month. Suppose we make it three? Here's pen and ink, and remember your boy is looking out on the battle-ships from his little bed up-stairs."

"You're right, Necker, he is in his little bed up-stairs and I've got to think of him." He turned to Balfe. "The President, Andie, just naturally expects me to tackle this new job?"

"I think he does, Greg."

"Then there's only one answer left, Mr. Necker. No."

"Wait again. Welkie, you've a God-given genius for concrete work. I came here to get you and I—sign now and I'll make it four thousand."

"No."

"No? Why, look here! Here's a check. See—I'm signing it in blank. I'm leaving it to you to fill it in for what you please. For what you please for your first year for us, and the contract to run five years at the same rate. Remember you've been trimmed once and you're likely to be trimmed again."

"Let them trim me and keep on trimming me! The work is here and I did it. They know it and I know it. If nobody but myself and my God know, we know. And no official or unofficial crookedness can wipe it out."

"But that little fellow up-stairs with his face against the screen?"

"It's that little fellow I'm thinking of. He'll never have to explain why his father reneged on a job he was trusted to do."

"But you haven't promised anybody in writing?"

"No."

"And, as I make it out, you haven't even given your word?"

"No."

"Then what right has anybody to—"

"He don't need to have any *right*. He just thinks I'm the kind of a man he can count on, and, in a show down, that's the kind of a man I reckon I want him or any other man to think I am."

"Then it is finally no?"

"No."

"No?"

"No. And let that be the end of the noes."

Necker smoked thoughtfully. Then, slowly gathering up his papers, he said: "I'm licked, Welkie; but I would like to know what licked me. It might save me from making the same mistake again."

"Why, I don't know's I know what you mean; but there is one thing, Necker: if it ever happens that a nation which don't like us comes steaming up here to get hold of this base, to batter it to pieces, say, she won't. No. And why? Because it's no haphazard mixture of water and sand. It's a good job, and if I'm no more than a lump of clay in my grave, I want to be able to roll over and say"—a flame seemed to shoot from his eyes—"'You sons o' guns, you can't get in, because what you've come to take was built right, and 'twas me built it, by God!'"

Necker studied him. "Well, if that isn't throwing a halo around your work, I don't know what is. I've met that before, too. But you've got more than that—what is it?"

"If I have, I don't know it." He paused.

"I know," whispered Marie in Balfe's ear—her eyes turned to the ensign on the table.

"But if there's anything else there, it must've been born in me, and so that's no credit. But if there is anything else there, I want my boy to have it, too."

Necker picked up his hat and cane. "He'll have it, never fear,

Welkie, and the more surely because he won't know it either. I'm off. Do you mind if I take another of Cabada's cigars?"

"Surely. Help yourself. Fill your case."

"Thanks." He lit up. "These *are* a smoke. I wish he'd let me have some, but he's like you something—he's only to be got at from the inside, and I guess I'm not on the inside. Good-by, Welkie. I hope you get your reward some day, though I doubt it. Good-by, Mr. Balfe. You're the first of your kind I ever met. You fooled me, but I'll be ready for you next time. Good-by, Miss Welkie. I forgot to say"—he smiled slyly— "there was a sixty-horse-power French car and a fifty-foot motor-launch went with that house. Good-by."

The pebbly beach crunched under Necker's receding feet. "Dear me," sighed Marie, "don't you feel half sorry for him, Andie?"

"Just about half. I'll bet he plays a good game of poker. But, Greg—" Balfe drew a square white envelope from an inner coat-pocket—"I was given a letter the other day to give you—in case you were still on the job here."

"On the job? Where else could I be?" He had taken the envelope and was about to rip it carelessly open, when his eye caught the embossed blue lettering on the corner:

WHITE HOUSE

He held it up in bewilderment. "Not from the President, Andie?"

"Why not? Read it."

Slowly Welkie read it. He took it over to the light at the little table and read it again. He dropped it on the table and gazed through the screen at the lights of the fleet. After a time he said in a low tone: "I must tell Sonnie-Boy," and, turning, went inside the house.

"Is it very private, Andie?" whispered Marie.

"No, no."

"Then I'm going to read it."

She read it. "Why, Andie!" she gasped, and, crowding to the light, she also read it again. Her face was alight when she looked up at last. "Andie, Andie, isn't it splendid! If Mr. Necker could only hear this:

"'It is a fine thing in these days of materialism that a man of your genius can set aside the allurements of money and fame, and exile yourself to a region where certain hardship and probable disease await you; and this only that your country may be served.' And the rest of it! O Greg!"

Welkie was back with his boy in his arms. He took the letter from his sister. "Look here, Sonnie-Boy, what do you think? Here's a man says your papa is the greatest man ever was in his line. Years from now you'll look at that letter and perhaps you'll be proud of your papa. Your papa's boasting now, Sonnie-Boy, but only you and your auntie and godfather can hear him, and they'll never tell. So that's all right. 'Our papa was as good as anybody in his line'—a great man said so. What do you say, little five-and-a-half, you'll be a good man, too, in your line some day, won't you?"

"Can I be a fighter, papa, on a big gun-ship?"

"Well, if you're bound to go that way, I don't see who's to

stop you, Sonnie-Boy. But if you are, whether it's a sword to your belt or a lanyard to your neck, here's hoping you'll never go over the side of your ship without"—he picked the ensign up—"you leave your colors flying over her. And now we'll go back to bed, Sonnie-Boy, and this time we'll go to sleep." In the doorway he stopped. "What do you reckon Necker would say to that letter, Andie?"

Balfe smiled. "He'd probably say, 'Welkie, you ought to publish that letter—capitalize it,' and think you were four kinds of a fool if you didn't."

"Well, I won't publish it or capitalize it. I'm going to frame it and hang it at the foot of your bed, Sonnie-Boy, where you'll see it mornings when you wake. Up we go, son."

Facing each other across the little work-table were Marie Welkie and Andie Balfe. She had said: "You surely have been my brother's friend, and, if you were not already so successful, I could wish a great reward for you."

He laid one hand of his gently down on hers. "Wish the reward, then, Marie. Do, dear, wish it, for I'm not successful. I played hard at my game, because playing it made me forget other things. Almost anybody playing a game long enough becomes half-expert at it. But successful? No, no, dear. So far I seem to have travelled only unending roads through bleak countries; and I'm dreading to go back to them alone."

Beyond the veranda screen the fireflies were flashing; farther out, the little green and red side-lights of the steaming launches, like other colored fireflies, were sliding by; to the mastheads of the battle-ships the red and white signal-lights were winking and glowing. The night was alive with colorful things. Closing her eyes, Marie could hear the lapping of little waves over pebbles, the challenging hail of a sailor on watch, the music of a far ship's band. She bent her head to hear it better—the sweetly faint cadence of that far-away band.

"And when was it you began to think of me, Andie?"

"Since those first days, Marie, when your brother and I bunked together in the old S.$1.$2.construction camp. He used to read me letters of yours from home. You were only a little girl then, and it was years before I saw you; but I knew what you looked like even before I stole your photograph—"

"Stole?"

"I did. Greg dropped it one day. I found it and never gave it back. There it is—after nine years."

She laughed when she saw it. "Why, I can't make out to see what I looked like then, Andie!"

"I know what you looked like. I've kissed the face away, dear, but I know. In nine years, Marie, I never shifted from one coat to another without shifting your photograph, too. If anything had happened to me, they would have found your photograph on me, with your address on the back. 'Then,' I used to say to myself, 'she'll know. And Greg won't mind my stealing it.'" He laid it face up between them on the table. "The miles you've travelled with me, dear heart, and never knew! Back in the days of the construction camp they used to find sketches of a girl's head in my note-books, a beautiful head badly done—drawn from that photograph. But after I met you—"

"And after you met me, Andie?"

"Then I needed no photograph, though look and look at it I

surely did. Steamers in western seas, battle-ships in eastern waters, balustrades of palaces—wherever it might be I was whirling with this old earth around, I've had your face to look at. And when I couldn't see for the darkness—rolled up in my rubber poncho, in no more romantic a place than the muck of a swamp, I've looked up through the swaying branches—or in the lee of a windy hill, it might be, with no more to hinder than the clear air, I've looked up and marked your face in the swirling clouds: your nose, your chin, the lips so shyly smiling. And if through the clouds a pair of stars would break, I'd mark them for your shining eyes, Marie."

"Poetry again, Andie!" She was laughing, but also she was melting under his eyes.

"If that's poetry, then I'm losing respect for it. It's a weak thing, Marie, and—"

"Sh-h—if somebody should be walking on the beach!"

"Let them, sweetheart. It's a fine night for a walk. What harm is truth?"

"But I don't want all the world to hear, Andie. For my poor heart was aching, too, Andie, and now it wants it all to itself, Andie mine."

* * * * *

It was taps on the battle-fleet. Over the mellowing, detaining waters of the bay the long-drawn bugles echoed. Good night, good ni-i-ght, g-o-o-d-n-i-g-h-t—they said, and gently, softly, whisperingly died away.

"He's asleep at last." Welkie was standing in the door. "And I don't know but we'd all better be getting to sleep, too. For to-morrow morning, you know, we—Wha-at!"

His friend was standing before him. "Shunt care for the morrow, Greg. Greater things than have happened are happening around you. The dream of years has come to pass. And we—we, Greg—"

He looked to her, and tremulous, vivid, she came, and with her at his side he was himself again. "Marie is to take me for Sonnie-Boy's uncle, and, Greg, we want your blessing."

TIM RILEY'S TOUCH

"A man outside—says his name's Riley," announced the youth who guarded the outer door. "A big husky!" he added when he saw the chairman did not look pleased.

The state chairman nodded round the table. "This is that new man the senator's been talking about." From a neat pile of letters the chairman picked out one.

"Here is what he sent in the other day. From it you can obtain an idea of the calibre of the man. Listen: 'As you ask me what I think about the crowd up here, I'll say that I think they've had their own way so long they've got to where they figure they don't have to make good. They seem to think that to be in politics is to be trying to fool everybody. They would rather—the most of them—get ten votes by faking than a hundred by straightforward work. They don't seem to see that nowadays people know more about the inside of things than they used to—that they're doing more thinking for themselves in political matters.'

"And"—the chairman reinserted the letter in the neat pile—"there's more drool of the same kind. I don't believe he ever wrote that letter. As I understand it, he's a coal-heaving sort who ought to have gone into the prize-ring and not politics; but, whether he wrote it or not, we will have to humor him

James B. Connolly

because of the senator, who is of course the boss"—he shot a glance round the table—"the boss now. We'll give this fellow a little rope. A couple of the boys up where he comes from tipped me off about him—and we'll let the senator see him for what he is. I've seen these wonders before."

"And I guess you don't have to see too much of a man to be able to size him up either!" This from a faithful one on the chairman's right.

The chairman's lips kneaded shut. "Well, in political life—I don't say this in a boasting spirit, you understand, gentlemen—if a man in my position can't size a man up fairly well at a glance he might as well get out. His letter alone would tell me that he knows it all, and the word I get from the county chairman up his way is that he is one of the turbulent, fighting kind. However, we'll have him in here and look him over. Show him in, George."

And Riley stepped into the room. From the moment of his entrance not a soul there had a doubt of the chairman's prejudgment; but, that his less acute associates might judge for themselves, the chairman allowed the man by his own words to portray himself, which, after all, was the most convincing proof of all. It was the senior senator's own way of doing it.

The new man—an agile, powerful figure—had bowed with a conventional show of pleasure to each in turn as he was introduced; but, that over with, he had faced squarely toward the chairman, waiting. And the chairman began:

"I take it, Mr. Riley, that you are not the kind of man who would stand up on a platform and dodge an argument with the most excitable of opponents?"

"Dodge? What from?"

"Not from the hoots and the jeers, or vegetables—or even the half-bricks—eh?"

Riley waved a contemptuous arm. "I'd rather see half bricks coming my way than be looking down on staring empty benches, or benches emptying swiftly when a man's at the height of his speech." Riley paused by way of emphasis. "It is to try a man's soul—a frosty greeting; but, a warm-blooded opposition—that's only to stir a man up."

The state chairman waited for the new man to leap into the air, knock his heels together and yell:

"Hurroo!" The new man did not do that. He gazed steadily into the face of the chairman. However, every specimen could not be expected to meet every requirement. No doubt of it—here was the made-to-order creature for clever manipulation; and there followed then the suggestion to visit New Ireland, with artful words to whet a fighting man's appetite for that kind of job.

"And now for one last little touch before we send the poor boob to his political extinction," whispered the chairman to his next at hand. Aloud he said:

"Yes, sir—I believe in frankness, Mr. Riley. And I will tell you now that we didn't poll many votes in New Ireland last year. I don't just remember how many—I have mislaid the figures; but I wish to tell you frankly—frankly, I say—that we did not poll many. What they need there, I think, is a determined man like yourself to pile into them hammer and tongs. That would be the way, I think. And you show me, Mr. Riley, a fair Republican increase in New Ireland—fifty out of five hundred, say—and you can lay out your own

James B. Connolly

itinerary for the rest of the campaign. Now isn't that fair?"

"Why, yes; that seems all right." As he said it, however, the new man, his eyes ever on the chairman's, had a feeling that it was not all right. And, as he was one of those intuitive ones with whom to feel was almost to prove, his attitude changed from the subjective to the objective. He had not liked this man a bit from the first, and he was liking him less and less; that finishing "Now isn't that fair?" was surely not meant for his benefit.

The new man left the committee-rooms with a disturbed soul, and on his way to the elevator he began to think things over. Among a dozen other things which flashed through his kindling brain he recalled the glint of what now he knew was mockery brightening the pale eyes of the chairman as the door closed behind him.

He pressed the button for the elevator; but before the upcoming car reached his floor he decided not to descend. He would have it out. He almost ran back to the committee-rooms and, brushing by the knowing but inefficient outer guard, made for the room where the leaders were. Already he could hear the laughter—yes, and the roaring at something or other; and as he placed his hand on the knob of the inner door he heard: "He's come here from the other end of the State, with a reputation for burning things up. Let him try to burn up New Ireland—and then go back to where he came from. Why, let his kind come butting in on us and soon we would all be out of jobs." The chairman's voice, that was.

Tim opened the door, and when they looked up and saw him it was as if they had all been clutched by the windpipes.

"Go to the devil—all of you!" exploded the new man. "Do you hear? Every mother's son of you!"

From out the silence some one at last said: "You mean, Mr. Riley, you are going to desert the party?"

Tim whirled on him.

"No; it doesn't mean I'm going to desert the party. Did ever you know a man who was any good to desert any party or anything, good or bad, under fire?"

"I'm glad to hear that." The chairman had come to life. "And not alone because we would lose you, eloquent though you are reported to be. So many of our people have maintained that no Irishman—"

"Cut that Irishman stuff! My chance to make a living, and my children's chance after me, I owe to this country."

"But, Mr. Riley, you are of Irish blood."

"Irish blood? You may be sure I am, and so proud of it that when I speak of it I slop over; but I'm an American citizen too. However, if you don't mind, we'll leave that for private discussion and not for political trading."

The chairman recovered.

"That's all very well; but when we ask your people to make sacrifices for the principles of our party—"

"Principles of the party—slush! Save that for your platform speeches. You're in the party because there's more in it for you. I'm in it because a man who gave me a square meal when I was starving asked me to join it. And, once in a fight, I stick. I stick because I don't know how to do anything else—and I'm going to stick now. And I'm going out now to New Ireland and talk to them."

The door behind Tim opened and a smooth, carefully trained voice said: "What's this about New Ireland?"

Tim knew the voice, even before he turned to greet him. It was the tall boss, the real boss, the senior senator, the man who ordered the State committee round even as they ordered the campaign speakers.

"New Ireland?" the senator repeated. "No, Mr. Riley. I can give you something better than that. That would be a waste of time. I'll change that right now. Here—"

"Excuse me, sir; but I'm going to New Ireland. I don't know what kind of a place it is or what kind they are there, except what the name tells me, and I don't care—I'm going there. No gang of men ever picked me for an omadhaun in the morning but found out they were mistaken before night. And I'll say further"—indignation in Tim always disposed him to classic periods—"if there are those who wave the green flag to tatters at every Irish meeting, and then betray her to those who hate her, there are also those who, though they have never made a sacrifice in their lives for this country, would prevent all but their own little kind from breathing the free air of it. As for me, I've come to this city to do something; and I'll stay here until I've done it. A while ago I agreed to go to New Ireland, and to New Ireland I'm going. Good day!" And the windows rattled with the banging of the door behind him.

"A proper bull-headed Irishman, that fellow," observed the chairman presently.

"Or is it he has convictions and is not afraid to voice them?" The senator had a habit of scratching his beard with his finger-nails, and again of drawing his chin in on his chest and looking over his gold-rimmed pince-nez. He drew in his chin now, and the chairman did not like it. He never did.

"A good fighter, I should say." The tall boss scratched his beard with his finger-nails. "An encouraging thing to meet a good fighter in these fat days; but let us see." He stepped over to where a blue-and-red-spotted map of the State was hanging and laid a finger on a blue spot: "New Ireland, which we can safely call the enemy's banner town for its size in the United States. If Riley can leave his mark on that place it will be proof to me that he can make breaches all along the line."

"More likely, I think, that the place will leave its mark on him. More likely they will crack his skull, I think. He may love a fight; but New Ireland is full of men who love fighting too—and they are not with us."

"That's true—they are not." The boss drew his chin in to his neck again. "Too bad they are not. Suppose we wait, however, and see how Riley makes out. His reputation is that of a most resourceful man. And if he does make an impression on New Ireland he can have anything I can give him in this State."

II

It is a good place—a moving train—for serious meditation. Tim Riley allowed the landscape to fly by, the while he considered matters. He knew the temper of the kind of people with whom he was to battle. They were so many more like himself. As for trying to bulldoze or browbeat them, or—if he was that kind—to bribe a single one, though they were the hard-working, unsophisticated kind—whisht! —like the wind they'd go the other way. And as for scaring the tough ones, he might be the strongest and toughest and scrappiest and quickest lad on his feet that ever was, but out there in that quarrying town would be a dozen or twenty or fifty just as strong and as quick and as scrappy as himself. And that kind—which was his kind—you might set them up in a row and knock them down one after another, and just as fast as one went down another would come bouncing up for the honor of the last word.

New Ireland! Tim viewed a town of two or three hundred small, square-planned wooden houses, with one green-painted house larger than most, labelled Kearney's Hotel; another, larger than that again, with a square cupola, which he knew would be the town hall; and yet one more, largest of all, white-painted, with a surmounting gold cross, which, of course, could only be the chapel. A mile or so beyond the town, on the scarred hillsides, stuck up the derricks of the quarries, which were the town's reason for being. Beyond the quarries were foot-hills, which gradually grew up into mountains. It was autumn, and in that high land the few trees were already bare; before the high wind the bare branches swayed.

It was not the most encouraging day of the year. Tim, with a warm fire and a hot meal in view, hurried on to the little hotel. Peter Kearney was the landlord, a companionable soul, who did not see the need of a register, and who, after a time, produced a lunch; and who, further, while Tim ate, smoked and gossiped of things a travelling man would naturally be interested in.

"And what kind have you here in New Ireland? Easy to get along with?" asked Tim, after the discovery of the quarries, the settling of the town, and the last explosion had been intelligently discussed.

"To get along with? The finest, easiest ever—of course if a man don't cross them."

"I wonder do you think I'll cross them?"

"And what would your business be that you'd be crossing 'em?" the landlord asked.

"I'm the Republican campaign speaker that's selected to address them to-night."

"Oh-h! Well, d'y'know, when I didn't see a sample case with you I had my suspicions; but when you said—or did you say your name was Riley?"

"I did. And it is. R-i-l-e-y—Riley, Timothy J. And there's any number of Republicans with names as good."

"I dare say, but not in New Ireland—nor likely to be while so many of your party put us down for a tribe of savages."

"Have patience, Mr. Kearney. There's a new order of things under way. Have patience. And tell me now how many Republicans should you estimate there are in New Ireland?"

"Estimate? Sure, and that's a large word for them. There's Grimmer, the cashier and chief clerk o' the savin's-bank. There's Handy, who keeps the real-estate office. And did ever ye notice, Mr. Riley, how, when a man has a soft-payin', easy-workin' job, 'tis ten to one he's a Republican?"

"I've spoken of it so often myself, Mr. Kearney, merely by way of humorous observation, that my party loyalty has been doubted. If you would never have your loyalty suspected, Mr. Kearney, you must never let on that you possess intelligence; but have patience and we'll have that changed some day—maybe. So those two are the leaders, are they?"

"Leaders, man! That's all of 'em."

"Two? Two out of nigh five hundred! Well, glory be, what kind are those two? The fighting kind?"

"Har-rdly the fightin' kind, Mr. Riley. They couldn't well be that in New Ireland, bein' Republican, and remain whole. Har-rdly! No, not if they were John L. Sullivans, the pair of 'em. Among five hundred quarrymen, d'y'see, Mr. Riley, and they mostly young men, there's always plenty of what a man might call loose energy lyin' round—specially after hours and Sundays and holidays; surely too much for any two, or two dozen, disputatious individuals to contend against. And yet, as I said, the easiest, quietest people living here—"

"Yes, yes; I'll bet a leprechaun's leap against a banshee's wail I know what peaceable kind they are. And I think I know now why I was—No matter about that though. Could you, Mr. Kearney, get somebody to pass the word to the quarries that the Republican speaker is here according to announcement, and that his name is Riley?"

"I'll send me boy. Dinnie!" called the landlord. No answer.

"Dinnie!" No answer. The landlord opened his lungs and roared: "Dinnie!!" Then he looked out of the dining-room window. "H-m! I thought as much. Look at him peltin' it on his bi-sigh-cle for the quarries! He heard you say Republican and 'twas enough. No fear now—not a soul in New Ireland but will know it before dark. And—but excuse me one minute, Mr. Riley."

The landlord stood up to greet a forlorn-looking old woman, who, with a man's overcoat wrapped round her, had appeared at the dining-room door.

"How are you to-day, Mrs. Nolan? About as usual? Well, don't be worryin'. Yes, you'll find Delia in the kitchen. Go in."

Tim nodded after the old woman as she went in.

"And who is she, Mr. Kearney?"

"A poor old creature who comes here once or twice in the week to have a cup o' tea and maybe a little to go with it, with the cook. A poor old soul dependin' on charity, and yet she won't take it from every one."

"Poor woman! Will you give her that?—not now, but when she goes out, Mr. Kearney." He slipped a silver dollar into the landlord's hand. "No need to tell her where it came from. I'll be going along now, I think, to have a look at the town. I'll be back for supper."

"Good luck to you!"

Tim had not left the hotel a hundred yards behind him when he met a Catholic priest.

"Good afternoon, Father," said Tim, and raised his hat.

"Good afternoon, sir. And is it"—the cane was shifted from the right hand to the left, and the hand thus freed extended to Tim—"Mr. Riley—isn't it?"

"It is; but how did you know, Father?"

"Oh, if Peter Kearney's long-legged Dinnie hasn't told half the quarries before this of your name and business 'twill be because he's burst a tire or broke his neck rolling down the steep hills. And so you're to speak to us to-night?"

"God willing, I am."

"And you're not discouraged?"

"And why should I be discouraged?"

"Why? You must be a stranger to these parts."

"I am."

"And no one told you of what happened to the last man your party sent here?"

"They did not. And what happened?"

"He was rode out of town on a rail."

"Well, well, Father. And what did he do, the poor man?"

"Oh, he only hinted at first that we were a lot of ignorant foreigners who were Democrats because we didn't know any better; but he warmed up as he went along. I don't know wherever they got him from. In the middle of it Buck

Malone gave them what they call his high sign—his right forefinger raised so—and every man in the hall got up and walked out. A few of them came back later and took him off. They didn't hurt him—no bones broken or anything like that; but they do say he never waited for the train when they turned him loose, but legged the thirty miles back to the city without a single stop!"

"He did? Well, it's fine exercise, Father—running; though thirty miles in one bite, to be sure, is a bit too much for good digestion, I'd say. This Buck Malone—he's the boss here, Father?"

"He is. And a famous one for surprising folks."

"Thank you for the information, Father."

"It's no information. The very babies here know of the last man here. If you see the children in the street smiling slylike when you pass, that will be why."

Tim pulled his lower lip with thumb and forefinger.

"And yet they'd laugh all the louder if I was to go away without speaking, Father. What kind is Buck Malone to look at and where does he hang out?"

The priest poked the end of his cane at Tim's chest.

"Is it fighting you'd be at, Mr. Riley?"

"It is not. I'm not for fighting—unless, of course, I have to. Isn't it only natural to want to know what kind your opponent is?"

"So it is—so it is. Well, then, about this time o' day you'll find him in that cigar-store with the sign out—below there.

He's a contractor himself, who furnishes labor for the quarries. A man about your height and breadth he'll be, but a trifle fuller in the waist. A stout, strong man, and not many able to look him down. An eye in his head, has Buck! I wouldn't want to see the pair of ye at it."

"Thank you, Father. And look—d'y'see that old woman coming out of the hotel? What's her story, Father?"

"The widow Nolan. A sad history, Mr. Riley, if you could get it out of her; but it's few she'll talk to."

"Poor woman! Would you give her this—a couple of dollars—Father, after I'm gone?"

"I will. And it's good of you. And you're bound to speak to-night?"

"I'll speak. And I'd like you to come, Father."

"Not I, Mr. Riley. Priests are better out of politics. Good day and God speed you!"

Tim strolled toward the cigar-store; and drawing near he picked out, standing near the glass case, a tall, powerfully built man, with intelligently heavy features and the unwavering eyes of a fighting man. As Tim entered this man was speaking. Before ten words had been said, Tim knew that his entrance had been forecasted and that this was Buck Malone.

"And he'll be up there on that platform all alone—not a soul with him, because these two dubs that ought to be standing by him, they've got cold feet already. And he'll be up there all alone, except for a pitcher of cold water and a glass, and a table and a chair; and he'll begin to spout. I dunno whether he c'n talk or not; but we'll let him run on for maybe ten minutes, and about the time he thinks he's making a hit I'll start up and I'll raise my forefinger like that—see? And that'll mean everybody get up and go out. No hurry, mind you— nor no hustlin'; but everybody just stand up and walk out and leave him talkin' to that picture o' that dago, or whoever he is, discoverin' the Mississippi on the back wall.

"And now you"—Malone turned leisurely to a stocky-looking young fellow in seedy clothes standing wistfully off to one side—"you go on and pass the word to 'em as they come out o' the quarries."

"All right," answered the stocky one in a hoarse voice, but without moving.

A meagre-looking man stood behind the cigar-case.

"Will you let me have," said Tim to him, "three good cigars?"

The man behind the cigar-case looked slyly at Malone.

"How good?" he asked.

"Oh, pretty fair—three for a dollar or so."

"Three for a—I got nothing like that here. Fifteen cents straight's the best I got."

"All right; they'll do."

The boss had not been smoking when Tim entered; but now he turned to look better at Tim, and he pulled a cigar from his vest-pocket, bit off the end, scratched a match, and leisurely lit it—all without taking his eyes off Tim.

Tim also leisurely bit the end off a cigar. The proprietor pushed three or four matches across the case. Tim, ignoring them, stepped close to the boss.

"Would you let me have a light?" he inquired politely.

"H-ff! h-ff!" The boss swallowed quite a little smoke, but recovered and passed over his cigar. Tim took his light from it, said "Thanks!" briefly, and—puff-puff—contemplated the boss's stout henchman in the rusty clothes, who was still standing irresolutely at one side.

"Smoke?" inquired Tim suddenly, and thrust a cigar at him.

"Wh-h—" stuttered the henchman, and then almost snatched it from Tim's hand.

"You gettin' hard o' hearin'? Thought I told you to get along!" snapped Malone.

"I am goin' along," returned the husky voice, "soon's I light up." In the curling of the smoke from the corner of his mouth, in the whoofing of it toward the ceiling, in the squaring of the thick shoulders as he passed out—there was a hint of rebellion.

"You may be the boss," thought Tim, "but your grip isn't too sure." And turning squarely on Malone he observed genially: "Fine day."

"H-p-p—" Malone stared fixedly at Tim. Tim stared back. Tim was rapidly developing a feeling of respect for the man. Tim knew the kind. A few years back he had been such an uncompromising one himself, who would have whipped off his coat, as no doubt Malone would now, and battled on the spot in preference to verbal argument.

"It is a fine day," responded Malone slowly; "but accordin' to my dope it ain't goin' to be half so fine a night."

From behind the cigar-case came a giggle, and from the boss himself came an after-chuckle and a pleased little smile.

"Why, it's not going to rain, is it?" asked Tim, and with an appropriately innocent manner he stepped to the door to look at the sky; and in looking he saw not the sky, but the widow Nolan, with some odds and ends of firewood, making her halting way against the wind.

"The poor creature!" murmured Tim; and while pitying her the plan came to him. "Gentlemen," he said over his shoulder, "I have to be off; but before going I cordially invite you and all your friends to the town hall to-night, to discuss the issues of the campaign. Good day, gentlemen."

And through the door, before it closed after him, he could hear the cackle of the man behind the cigar-case: "Is it going to rain! Say, Buck, you won't do a thing to him to-night, will yuh?"

III

With his greeting of "Good afternoon to you, Mrs. Nolan!" Tim stowed the widow's little bundle under his left arm.

"And good afternoon to you, sir; but you'll be sp'iling your fine clothes, sir!"

"And if I do it's small loss." He gripped her right elbow. "It's the hard walking it is, Mrs. Nolan—what with the wind and the steep hill and an old lady of your age."

"Oh, yeh, it is—coming on to seventy-five."

"Seventy-five? And you still hopping about active as a grasshopper! A great age that. 'Tis little, I'm afraid, many of us young ones will be thinking of climbing steep hillsides when we're coming on to seventy-five. 'Tis you was the active one in your young days, I'll wager."

"'Tis me that was, sir; but oh, I'm not that now."

"It's sad it must be to be looking back on the bright dancin' days o' youth, Mrs. Nolan."

"Sure and it is, sir; but why—the fine bouncin' lad ye are— why should you be sayin' it?"

"Ah, sure, youth has its trials and tribulations too, ma'am, sometimes. And is this your little place?"

"It is. An' will you come in, sir?"

"I will and thank ye kindly, ma'am. 'Tisn't every day a lady invites me into her place."

"Whisht! There are ladies enough to be pleasant to a fine strappin' lad like you, with nothing on earth to be botherin' you."

Tim laughed as he sat down.

"Nothing? Oh, ma'am—"

"And what is it can be worryin' you, sir?"

"What is it? Well, if you had my job, Mrs. Nolan, I'm thinkin' you'd be worrying, too; even if 'twas big and strong and a man you were, and but thirty years of age. I'm the Republican speaker, ma'am, that has been sent to ye here. And for why? To convert ye, ma'am."

"And so you're a Republican, sir? Well, well—but, savin' your presence, you don't look it or talk it. Sure, you're as Irish as myself!"

"I'm that Irish, ma'am, that if you were to take the Irish from out of me it's faded and limp as a mornin'-glory at two in the afternoon I'd be."

"And what's your name, may I ask?"

"Riley, ma'am. Timothy Joseph Riley, to be exact."

"Riley—Tim Riley! Well, you're the first Riley ever I knew was a Republican. That thin-necked one in the bank, and that other one, the fat-necked one in the real-estate place—sure, you don't favor them no more than—Yet there must be good men Republicans, too. Will you have a cuppeen o' tea? 'Tisn't much; but 'twill war-rm you, maybe, on the chill day."

"Thank you; and 'twill taste fine—a cup o' tea on a chill day like this. And like to be chiller, Mrs. Nolan."

"True for ye. And gen'rally I feels it; but not so to-day, sir. Mr. Kearney gave me a dollar, sayin' it was from a stranger and I wasn't to mention it—and I won't; but"—she shot a quick, warm glance at Tim—"God guard the kind heart of him, whoever he is. To-morrow I'll be orderin' some beautiful groceries with it. Tis a gran' sinsation to be goin' into a store and orderin' things."

She stooped for her little bundle of fagots, but Tim forestalled her. He undid them, arranged them craftily in the stove with rolls of old newspaper beneath, and touched a match to the fire.

"There, ma'am."

"We'll have the little kittle b'ilin' in a minute now, sir."

"And what will you do against the cold winter comin', ma'am?"

"Oh, yeh! I'll do, no doubt, what I've done every winter since I come here—live through it."

"With the cold wind coming through the wide cracks and the snow piling high on the wintry mornings, it won't be the tightest place in the world, ma'am."

"Thanks be to God I have it—the same little cabin!"

"Thank God you have! Whisht, ma'am"— Tim laid a restraining hand on hers as she spooned the tea out of the can—"you won't be leaving yourself any at all."

"Sure, there's enough for the breakfast. And if we could

always be sure of our breakfast it's little we'd have to complain of. And now let me get out my cups and saucers. I have two of each, thank God!"

"Let me, Mrs. Nolan—I see them."

"Well, well—but 'tis the spry lad ye are! Sure, you're across the floor in one leap—like a stag just."

"Oh, sure; my legs are young. And one spoonful o' sugar is it, ma'am?"

"One—yes. And now sit down. And so it's a Republican ye are? And an Irishman, too? Well, well—they do be queer happenin's in the world!"

"Queer enough. And from what part of Ireland are ye, ma'am?"

"Galway."

"A fine place, ma'am. I know it."

"Do ye now? But you're not Galway?"

"I wouldn't lie to ye, ma'am, though I'm tempted—I'm not; but I had an uncle, as fine a man as ever lived, who died there. I went to see him there once, and a grand time I had with salmon-fishin' in the loch and fishin' with the Claddagh men in the bay—and on a Saturday night the little boys singin' the old Irish songs in the streets and before Mrs. Mack's hotel door. And was it in Galway the last of your people died?"

"It wasn't. And they didn't die—they were killed, God rest their souls!"

"Amen!"

The sticks in the little stove crackled; the water in the little kettle spluttered; a gaunt black cat crowded his way through the poorly fastened door and rubbed himself against Tim's legs, whereat the widow threw a stick of wood at him.

"Out o' that, you with your mud on you from the quarry pools sp'ilin' the gentleman's fine clothes!"

"Small harm he'll do, ma'am."

"It's better manners he ought to be havin', though 'tis fine to see a man like yourself hasn't too much conceit of his clothes. But now have your tea, avic."

"I will. Ah-h! and the fine tea, it is, too. And isn't it a queer thing now, Mrs. Nolan, that I can go to the finest hotels in the land and not get the like o' this for tea? The finest of hotels—yes; and here in a little cabin, with the wind blowing through the cracks, I'm havin' tea that for its equal I'd have to go—well, to China itself, I'm thinking. But tell me, Mrs. Nolan—it's as a friend I ask—what misfortune was it brought you to be living in a little shebeen on this rocky hillside?"

The old woman made no response, except to add three or four little sticks of wood from her pile to freshen the fire. It was still chilly and outside it was windy, and Tim drew the man's worn coat about her shoulders and made her sit closer to the fire. And by and by she told him.

When she had done the twilight was on them and the fire long gone out. Through the one little window of the cabin they could see the increasing lights in the town below, and from the road they could hear the tramping of heavy-booted men.

"They'll be hurrying home from the quarries now. And 'tis not a lonesome home they will be finding."

"True, ma'am."

And Tim sat there smoking the last of the three cigars he had bought that afternoon, and thinking—thinking—sometimes of the evening's work before him, but mostly of the old woman's story.

"Oh, yeh; if it was but a stone I had to put on their two graves in the cemetery below!" she said after a long silence.

"And why shouldn't you have the stone to put over them?" Tim jumped up and patted her white, straggling hair. "And you will have it, Nanna. Come with me to-night and I'll guarantee you'll have it."

"And where will I go?"

"With me and have a fine, hot supper at Kearney's—and then to the town hall to hear me speak."

"Indeed and I'd like that fine, Mr. Riley; but they don't be invitin' women—old women—to any rallies."

"'Tis me is giving the rally, and I'll invite whom I please—I mean, if you're not afraid of the rioting when they don't like, maybe, what I'm going to say to them."

"Me afraid? Of what? Sure and they could be liftin' the roof itself from the town hall and a lone woman like myself would be safe among them. But why should you be wanting me there?"

"Why? I'll tell you, Nanna, and you must take it for the true reason until I can give you a better. And who knows it isn't the true reason? I'm that vain, Nanna, that I want some one soul there that isn't against me—some one that, before ever I begin, I know will hear me out. If you're there I know whose heart will be warm to me while I'm speaking. For 'tis terrible discouraging to see nothing but cold faces staring up from the benches and your heart bursting to tell them what's in it."

"Sure and it must be, avic. The cold heart—'tis an awful thing. A bony black cat itself is more company in the house than one of ourselves when the heart is ice. But whisper"— she leaned doubtfully toward him—"d'y' think there'd be hope of you turnin' Dimicrat?"

"I'm afraid I'm fixed where I am. I'm not easily turned, Nanna."

"Oh, yeh! Well, well—in one minute, Timmie avic, I'll be along with you."

And she dusted the hearth and gathered up her cups and saucers, which, as she washed, Tim dried. And presently he was guiding her halting steps down the hill.

IV

At eight o'clock that night Tim was facing his audience, and
a fine, large audience it was—not a hand's width in a single
bench vacant; from the front row, where sat Buck Malone,
almost smiling, to the back wall, where De Soto with some
Indians and mailed companions was discovering the
Mississippi—from stage to entrance, not a vacant seat. What
hopes for a man in a fighting audience like that if he could
but win them to him!

Tim was alone on the stage.

"Gentlemen," he began, "the Republican party in New
Ireland seems to be very busy to-night. One-half of it has to
attend a conference of bank cashiers over in Rocktown; and
Rocktown, it appears, is four miles in a buggy over a rough
road. That rough road and the buggy are, of course, an
incontrovertible argument, gentlemen. And the other half has
a rich prospective customer for a couple of town lots—also
over in Rocktown. A busy little place that Rocktown must
be! I don't wonder you're smiling. I smiled myself when they
told me.

"But if they are not here, gentlemen, to accredit me, I am
here to speak for myself. And, as you see, there is the table,
the chair, the ice-water pitcher, the empty glass, all as"—he
smiled down at the boss in the front row—"as Mr. Malone
said it would be. 'Twas this very afternoon Mr. Malone
spoke of it; and, myself happening to hear him, I would not
for a lord lieutenant's income disappoint him. 'Twas my good
old mother—God rest her soul!—who used to say—and
many's the time she said it: 'Timmie dear, don't never
disappoint people if you can help it.' And I never do—
especially when it don't cost me anything; for water is the

only thing I had to bring into the hall to-night—and water, gentlemen, is cheap."

"Yes, an' talk's cheap, too!"

Tim bowed to the voice and smiled with the laugh that followed.

"God knows it is cheap. If it wasn't 'tisn't the likes o' me could afford to be handing it out to you to-night, and no charge for admission at the door."

"Say, Buck, his ten minutes'll be used up before ever he gets started!" came a voice from midway of the hall.

"True for you, boy. And so I'll be introducing myself. My history is short. Riley is my name, Timothy Joseph Riley—baptized by Father Kiley, in the parish of Ballymallow—and I'm a Republican."

"And there's what we'd like to have you tell us, Misther Riley—how came you to be a Republican?"

"Yes, you blarneyin' turncoat—how came ye?"

A man in the front row stood up to say that last, a rugged-looking man, who looked as if he would like mighty well to jump up on the stage and haul Tim down off it. Toward him Tim stepped, leaning over the edge of the stage so that the belligerent one would not miss a syllable.

"I'll tell how I came to be a Republican. When I landed in this country and before I was fairly out of Castle Garden some thief of a pickpocket or worse stole the few little dollars I had to keep me until I could get a job. I was a seventeen-year-old boy, and that shy I couldn't beg. For two days not a morsel of food went into my mouth. And there I was, jumping sideways with the hunger, when a man comes along and saw me and brought me into a grand restaurant, 'And how'll I ever pay you?' I asks when I'd eaten my fill. He was a butcherman, with a white smock on him. And he laughs and says: 'You can't now; but by and by, when you get a vote, be sure and vote the Republican ticket.' And I says: 'Why the Republican ticket?' And he says: 'Oh, just by way o' variety—just to show that you people don't all go one way.'

"And"—Tim straightened up—"I took his hand, and 'Sir, I will!' I said. He was joking, maybe; but I wasn't. And I did vote the Republican ticket; and I'm still voting the Republican ticket. And I'm saying to you all to-night—the one Republican among five hundred of ye—that I'm not apologizing to any man in this hall or any other hall for it. And I'm saying to you"—in the face of the inquiring man in the front row, in the face of Buck Malone, in the face of the whole hall, Tim clinched his fist—"I'm saying that the man of Irish blood who ever forgets the promise that he's made to the one that befriended him—I say to ye all, and I don't care whether ye like it or not—his blood's been crossed somewhere; he's no Irish in him! No—nor fit to be called a man at all!"

Tim stepped back to pour out a glass of water; a form rose up midway of the hall, and a voice roared out:

"Say, you Riley man, your politics are the divil's own, but you're Irish all right. Go on!"

Tim held the glass toward the speaker.

"And, ma bouchal, 'tis you has the Irish heart in you, too. Here's to you! You stubborn, unconverted, hereditary Democrat, here's to you!" He drained the glass.

"Go on! Tell us more!"

"Yes; go on—talk up!"

"You'll get a show here. Go on!"

Tim glanced down at Buck Malone, swept the benches for the sight of a more cheerful face and caught the friendly eyes of Peter Kearney. Also he suddenly recognized the face of Malone's henchman—the man to whom he had given the cigar. He was wagging his head encouragingly.

"Gentlemen, I will go on—and thank you for the chance. And, with your permission, gentlemen, I'll speak of something besides politics. It is of charity. Gentlemen, a great quality is charity. Only because of the spirit of charity in you, gentlemen, am I allowed to speak to you here to-night; but it's another phase of charity I'd like to speak of. I will put it in the form of a story—and, gentlemen, not too long a story.

"There was an old lady in the old country, who received a letter from her oldest son, John, with passage-money for her second son, Pat, to come over and join him. She gave her consent. Why wouldn't she—when the living was so hard? Pat went, leaving his mother of nigh seventy and the last of his brothers with her. One son had already gone to South America and another to Australia; and now only a boy was left to her—and him with one leg gone in a railroad accident, for which they'd never got a farthing."

At this point Tim heard the side door softly open and close. He took a quick backward peek. Dinnie and old Nanna Nolan were waiting in the wings. Tim signed to them to remain there. He stepped to the front of the stage then, just in time to see Malone, whose every move he was watching, uncross his legs and half rise in his seat. Tim looked at him steadily and waited. Malone did not move farther, and Tim resumed:

"Well, the two sons in America, strong and willing, worked side by side, earning their dollar and a quarter and their dollar and a half a day, with now and again a day's or a week's layoff to set them back, but managing always between them to save four dollars in the week and send it over every month to the old mother—until by and by, she scrimping and saving, too, there was passage-money for herself and the lad to come to America. They took the steamer at Queenstown; and 'twas like a grand dream to them—until one day there came a great storm and the ship leaped and jumped, and the poor, helpless, crippled boy was thrown down an iron ladder; and when some one thought to help the poor mother pick him up he was dead. Well—But, gentlemen, maybe I'm trying your patience?"

"Go on!" came a voice, and "Go on!" came another; and then three, four, a dozen voices called for him to continue.

"Thank you. Well, gentlemen, a tempest in the great ocean, with its tremendous winds and mountains of seas, must be a terrible sight; but surely a more terrible sight is to see that same ocean, as smooth as oil, and the blue heavens smiling down, while the body of one that's dear to you is lowered into it! So it was. With loose, wide stitches they'd sewed the boy into canvas; and to the one foot of him they tied a piece of an old grate-bar, and dropped him into that great ocean."

Tim saw Malone shoot a furtive glance sideways to learn how they were taking it in the front row. Plainly he was not liking it, for he stood up straight then and surveyed the rows of voters behind him. Tim waited, and every man there knew why he waited. There was an indrawing of breaths all over the hall. Malone, without showing the ordering forefinger, sat down again.

Tim bowed to him. "Thank you, Mr. Malone, for that fighting chance," which remark brought out a quick burst of applause.

"Well, gentlemen, that poor old woman landed in the strange country. Grief-stricken she was, but not yet utterly discouraged. The son Pat was to meet her at the dock. He was not there. Well, she could see a good reason for that. They could not leave their work—sometimes the bosses were strict—they had often written so in their letters. No matter. With not much left of her little savings, she bought a ticket and took the train for the town where her two sons were working. Well, neither was Pat at the station to greet her—but by and by she learned why.

"There had been a premature explosion in the quarries, and a fall of rock had knocked Pat senseless; and as he lay there, unconscious, a second blast came and killed him. Well, that was an awful thing; but still there was the son John. And they had then to tell her of John. Well, while Pat lay there helpless, another man had run in to carry him out of danger. He was a brave man, that second man, for the flame of the second fuse was then almost to the charge; but he ran in and he had the injured man in his arms when the second explosion came. They were killed together. That second man was her other son, John."

Tim paused; but he no longer had to ask their leave to speak. He was in full swing; and out there, beyond the ends of his nervous, spreading fingers, they were swinging with him. Sitting up straight and still they were—or leaning forward, bent and eager.

A potent gift, the orator's. A writer may never hope to achieve instantly his great intention. He is limited to monotonous-looking black words on a blank page. But a speaker! Added to the words are eyes, lips, hands, head, body, and the immeasurable force of personality. Tim's voice softened and deepened, halted and quickened, rounded and trembled; the ruddy cheek took on a ruddier color; his deep-set eyes grew deeper and darker, and by and by they flamed. He grew taller; his body expanded. He spread his hands—fine, shapely hands, with nervous, expressive fingers—and as he gestured he quivered to his very finger-tips, and down there on the benches they quivered with him. The cold words—he warmed and revivified them. Under the caress of his beautiful, barely perceptible brogue the commonest, harshest lines took on smoothness and roundness; and from out his mouth the fine, tender words bloomed like summer flowers; and the larger, colorful words flashed like gems.

Tim, in short, was an orator. And when he said: "There, gentlemen, you have the story—and you know whose story it is. Poor old Nanna Nolan's—yes:" when he had said that, with arms and hands no longer gesturing, but drooping straight and motionless by his side, no one stirred—but a great sigh went up.

And not till that moment did Malone wake up to it that he had waited too long; but that moment he desperately chose to take his position at the end of the aisle and face his hitherto unbroken constituency; and while Malone was doing that Tim was motioning to Dinnie in the wings; and now Dinnie was leading her out—old Nanna Nolan, halting and bewildered, blinking at the audience—as Tim held up one hand for a last word.

"Here she is! I've tried to tell you her story, gentlemen; but there's only one living person can tell that story right, and I'm not that one. If you could have heard her telling it—she in her little cabin on that windy hillside, before her little stove, with the dark coming down and the lights beginning to shine through—"

And that instant, while Tim's arm was across her poor thin shoulders, covered as ever with the worn man's coat—that instant Malone, whose back was to the stage, chose to raise his fateful forefinger.

And Tim waited. And Malone waited.

Not a man left the hall.

Malone turned and faced Tim.

"You win," he said; "but that two-faced chairman of yours— and he ain't any friend of yours—he never tipped me off you could fight any way except with your hands. Speak the rest of your piece. You win!"

* * * * *

Back at headquarters the state chairman had been for an hour trying to extract a little comfort from the newspaper story of the New Ireland upheaval when the tall boss came in. To the boss, of course, he had to make some comment, and he made it.

"This man Riley," he began cautiously, "I've been trying to discover whether he's a Republican or a Democrat by what he says here."

"How's that?"

"He says: 'Take your leaders: and if they don't carry out your will fire 'em out! If the men you have set on high betray you,' he puts it, 'lasso 'em off their pedestals and set 'em on the street level again!' If that isn't—"

"—government by the people?"

"I wasn't going to say that, sir."

"Why not? Isn't that what it amounts to? Let me see your paper, please. H-m! I don't see what there is here to object to. He is not against a party government; in fact, he's all for party. Only make sure the party leaders are honest, he says, in politics, religion, business—in everything; and if they do not live up to their promises read them their lesson. Well, why not? I think he's right. The people know more than they did and we might as well reckon with that new knowledge. The men who don't do that might as well give up the leadership!"

There was a whole page of it in the New Ireland *Record* about Tim. The senator read it all. When he at last looked up he murmured:

"Raised twelve hundred and odd dollars for the widow Nolan. That was surely well done! Two hundred and fifty votes pledged to him before he left the hall. He surely has the touch! And Malone says he's going to stick to his contracting hereafter. Good idea!"

The senator read on: "And Malone also says—also says— H-m!"

The chairman was startled out of his silence.

"I set Malone on to Riley—to fool him."

"You did!" The senator scratched his beard with his finger-nails, drew his chin in to his neck and looked over his pince-nez at the chairman. "Too bad he misunderstood you—wasn't it? It would be so nice if we could give you the credit; but I'm afraid we'll have to hand it to Riley."

It was not said loudly; but the tone and the glint of the eyes—and the cultured boss stirred into using slang! The chairman knew that he might as well pick up his hat and go.

And he did; after he wrote out his resignation with the big boss dictating it over his shoulder.

IN THE ANCHOR WATCH

The battle-fleet, home from foreign waters, now lay, within a mile-square, emblazoned quadrangle, to placid moorings in the bay.

From the after bridge of his own ship Lieutenant Wickett had been observing in silence the night life of the fleet, but when from some happy quarter-deck to windward there floated down the opening strains of a mellow folk-song, he lifted his chin from arms crossed on the bridge top-rail to say to his shore-going friend beside him: "Were you ever able to listen to a ship's band over water, Carlin, and not get to feeling homesick?"

"Still the kid, aren't you? How can you be homesick and you home?"

"I'm not home—not yet."

Just below them the officer of the deck was roaming the quarter-deck. A ship's messenger stepped up to him, saluted and said smartly: "Two bells, sir."

"Strike 'em," came the sharp order; and as the two bells were striking, from other ships, from windward and leeward, came also the quick, sharp-toned double stroke.

James B. Connolly

"Why," asked Carlin, "couldn't they strike those two bells without bothering that deck officer?"

"Regulations."

"They're the devil, those regulations, Wickett."

"Worse—sometimes. You can steer clear of the devil if you want to." He paused. "And yet it would soon be a devil of a service without 'em."

A sailor stepped up to the officer of the deck, and, saluting, said: "Anchor lights burning bright, sir."

A man in a chief petty officer's uniform stepped up to the officer of the deck, whereupon Wickett, sitting up, said: "That's our wireless operator."

"A message for Mr. Wickett, sir," came the operator's voice.

"You'll find Mr. Wickett on the after bridge," the officer of the deck said; and the wireless man came up the bridge ladder and saluted:

"You raised the *Clermont*, Wesson?" Wickett's voice was eagerly anticipatory.

"No, sir, I could not. She has no wireless."

"Oh-h!"

"But I raised the Cape station, and they reported she passed there on schedule time."

"On time? Good! Thank you, Wesson; that's all."

"Were you expecting somebody on the *Clermont*?" asked Carlin, when the wireless man had gone.

"Not really expecting. My home is a thousand miles from here, and my pay won't allow of my family travelling around everywhere to meet me. But I like to dream of rosy possibilities, don't you?"

A cool night breeze was blowing. Wickett bared his head to it. Presently he began to hum:

> "And it's O you little baby boy
> A-dancing on my knee—
> Will it be a belted charger
> Or a heaving deck to sea?
> Is't to be the serried pennants
> Or the rolling blue Na-vee?
> Or is't to be—"

He turned to Carlin. "When I hear myself singing that, in my own quarters ashore, then I'm home—and not before."

He set to humming softly again:

> "And it's O you little baby girl
> Athwart your mother's lap—"

Suddenly he asked: "Were you ever away from home sixteen months?"

Carlin emphatically shook his head. "No, *sir*. A year once. And I don't want to be that long away again. Were you— before this cruise?"

"Five years one time."

"F-i-i-ve! Whee-eee! Pretty tough that."

"Tough? More—inhuman. A man can get fat on war, but five years from your family—!" He raised his face to the stars and whoofed his despair of it.

"My year away from home," said Carlin, though not immediately, "was in the Philippines—where I first met you—remember? The night you landed from the little tug you were in command of and a bunch of us—war correspondents we called ourselves—were gathered around a big fire."

Wickett nodded. "I remember. And pretty blue was I?"

"Not at first. I thought you were the most care-free kid I'd met in months as you sat there telling about the funny things that had happened you and your little war tugboat. But towards morning, with only the two of us awake, I remember you as possibly the most melancholy young naval officer I'd ever met. You started to tell what a tough life the navy was for the home-loving officer or man, and I had a special reason for being interested in that. I had—I still have—a nephew with his eye on Annapolis. But just then reveille blew the camp awake and you went back to your tugboat."

Wickett smiled, though not too buoyantly, as he said: "Well, on my next cruise to the East I could have added a chapter to the story I might have told you by that overnight camp-fire. And I will now—but wait."

A ship's messenger was saluting the officer of the deck. "Taps, sir."

"Tell the bugler to sound taps," was the brisk command.

The ship's bugler had already taken position, heels together and facing seaward, in the superstructure bulkhead doorway. Looking straight down, Wickett and Carlin could see him, as, shoulders lifting and blouse expanding, he put his lungs into the call. From other ships, as he called, it was coming also—the long-noted, melancholy good night of the war legions.

When the last lingering note drooped out, only one ship, and she a far-away one, remained; but from her, finally, on the wings of the night breeze, the last notes drifted—gently, sweetly, lonesomely, to them.

* * * * *

"What was keeping me walking the deck or sitting up around camp-fires nights in the Philippines wasn't Filipinos," began Wickett. "I'd been in the East a year that time we met, and I put in another year on top of that in China. A terrible two years. But even two years in the East with your heart at home must have an ending. After all, the earth can only revolve so many days in one year, though at times I used to believe she'd quit revolving altogether, had stopped dead, was only marking time—'specially nights—and that the astronomical sharps weren't on to her changes. However, at last she'd rolled her sun up and her sun down the necessary seven hundred and odd times and I was headed for home.

"I went out a middy and came back an ensign—which is very important. An ensign may not rate many high rights in the service, but he does rate a leave of absence. And when my leave came I flew across the bay to the fort, where Colonel Blenner—Doris's father—was commandant. And on the way over I had a thousand visions, dreams, hopes, with of course a million misgivings, fears, doubts, and so on.

"When I met her I set it down right away that my misgivings

had come true. A fleet of young artillery officers were manoeuvring within shelling range of her, and while I didn't expect her to bound half-way across the drill-ground and throw her arms around my neck, or anything like that, because she never had bounded down and thrown her arms around my neck, and wasn't the bounding-down-and-throwing-her-arms-around-your-neck sort of a girl anyway; but what I did sort of hope for was that after a polite little interval she'd turn the red-caped chaps adrift and say, 'Come on, Dick, let's sit down here in the corner by ourselves and have a good talk,' and perhaps later, before the evening got too old, go for a stroll on the long walk, same as she used to.

"But she didn't turn any of them loose. She kept them all about her while she drew me into the middle of them. But poor me! I'd had no service at all in the civilized ports and hadn't seen more than a dozen white women in the whole two years I'd been gone, and of that dozen had spoken to only three, while as for these artillery chaps—! They made me feel like a six-pound shell in a big turret magazine. Any one of them could talk the eye out of my head the best day I'd ever seen. And the day I came back to her wasn't the best day I'd ever seen—not for talking purposes. I looked at and listened to them, and kept saying to myself: 'I wonder if they realize what a lucky lot they are to be able to stay all the time around where civilized women live?' But I don't believe they did. They took everything as if 'twas no more than small-arms ammunition was being served out to them.

"In my room in the hotel that night I began to chart a few new courses for myself. Before I left for the East Doris was terribly young and there'd been no other war heroes hanging around. She and her mother were then living in a quiet hotel near my house while her father was off on some board mission in the West. But now it wasn't any isolated little country hotel. It was post quarters, with her father the commandant, and a parade of young army officers in and out of those quarters, with squadrons of two and three-stripers steaming over pretty regularly from the navy-yard across the bay. And she was two years older—a terrible advance, eighteen to twenty, and I'd been two years gone.

"You said a while ago, Carlin, 'What a kid you are!' and perhaps I am, though I think I'm an old, old party myself; but about the time I came back from the East that first time I must have been a good deal of a kid. I know now I was. That first night at the hotel, after I'd been to the fort all day, I talked to myself in good shape. And I wound up by saying: 'Well, what do you care? There are forty nice girls between this hotel and the post.' But there weren't forty. There were a hundred, as far as that went, but there was only one that I wanted to see coming over the side of my ship, and next day when I went to see that one again I set out to win her. And I'm not going to give you any history of the courtship of Doris. I couldn't tell it right if I wanted to, and I don't want to—it's our own private story, but she wasn't trifling when she told me she'd never forget me before I went East. In a week it all came back, and once more we were walking under tall pines and sailing in a beautiful bay. In another week it was as when I left her—I had hopes.

"And then came the morning of the last day of my leave, and as an ensign doesn't rate any shore duty I knew that next day it would have to be back to my ship for me; though that same ship being slated for a neighborly berth with the North Atlantic fleet, I didn't feel too discouraged. I'd be within wireless distance at least. But I did not want to go without a promise. The night before I couldn't get two minutes together with her—there being a reception in her father's quarters to somebody or other—but when I was leaving for the night she had said yes, she'd come sailing with me in the morning after breakfast. And I left the hotel at sunrise and went down to the boat-landing to overhaul the hotel's little twenty-one-footer to make sure everything would be all ready for our sail after breakfast.

"I went through the post grounds to get sight of her window in passing, and there she was—all dressed, and looking out across the bay from their veranda. 'I was just wondering if you, too, would be up early this morning, Dick,' she said. 'Do you think it is going to storm?' And I told her no, and if it did, what matter? And without waiting until after breakfast we went off for our young cruise in the bay.

"I was half hoping it would storm, so I could show her what I could do with that little boat. But there was no storm or anything like it. There did come a squall of wind and I let it come, wearing the boat around, and letting the main-sheet run. And she zizzed. And I let her zizz. Nothing could happen. She was one of those little craft with a lead keel that you couldn't capsize, which I explained to Doris, while down on her side the little thing was tearing a white path in the blue water. But Doris's people had been always army people, and she hadn't much faith in floating contraptions. She clung closer to me; and the two of us sitting together and nothing to do but watch the boat go, why—well, we sat together and let her go.

"The breeze died down until there wasn't enough of it to be called a breeze, but that was no matter. We were still sitting close together and while we sat so, I found courage to tell her what had been flooding my heart through all those nights and days in Eastern waters. And we came back to breakfast engaged. And after breakfast—" Wickett unexpectedly turned to Carlin and said, half shyly: "I suppose you still think I'm a good deal of a kid to be telling you all this?"

Carlin nodded in serene agreement. "I always thought you

were a good deal of a kid. I hope you always will be. God save me from the man who isn't still a good deal of a kid at thirty. What did you do after breakfast?"

"After breakfast I went up to see Colonel Blenner, and found him on his veranda smoking his after-breakfast cigar before he went over to guard-mount. He was genial as ever; except that he put his foot down on an engagement. 'An engagement means a marriage, or should,' he says, 'and how can you marry on an ensign's pay? You with your mess bills and other expenses aboard ship, and Doris with her quarters ashore—you would never meet your bills.'"

"I agreed with him, but also argued with him, and shook him some, but could not quite upset him. I left him to run back to the hotel to throw my things together. And there I found a new complication—orders were waiting me. I was to be detached from my ship and to take command of the gunboat *Bayport*—and a rust-eaten old kettle of a *Bayport* she was, famous for her disabilities; and I was to sail for Manila next morning at eight o'clock. Manila! Another jolt. I sat down and thought it out.

"And when I got talking to myself again, I said: 'Doris Blenner, you're a great girl—the best ever; but you're not superhuman. No man has a right to expect a girl to be that. You're too lovable, too human, Doris, to be the superhuman kind. I'll be away in the East Lord knows how long—another two years perhaps—and there's all those army chaps always on the job. We'll just have to be married, that's all there is to that, before I leave.'"

"I was back to the post in time to join a riding-party after lunch. It was no use my trying to see her alone riding. But after the ride we slipped out onto the ramparts of the fort, and there, the pair of us sitting hand in hand and a sentry a

James B. Connolly

dozen paces away trying not to see and hear us, I told her of my orders and then entered my new plea. 'All for myself, Doris,' I told her. By that time the sun was low behind us and throwing our two shadows onto where the water of the bay came gurgling up against the walls of the fort, and looking down on our shadows from the fort walls, she said at last she would marry me before I left, if papa agreed—and glad one minute and sad the next, we walked back in the twilight.

"Colors had sounded when we got back, and the colonel was dressing for dinner; but after dinner I took him out for a walk. Three laps we made around the drill-ground and then, halting him under the clump of willows down by the outer walls, I plumped it at him—what it meant to be away for months and years from your own people.

"And he heard me through, and said: 'Why, that's part of the hardship, Richard, in both arms of the service. In my day, Richard—"

"'Pardon, Colonel,' I butted in, 'pardon me, Colonel, but in your day the army people never left the country. Even when you were fighting Indians on the frontier, after all it was only the frontier and never more than a couple of thousand miles at the most to get back home. And when you were through campaigning and back in garrison, your people could come to see you. But twelve thousand miles! It isn't as if a man's within telephone call then. And when you're not to see your people for that length of time, there's danger.'"

"'Danger?' He stiffens up and takes a peek at me."

"'Danger, yes sir,' I said. 'I've been out there in the islands, in a tugboat with her engines broken down and she drifting onto a beach where four hundred squatting Moros with Remington rifles were waiting hopefully for us to come ashore. Four hundred of them and five of us all told. But that's not danger, sir,' I hurries on, 'of the kind to scare a man, though it did sicken me to think I'd never see Doris again, and that perhaps it would shock her when she heard of it. But otherwise, sir, that's no danger. But when a young officer goes a thousand miles up a Chinese river in command of a gunboat, as I was this last time—gone for months on it—and being commander was everywhere received as the representative of a great country by all the governors and topside mandarins along the route. And they haven't our idea of things—a lot of things that seem wrong to us seem all right to them. They mean no harm. They intend only to be courteous and complimentary, and so they strew a fellow's path with the flowers of ease and pleasure—if he forgets himself, there's danger, Colonel,' I said. 'I sail at eight in the morning, sir. I'm to be gone I don't know how long, perhaps another two years, and—Colonel—I want a home anchor.'"

"He said no word till he had finished his cigar. When he does he drops it at his feet, steps on it to put out the light, and says: 'A good argument for yourself, Richard, but what of Doris?'"

"'Doris has probably done a lot of thinking in the matter, sir. Why not leave it to Doris, sir?'"

"'Of course,' he said, dry as powder, 'Doris would be disinterested in this case!'"

"'Then leave it to her mother, sir.'"

"'I see neither logic nor prudence in your argument, Richard,' he answers at last, 'but I will leave it to her mother.' And when he said that, I knew I had won; for, without her ever telling me, I knew her mother was with us. If I had told him that, I would only have been telling what he already guessed,

James B. Connolly

as he told me that same night, later.

"Anyway, after a minute with Doris and her mother, I jumped over to the hotel, and from the side of a most billowy waltz partner I detached Shorty Erroll to get the ring and the smaller stores for a proper wedding, and then I went out to bespeak my own ship's chaplain. I found him lying in his bunk in his pajamas with a History of the Tunisian Wars balanced on his chest and a wall-light just back of his head, and he says: 'Why surely, Dick,' when I told him, but added: 'Though that old sieve of a *Bayport*, I doubt will you ever get her as far as Manila,' after which, carefully inserting a book-mark into the Tunisians, he glides into his uniform and comes ashore with me.

"And without Doris even changing her dress we were married—in the colonel's quarters, with every officer and every member of every officer's family on the reservation—even the children—standing by. And the women said, 'How distressing, Mr. Wickett, to have to leave in the morning!' and the men said, 'Tough luck, Dick'—and be sure I thought it was tough luck, and it would have been tough luck only by this time the entire post had got busy and got word to Washington, and at eleven o'clock, while we were still at the wedding-supper, word came to delay the sailing of the gunboat for twenty-four hours. And that was followed by a telegraphic order next morning to haul the *Bayport* into dry dock and overhaul her."

Wickett, who had been talking rapidly, came to a full stop, while three bells were striking throughout the fleet.

"Nine-thirty," said Wickett. "I thought I saw a steamer's light beyond the breakwater."

Carlin looked where he pointed. "I don't, but I haven't your eyes. How long was the respite?"

"In ten days they had her afloat again. I thanked my God-given luck for every flying minute of those ten days."

"And did she stay afloat long enough to get to Manila?"

"Oh, yes. She wasn't half bad. Needed a little nursing in heavy weather, but outside of that she wasn't hopeless at all."

"And what of Mrs. Wickett?"

"She was to come to me just as soon as I cabled where in the East the gunboat would fetch up for any sort of a stay. But I was never in one spot for long. We cruised from Vladivostok to Manila and back again, never more than a week in any one place. Even so, as soon as I'd saved enough out of my ensign's pay, she was to come—and she would have—to meet me; but before enough months of saving had passed she wrote me. There was a baby coming, and then I wouldn't let her come. I did not want her jumping from port to port in foreign waters before the baby was born, and she would soon be needing every cent of my ensign's pay that I could save.

"And the months rolled around and the cable came which told that the baby had come, and that Doris and everything was fine; and I was as happy as a man could be with a wife and boy he was crazy to see, but couldn't. She wanted to come out and join me right away, but I said no.

"Well, when the baby was big enough to stand travel she was coming, anyway, she wrote; but I reminded her that before a great while now I ought to be on my way home. And one day in the China Seas I saw the sun between us and the shore setting under a thousand golden lakes and pools and purple pillars, and a home-bound pennant of a full cable's length whipping the breeze in our smoke astern."

Wickett paused, and resumed: "That was a great night. It was two years and three months since I'd left Bayport. The first thing I did in the morning after turning out, and for every morning thereafter, was to step to the calendar on the wall of my room and block out that day's date with a fat blue-leaded pencil I'd got from the paymaster for that purpose alone, and then, estimating the run on the chief engineer's dope, count how many days were left."

Wickett was silent. He remained silent so long that Carlin thought that that must be the end, abrupt though it was, to the story. But it was not that. Wickett was pointing across the bay.

"See, Carlin—the flag-ship of the second squadron has just sent out an order for its first division to prepare for an emergency signal drill. And the first division are to have a torpedo drill at the same time. Wait—in half a minute it will be on. There—look!"

From the mastheads the red and white Ardois lights were winking even as the illuminated arms of the semaphores were wigwagging jerky messages from bridge to bridge; on shore, on the water, on the clouds, the great search-lights swept and crossed endlessly. It was dazzling. Suddenly it ceased. "Oh-h!" protested Carlin.

"Life is just like that, isn't it?" said Wickett; "all light and play and color for a spell, and then—pff—lights out."

"Maybe," admitted Carlin, "but don't impede the speed of the story. Your ship was racing for home."

"Our orders were to proceed by way of Suez and to

rendezvous with the battle-fleet at Guantanamo, Cuba. We got into Guantanamo the day before the *Missalama* arrived from the North. The *Missalama* had orders to proceed to the West Coast. Half a dozen of the officers already in Guantanamo were ordered to her. I was one of them."

"Good night! But that was a jolt!"

"That's what it was. But that's the service."

"And couldn't you do anything about it?"

"What could I do? There were my orders. A couple of the fellows came as near to being politicians then as ever they did in their lives. They tried to reach people in Washington—bureau chiefs, senators, influential congress-men—to have me detached and ordered home. But next day was a holiday and the day after was Sunday, and the ship had to sail by Sunday. And she did, and I with her."

"And how do you account for your being shunted off like that? Somebody have it in for you?"

"No, no—not that. Simply the politicians. I don't suppose the service will ever be free of the near-politicians. The navy has them—fellows who are not good enough officers to depend upon themselves alone, and not good enough politicians to go in for politics altogether. Somebody with a good shore billet somewhere was probably due for sea-duty, and not wanting to let go of a good thing, and having the pull, somebody else went instead. And somebody else for that somebody else, and somebody else again, and so on till at last the somebody else who could be made to serve a turn happened to be me.

"'Hard luck, Dickie,' said the ward-room mess. 'But cheer

up—in three months you'll see the Golden Gate, and by then you'll be ready for a little duty on your home coast. Then your lieutenant's straps and shore duty, and your wife and baby to yourself for a while.' I had that thought to cheer me through the night-watches around South America, but at Callao we got orders to proceed to Manila, and after six months out that way it was off to the Island of Guam, and from there to make a survey of some islands in the South Sea. No way I could fix it could I tell my wife to come and meet me at any certain place.

"But no task is endless. We were homeward bound at last. I remember how I used to say at mess that I was never going to believe I was home, till with my own eyes I saw the anchor splash in a home port. But there it was now—the anchor actually splashing in Bayport. I had the bridge making port, and I remember what a look I took around me before I turned the deck over to the executive. From the bridge, with a long glass, I could see above the tree tops the roof of the colonel's old quarters. I pictured him on the veranda below with the baby and Doris waiting for me. I'd sent a wireless ahead for Doris not to risk herself or that baby out in the bay with a fleet of battle-ships coming to anchor. And the baby! I dreamed of him reaching up his little hands and calling, 'Papa, papa!' when he saw me.

"Well, everything was shipshape. We were safe to moorings and I was relieved of the deck and about to step off the bridge when the word was passed that somebody was waiting to see me in the ward-room. And with no more than that—'Somebody to see you, sir'—I knew who it was. The fort boat had come alongside and people had come aboard— officers' wives and families, I knew, but not just who, because the boat had unloaded aft while I was on the bridge forward. But I knew.

"The messenger smiled when he told me. The men along the deck smiled when they saw me hurrying aft. The marines on the half-deck smiled as I flew by them. Everybody aboard knew by this time of my five years from home and the little baby waiting. Good old Doctor and Pay, going up to take the air on the quarter-deck, said: 'Hurry, Dick, hurry!' Hurry? I was taking the ladders in single leaps. At the foot of the last one, in the passageway leading to the ward-room, I all but bowled over a little fellow who was looking up the ladder like he was expecting somebody. I picked him up and stood him on his feet again. 'Hi, little man!' I remember saying, and thinking what a fine little fellow he was, but no more than that, I was in such a hurry.

"And into the ward-room, and everybody in the ward-room that wasn't occupied with some of his own was smiling and pointing a finger to where, in the door of my stateroom, Doris was waiting for me. And I dove through the bulkhead door, leaped the length of the ward-room country, and took her in my arms. For a minute, five minutes, ten minutes—just how long I don't know—but I held her and patted her and dried her tears.

"'And where's little Dick?' I asked at last."

"'Why, that was Dick you stood on his feet in the passageway,' she said, and laughed to think I didn't know him. 'But that's because he looks so much like you and not me. No man knows what he looks like himself,' she said, and ran and got Dick, and brought him to me, and said: 'Dick, here's your papa.' And Dick looked at me and he said: 'No, mama, that is not my papa. My papa has no legs,' just as I was going to fold him in my arms and hug him to death."

"And—will you still think I was only a kid?—I stepped into my room and drew the curtains, and sat down by my bunk

James B. Connolly

and cried. After five years! And Doris came in, and perhaps she wanted to cry, too, but she didn't. She drew a photograph from her bosom and showed it to me. It was the only one of me that ever suited her, and it happened to be only a head and shoulders, and every day since the baby was old enough she had told him: 'That's your papa, dear, and some day he'll come home in a great big war-ship with guns and guns, and then you'll see.' And the poor little kid, four years and three months old, had never seen any legs on the man in the photograph; but he had seen his mother cry almost every time she looked at it, and he supposed that was why she cried—because papa had no legs. And so the poor kid was waiting to see a man with no legs."

Wickett was silent. Carlin asked no more questions. In silence he, too, studied what was left of the night-life of the fleet. Only the white anchor-lights of the motionless battle-ships, the colored side-lights of the chugging steam-launches, were now left.

Carlin pointed out to Wickett a green light coming rapidly in from sea. "Another battle-ship, Wickett?"

Wickett shook his head. "No. I've been watching her. It's the *Clermont*. She's due. And I'm half afraid to go and board her."

"Why?"

"If my wife's aboard, she'll have with her a fifteen-months-old daughter that I have never seen. Suppose she, too, greets me with—She's swinging back—to her anchorage—look."

The green light rolled in a great half-circle inshore, and disappeared. A red light curved into sight.

Wickett jumped up. "Come on, Carlin, I'll get permission to leave the ship. We'll be there before she lowers the port ladder."

"No, but drop me at the landing on the way and I'll see you in the morning at the hotel. How's that?"

* * * * *

Carlin saw him before the morning. He was in the lobby of the hotel when Wickett with his wife, a fine big boy, and a lovely little baby girl, got out of the hotel 'bus. The boy was clinging to Wickett's hand, all the while talking rapturously of the trip of the *Clermont*. With his free arm Wickett was carrying the baby, which was murmuring, "Papa, papa, papa!"

Carlin would have known Mrs. Wickett without an introduction or the presence of the boy and the baby. Merely from the way she looked at Wickett he knew that this was the girl who had gone sailing with him in the dawn and become engaged before breakfast.

"It's all right," smiled Wickett, with his cheek against the baby's. "This one can't seem to say anything but papa!"

Carlin nodded, and whispered: "And you couldn't afford it?"

Wickett grinned. "We couldn't; but we did. We always do."

"And how about the service—going to quit it?"

Wickett stared at Carlin. "Quit the service!"

Suddenly he recalled, and laughed, and whispered: "Sh-h—! I'm due for a year and a half of shore duty. But don't mind if

　　　　　James B. Connolly

I hurry along, will you? I got to get these children to bed."

"Go on—hurry—and good night," said Carlin. "Good night, Mrs. Wickett," and handed her into the elevator; and smoked two thoughtful cigars on the veranda and then went inside and sat down and wrote a long letter on the subject of the navy as a profession to the mother of a young lad back home.

There was much detail, and then:

> As to being away from home for long periods: Married officers tell me that it is hard at times. But judging by what I saw awhile ago here, the home-coming almost offsets the long absences. The kind of a woman they marry probably makes a lot of difference. I'd say, let him go if he wants to. Good night.

> Your affectionate brother,

> SAM.

CROSS COURSES

Hearing the boys in the office talking of a lecture at the Sailor's Haven a few nights ago was what set me thinking to-day. It was on superstition, and the speaker digressed to expend ten minutes, as he put it, on sailors. A most superstitious lot, sailors.

He had a lot of fun with the sailors, and a crowd of old seafaring men sat there and let him, until a boss stevedore from our wharf who'd been one time mate of a coaster, with the preliminary contribution that this was sure the wisest party he'd listened to in all o' seven years, rose to inquire of the gentleman how long he'd been to sea.

Well, he had been to sea quite a little. Twice to Europe and return, once to Panama and return, once to Jamaica in the West Indies and—

"—return?" finishes our stevedore. "Sure you returned each time? 'N' in what sortivver craft'd you sail to them places—and return—in?"

"Why, steamers," answers the lecturer.

"Passinjer?"

"Passenger? Certainly."

"Excuse *me*!" says our stevedore. "I oughter known better. O' course, *you know* all about sailors," and sits down.

The lecturer was all right. He was doing the best he knew, with the finest and fattest of words he could pick out, to make things clearer to his audience; and his audience, appreciating that, let him run on, until he said that there was not one mysterious thing which had ever happened that could fail to be proved very ordinary by mathematical, or historical, or logical, or physical, or some other "cal" deduction; which bounced our watch-dog out of his seat again.

"How d'you 'count," he growls, "for th' *Orion* 'n' *Sirius*?"

Well-l, he could not account for it, for the simple and overwhelmingly conclusive reason that, previous to that very moment, he had never heard of the ships named.

"Then s'pose you hear 'f 'em now," says our stevedore, and starts in and delivers the lecturer a lecture on the *Orion* and *Sirius*, and it wound up the show; for when the lecturer started to butt in, all the old barnacles, who before this had been clinging warily to the edge of their seats, now rose up and rallied around our stevedore to finish his story, which he did; and the old fellows, on leaving the hall, said that the credit of the proceeds for the Sailor's Haven fund, for that night, anyway, ought to go as much to their old college chum from the coal wharf as to any imported lecturer with his deckload of lantern slides.

But our stevedore didn't tell all there was of the *Orion* and the *Sirius*. The lecturer went home thinking he had been told all about it, but he hadn't. Here it is as it was.

I

In the fleet of big coal schooners, which at this time were running from the middle Atlantic ports to Boston, the twin five-masters, the *Orion* and the *Sirius*, were notable.

They were twins in everything: built from the one set of moulds in the one yard at the one time, launched together, rigged together, sailed on their maiden trips together, and were brought home with their first cargoes of coal together by two masters who were almost as twinlike to look at as their vessels.

It was the history of these two big schooners, that they seemed always to be wanting to get together. Their crews used to say of them that if left anchored at all near each other in the stream, they would start right away to swing toward each other. Even if it was slack water they would. Yes, sir.

I can't speak from personal knowledge of that tide-swinging trick, but I do know that I saw them a few hours after they had twice smashed into each other—once under sail off the Capes and once in tow up Boston Harbor; and it was not to be doubted that in both cases they had more than drifted into each other. And of their near-collisions! A day's loaf along the water-front would yield gossip of a dozen or more.

Now, these next few lines are from out of the sailors' book of gossip of mysterious happenings at sea; and it is true that the more sailorly the gossip, the more likely will it be to try to account for unusual accidents at sea in a natural way; and the most usual reason given is inefficiency—lack of seamanship. As to that, it is true that lack of seamanship or of sea instinct has accounted for many calamities at sea, and the same lack would probably account for many another not so set down on the public tablets; but lack of seamanship won't account for all the queer happenings at sea. Every now and then comes a ship which no earthly power seems able to keep up with. From out of our superior shore knowledge we may deduce that the builder or designer was in fault, that there must have been an asymmetry in her hull, or that her rigging lacked balance, such defects tending to render her uncontrollable under certain conditions. Maybe; but there she is, as she is, with the malign fates seeming to be working double tides to get her.

"Hoodoo ships," sailors term such, and "Hoo-doos, both of 'em," the crews of the collier fleet early labelled the *Orion* and the *Sirius*. Yes, *sir*. And some day the pair of them were going up—or down—in a whirl of glory. If only they would smash only each other, and not go to putting poor innocent outsiders out of commission when they did go!—that was all they'd ask of *them*.

The master of the *Orion* was Oliver Sickles; of the *Sirius*, Norman Sickles; and they were from the same little hamlet in that Cape Shore region whence come so many capable sailormen. Each was named for his father, and their fathers were brothers who hated each other and brought up their children to hate each other.

It was curious to see them—two master mariners commanding sister ships for the same owners—passing each other on the wharf, brushing elbows in the office, putting to sea time and time together, sailing, again and again, side by side for days together, and yet never seeming to see each other. Indifference was the word; but if by any chance a third person referred to one in the presence of the other in anything like complimentary terms, that third person was soon let to know that he wasn't making any hit with whichever Captain Sickles it was who had to listen. If it was

Norman of the *Sirius*, he would shift his feet and start to stare intently at the ceiling or the sky; if it was Oliver of the *Orion*, with a snarl of disgust he would get up and walk off.

I had heard a lot of the Sickles cousins, but had never had more than a hailing acquaintance with either of them, until this early fall when my firm chartered, among others, the *Orion* and the *Sirius*, and sent me down to Newport News to see that they lost no time in loading and getting out. It was the time of a threatened coal famine in New England, with coal freights up to two dollars a ton, and my firm chartering everything they could get hold of to take the coal from the railroads at Newport News and rush it east.

In our two new schooner captains, Norman and Oliver Sickles, I found, when I came to have dealings with them, a pair who knew their business. Implacable toward each other they surely were, but so long as their feelings weren't delaying their sailing days, that was their own business. Tall, broad, powerful chaps they both were, twenty-eight or thirty years of age to look at, slow in thought, heavy in action, but competent sailormen always. I had no need to know their records, nor to talk with them too many hours, to find that out. Not much about a schooner, be she two or five master, nor much about the North Atlantic coast, that they didn't know.

I had been three months in Newport News, Christmas was at hand, and the railroad people were telling me that they would have no more coal for my firm until after New Year's. There were twenty thousand tons not yet gone; but if my four four-master schooners could sail next morning, and the five-masters, *Orion* and *Sirius*, get away the morning after, that twenty thousand tons would be cleaned up.

I hunted up the Captain Sickles of the *Sirius* and put the

question to him: "Captain Norman, if I can get you loaded and cleared by the morning after to-morrow, what's the chance of your making Boston by Christmas?" And he answered, after some thought: "It's a westerly wind with a medium glass to-day. It ought to hang on westerly and dry for another four or five days. Clear me by the morning after to-morrow, and I'll lay the *Sirius* to anchor in Boston Harbor Christmas Eve, or"—he was a man of serious ways, and spoke most seriously now—"or I'll give you a good reason why."

I hunted up Captain Oliver Sickles of the *Orion*, and I found him having a drink in the bar of the Tidewater Cafe. He looked as if he'd welcome a quarrel, but that was nothing strange in him. I put the same question to him that I had put to his cousin, and the answer came in almost the same words as to the medium glass and the westerly wind, but at that point he looked sharply at me.

"And when does the *Sirius* sail?" he asked.

"The morning after to-morrow."

"And"—suspiciously—"who first that morning, the *Sirius* or me?"

"I don't know. You'll be loaded and cleared together—it's for yourselves to say who sails first."

"And what did he say?"

Captain Oliver had a hectoring way about him which used to make me promise myself that some day, after he'd done hauling coal for my outfit, I'd tell him what I thought of him. "What did who say?" I asked him now.

"Warn't you talkin' to my cousin awhile ago about the

same thing?"

"I was, though I don't remember telling you about it."

"H-m," he sneered, "I thought so. Y' always go to him first."

"Yes, I do!" I snapped at him. "And why? Because he knows his mind. And he's a man to give an answer without using up an afternoon talking about it. He said he'd have the *Sirius* to anchor in Boston Harbor by Christmas Eve or give me a good reason why."

"He did, did he? Then set this down in your log"—with the end of a prodigiously thick forefinger he was tapping the bar as he said it:—"The *Orion* will be laying to anchor in Boston Harbor by Christmas Eve or there'll be a *damn* good reason why."

Right here I should say that there was more than a rivalry of craftsmanship between the Sickles cousins. Once, thinking it was the *Sirius*, Norman Sickles's sweetheart, a very pretty and a very good girl, had gone aboard the *Orion* as it lay in Boston Harbor. Oliver at once locked her in the cabin, put to sea, and carried her to Philadelphia, where, urged by her mother, and to save her good name as she thought, she married Oliver. But that her heart was still with Norman was current gossip in the fleet.

Because he had lately heard that I had been free-spoken in my comment on that exploit was why Captain Oliver now— his forefinger tapping the bar and he eying me from under his hat-brim—added to his "good reason" the word that, no matter what my firm or any other firm thought of this or that, which warn't none o' their business anyway, he wanted 'em all to understand that he was as capable of getting a quick passage out of a vessel as any Norman Sickles that ever walked; which gave me a fine chance to say: "Well, the place to prove that is at sea, and not in a barroom ashore."

Not very delicate—no; but it sent him almost on the run down aboard his vessel, to clear his decks for loading, which was mostly what I was after.

And I let it leak out—the answer of the two cousins about being in Boston before Christmas. A little rivalry of that kind doesn't do any harm; and I wanted to walk into the office on Christmas Eve and say, "The last of that Newport News coal is lying out there in the stream waiting to dock," and then go home, even as many of the crews would want to go home, with an easy conscience for a Christmas holiday.

II

People in my line used to say that I was pretty young for my job, and some of them to warn me about allowing the underlings to get familiar with me. Well, perhaps I was too young for my job, or for any other job of any account; but as to the other charge I never noticed anybody getting over-familiar with me. Friendly, yes; but even the head of the firm himself couldn't get over-familiar unless I let him.

Part of my job, as I figured it, was to know freights and ships and the masters of ships; and where it hurt the firm's interests if I knew the crews as well, I couldn't see. Some would tell me that the further away I kept from them the more highly they would respect me, and the more highly they respected me the more they would do for me, which would have listened well if their vessels were getting in and out of loading ports any faster than mine did; but nobody noticed that they were.

And beyond that: I could never see where a little friendliness to anybody did any harm. I may have been too young for my job, but I wasn't too young to know that the world is alive with unassuming little fellows who are full to the hatches with knowledge of one kind or another that they will cheerfully unload to anybody who has time for them. Not that I want anybody to think I am so long-headed or forehanded a chap as to spend time only with people who could tell me things! I didn't do any thinking about it one way or the other. Any man that had time for me, I had time for him.

I had time for Drislane. He was one of the crew of the *Sirius*, and I had been seeing quite a little of him while I was in Newport News this fall on the coal. The *Sirius* would load,

James B. Connolly

sail, and return; load, sail, and return; and between trips Drislane and I would have sessions.

I'd seen something of Drislane before this in Boston. His mail used to come addressed to our Boston office, where everybody knew that twice a year, toward the end of June and just before Christmas, a check would come to him from his home in the West. When he came up from the vessel after a trip and found that home envelope awaiting him, he would step around to his room, clean up, and in his shore-going suit of clothes come back, have us cash his check, and then, according to our office force, it was—Good night! for two weeks.

The check, always the same—for twelve hundred dollars—would have given him a good two weeks' whirl in highly-rated, expensive places, if he cared for splurge, but I guess he never was influenced much by regulation ratings. Any place he liked the looks of would do for him—and some perhaps that he didn't like the looks of.

It was no use to try to tell the office force that Drislane hadn't a weak joint somewhere. Man, they *knew*! and holding no berths for the purely spiritual, with but one suspicious and unexplained action to work from, would build you up a character of any depth of depravity you were pleased to have. Three guesses, no more, was all they needed for Drislane's case. It was rum, or women, or rum *and* women. If neither, then there was no hope for him at all—he was insane.

And certainly his judgment in women was something fierce. I'm setting down now the diction, as well as the judgment, of the office force; this last judgment being based on the evidence of the two illuminated occasions when he had come in to cash his check, and each time brought with him a young woman. Naturally, on his departure, the lads in the office had a word to say. The only way they could account for his selections—well, they couldn't account for them. It must be a genius he had—something was born with him—to pick the homely ones.

There wasn't the least evidence to show that there was anything wrong in these companionships of his. My notion of it was—he would never speak of it—that he picked up any kind of people in any kind of place, and made them as happy as he could while his money lasted. He certainly never went off for any two weeks' jamboree. Whatever his experiences were, they seemed to leave him in good shape physically, anyway. At least the marks of too many lonesome hours seemed to be ironed out of his face when he came back.

The man was so everlastingly unconscious that he was different from anybody else that it was refreshing. But there was more than that—to me, at least. I always looked on him as a touchstone, one of those men by whom you may gauge other men. Drislane was sensitized to crooks. He had only to stand in the same room with them to get their moral pictures. If I heard of Drislane distrusting a man or of a man disliking Drislane, I would at once set that man down, knowing nothing of the man, as having a rotten spot in him somewhere.

That was the Drislane who met me this night before the *Sirius* and the *Orion* were to sail for their last coal trip of the year, and asked me to have supper with him. And he took me to that same place where I'd had the words with Captain Oliver Sickles the day before—that is, the Tidewater Cafe—where was a drinking bar in front and a restaurant in back, a common enough sort of place, where women of the street could—and did—bring drunken sailors, and they served you pie with a knife.

I speak of that item of serving pie with a knife, not by way of poking fun at anybody; but here was a man five years away from his inland hills, for a whole year owner of an eating-place in a good-sized seaport city, and had not yet noticed that some people ate pie without a knife. By it I fancied I could gauge the man's social inheritance. And there were other customs of the place in keeping with the pie and knife. I used to speculate on what primitive sort of an upbringing he had that he was so slow to adopt the most ordinary civilized customs.

Drislane seemed to be at home in the place. So was I for that matter; by which I mean I felt safe enough. Several times before this, in my inquisitive ramblings about the port, I had looked in there. So far as that goes, there are not many places where they bother a man who doesn't bother them, always excepting, of course, that he doesn't get drunk and disorderly, and isn't naturally foolish.

While I was studying the place and the people, Drislane ordered supper. I paid no attention to him until he joggled my elbow. "What do you think of her?" he asked.

"Which one?" I asked, and looked about me afresh to note what worshipful creature it was I had missed.

"You didn't notice," he said, plainly put out with me, "the girl who is waiting on us?"

I had noticed her; but when she reappeared with the first part of our order, I noticed anew. A tall, full-bosomed girl she was, and as she walked across the floor toward us, a load of table things in each hand, she swayed from her hips like a young tree in the wind.

The physical force and poise of the girl was the notable thing about her. She carried her armfuls of dishes and food as if they were handfuls of marshmallows. She must have spent years working like a man in the fields to have developed such physical power. As to her face—it was innocent as a child's.

He introduced me when she had set down her dishes. "Miss Rose"—I didn't get her surname, and it doesn't matter. "Rose's uncle owns this place," he added.

"Poor girl!" I thought.

She met his enchanted gaze with a slow, red-lipped smile. To me she gave an embarrassed, half-sidewise glance. Strange men as yet were evidently disturbing items in her life.

He watched her when she left us, until she had passed through the kitchen-door and beyond sight. "I'm going to marry and settle down," he said.

"This young lady?"

"If she'll have me. I haven't asked her yet." He was fiddling with his bread and butter. Suddenly he burst out with: "If you knew how lonesome I used to get, and the things I was tempted to do to forget it!"

"A man doesn't need, son, to be entirely exiled from his family to believe that; but when you're married will you go to sea just the same?" I asked.

He did not answer.

I felt sorry for him. She looked to be a good girl, but I foresaw her troubles in a place like this while he would be away to sea. It would be a constant fight. She was possibly nineteen; she didn't look like a girl who had been tempered by temptation's long siege, and Lord knows what resisting power she would develop when so tempted.

From the fragments Drislane fed me with while she was coming and going, I learned that both her parents were dead, that she had been in the city only three months, that her uncle didn't seem to see anything strange in her employment in his place, and that Drislane was the first man who had shown an honest interest in her. "I take her to the theatre regularly," said Drislane. "I would to-night, only I want to sit in somewhere and have a long talk with her. You'd be surprised the things she doesn't know about the world."

"I wonder," I thought to myself, "if you realize the things *you* don't know about the world," and began to wish then for his own sake that he'd hurry up and take to looking at life through the same glasses other people used.

She was living in sordid quarters in a section where a woman was any man's who could get her, and on any terms he could get her; and she was of the type and at the age which has always been held most desirable by the primitive male; and it was to be doubted if she had had the religious or home training needful to an emotional nature. In a good home, in a community where a woman was respected because she was a woman, all would have been fine; but here—they married, and he most of the time at sea—I felt sorry for her as well as for him.

"Take her out of here when you marry," I said to him before parting.

He shook his head. "No, I had a scrap with my people leaving home. They're all right at home—the best—but they want me to get down on my knees to them."

"Better be on your knees of your own will to your own people than against your will to an enemy," I said, but it had no meaning to him; and I left him to his Rose, almost wishing that something would happen to him soon to shake him up, even if, shaking him up, it shook off a few of the purple blossoms that he thought so necessary to the tree of life. Thinking of him I almost talk like him in his absent-minded moments.

III

I left Drislane to go to the theatre with Captain Norman Sickles. The theatre over, he went with me to my hotel to get a few ship's papers I had for him. After that we sat in for a smoke and a chat.

Not that there was much chatting on Captain Norman's part. He never did have much to say of himself, nor too much of anybody else, though he could praise a man if he liked him. It was the first time I had ever spent more than an hour together with him except on pure business, and I was curious to know just what he thought of a lot of things; among others, of his cousin. I gave him two or three openings, but he didn't rush in. What he did have to say of him he said at one gulp. It was: "Where I was raised 'twas common talk that after you'd been getting naught but fair winds for a long course, it was then a good time to keep a watch out. The headwinds have to come some time, and the longer they be in coming the longer they'll stay with you when they does come. Oliver Sickles's been runnin' with a free sheet so long that I calc'late he's forgot there's such a thing as headwinds this side the Western ocean."

Even as Drislane, so did Captain Norman look like a terribly lonesome man at times. He probably was not yet over losing that girl who had been tricked into marrying his cousin. His cousin seemed to have got over it. There was gossip enough between Boston and Norfolk to hang more than a suspicion of that on—for that and the belief that not so much in marrying her as in getting the girl away from his cousin was where Captain Oliver had most likely achieved his main desire.

We talked until Captain Norman thought it was time for him

to be getting back aboard his vessel and turning in. As he stood up to go, he said: "'Tis said you like a little sea trip now and again? Why don't you go home with me in the *Sirius*?"

I was pleased at that—he was known to be not over-free with his invitations—and I thanked him, but on my not saying yes or no at once he looked chagrined; seeing which, I explained that early that fall his cousin had invited me, if ever I cared to return to Boston by water, to take passage with him on the *Orion*.

He tried to smile. He was a whale of a man, bashful in his ways. He smiled like an overgrown boy who had done something there was no harm in but of which he was ashamed. "He always appears to be gettin' in ahead o' me, don't he?" he said, wistfully-like, after a moment, which hurried me into saying: "But I never said I'd go with him, captain, and he probably thinks he knows me too well to ask me now. I want to go with you, captain, and"—I made up my mind then and there—"I will—and proud to have you ask me."

"Good!" 'Twas a real smile now. "And if the *Orion* hauls out with us you may see a wet passage, and maybe a bit of excitement of one kind or another before we make Boston Light."

We shook hands on the hope of a fast run to Boston, and then, drawing from my suit-case a package of receipts, coal memoranda, and so on, I held them up. "For the *Orion*, captain. Where do you suppose I'll find your cousin this time of night to give them to him?"

"Where but the Tidewater where that girl is?"

I stopped to put one thing to another. "And he is after that red-haired Rose, too?"

"What else?"

"But doesn't she know, or doesn't her uncle know, that he's a wife in Boston?"

"Her uncle!" he snorted. "He's no more wit than my ship's cat."

"But Drislane knows—won't he tell her?"

"He don't seem to. A proud one, Drislane. Six months he's been with me now in the *Sirius*, and if she isn't sure she wants him above anybody else on this earth, then she needn't have him, that's all; or leastwise, that's how I sense him. He wouldn't take no odds of the devil, that lad."

I could believe that; and it set me to thinking.

"Maybe you're thinkin' now," he went on, "that she should be able to see for herself what my cousin is? But what training has she had to judge o' men? What other kind does she see aught of in her uncle's place? Indeed, with her bringing up and what brains the poor girl has, she's done very well, I'm thinkin', to ha' kept off the rocks as long as she has. A hundred to one you'll find my fine cousin at the Tidewater to-night. But I must be going. Good night to you."

* * * * *

Only the bartender was in the front room of the Tidewater, and he was so busy peeking through a slide in the wall, the same through which he passed the drink orders from the restaurant, that he did not hear me come in. The door to the inner room was closed, but the low-powered roars of people trying hard not to be noisy were oozing through.

"What's doing?" I called to the bartender. I had to call it twice to make him turn around.

"It's the big captain of the *Orion* and that little deck-hand Drislane."

Anybody taking Drislane for a joke always did get my goat. "He's not a deck-hand!" I bit out, "he's a seaman, and a good one. But what about him and Captain Sickles?"

"It's about him an' the boss's Rose. The captain begins to abuse Drislane somethin' fierce, an' he comes back at him. Then the captain brings her into it. 'What would a girl be wantin' with a little runt like you?' he says; and after that, 'I dunno but I'll take her to Boston with me this trip,' and said it like he meant it. An' the little Drislane he jumps into him two-handed, an' they're hard at it now."

I squeezed inside the door of the inner room. "Man-to-man fashion!" I could hear, in the powerful voice of Captain Oliver, while I was crowding through the ring of people to the open space in the middle of the floor. "That's it—man fashion wi' the naked fists!" some scattering voices echoed.

Man-to-man fashion! As if man could invent an unfairer scheme to settle private quarrels! Give a man heavy muscles and huge knuckles, tough hide and thick skull, add half the courage of a yellow dog, and how can he lose at that game? The old-time duellists with their swords were a hundred times fairer. A long sword to his wrist and the smallest man had a chance; which is as it should be, or else we might as well pick some seven-foot, solid-skulled savage from out of the jungle and set him up for king.

Man to man! Drislane was five foot six and weighed, possibly, a hundred and thirty-five pounds, and was no boxer. Sickles was six foot three and weighed two-fifty. He had enormous muscles and knuckles of brass. His hide was thick and hard as double-ought canvas. Drislane could have stood off and pounded on his ribs for a week and hardly black-and-blued them. He could have swung on him for a month and not knocked him over.

It was the old-fashioned style of stand-up fighting. No regular rounds with a rest between. The men rushed and slugged and clinched and tugged, and when they fell, got up and went at it again. Always, when they went to the floor, Sickles let his two hundred and fifty pounds drop limp and heavy on Drislane. Drislane would almost flatten out under it. Standing up, when Sickles's fist landed on him he would wince all over. He felt pain like a girl.

It was slaughter. Blood, blood, blood; and the blood all on one side. For perhaps twenty times Drislane was knocked flat. If Sickles had only the explosive spark to go with those tremendous blows he wouldn't have had to hit Drislane more than once. But he could only continue to knock the little man flat; and knocking him flat often enough, the pounding finally told.

The time came when Drislane could not rise to his feet. He worked himself up to one knee, with the big man waiting for him to look up so he might deliver the blow more sweetly. Drislane, knowing to the full what was coming, looked up and took all there was of it.

This time he lay flat and quiet. The triumphant Sickles bent over him. "Y'are satisfied, are yuh?"

Sickles wasn't going to stop with beating him up. Drislane

must proclaim his conqueror's victory and his own defeat. Possibly he wanted the girl Rose to hear it. She had been standing back on a box in the kitchen doorway and must have seen most of the fight. I was wondering how far the joy of battle would mount in her primitive nature; but when I looked up to note that, and how she took Drislane's beating, she had gone.

"Are yuh? Speak up!—are yuh?" bellowed Sickles.

Drislane by now could open his eyes. He looked up at his conqueror but would not say the word. Sickles dug the toe of his shoe into his side.

I had been waiting, half sick to my stomach, for a good excuse to butt in. I had marked, when I first came in, a piano-stool setting upside down atop of the piano to one side of the room. In these possibly rough-house wind-ups it never does any harm to note where a few little articles of warfare may be picked up in a hurry. This piano-stool had a two-inch oak seat.

"You wunt, heh?" Sickles lifted his foot.

"No, he won't!" I butted in, and as he straightened up to see who it was, I went on: "And don't think I'll be foolish enough to go staving in my good knuckles on you. See this little wherewithal I'm holding, and not too loosely, by the wind'ard leg? You've a fine thick skull, but this is thicker. One cute little wallop o' this amidships of your ears, and it's little you'll care whether you take the *Orion* out on the first or the last of the flood-tide to-morrow. Let him be!"

Now, don't let anybody think I was making a play for any Carnegie medal thereby. I knew Oliver Sickles, and even better did I know his kind, who only go to battle when certain victory lies before them. The only chance I was taking was with my firm's interests. It might be that he'd have such a grouch against me that he'd carry no more coal for my firm than he could help in future.

He let him be. He put on his collar and coat, and received as his due the applause of that crawling breed which are never by any chance seen shaking hands with anybody but a winner. While he was still at the hand-shaking I threw him his ship's papers.

I had the bartender order a carriage, and while waiting I tried to cheer up Drislane. I told him that he must not think of going to sea next day, that I would see Captain Norman Sickles and get him off, and later go with him to Boston by rail.

He shook his head. He could hardly part his swollen lips to talk; and then could only half whisper. "I'll sail to-morrow on the *Sirius*," he said; and rolled his head over to see what Sickles was doing.

Sickles was just then stepping through that kitchen doorway where but two minutes earlier Rose had been standing. Drislane closed his eyes; and then, as if he thought he had to show me he wasn't beaten, he opened them and smiled. After I'd fully taken in that smile, I wished he had cried.

The bartender called through the slide that the carriage was waiting. I carried out Drislane, drove him to my hotel, and called in a doctor. Between us we gave him a hot bath, salved and plastered him, and put him to bed.

I turned in on a cot which I had had brought in. Hours after I heard him groan. I switched on the light and went to him. He was lying on his side with his head on one arm. His hands were clinched.

After a moment he said: "She is in trouble somewhere." That was another one of the things he believed in—telepathy.

He may or may not have had it right; but it certainly wasn't going to do him any good to let him lie there and be torturing himself. "Sh-h—go to sleep, son. Don't imagine things. You'll find everything will be all right to-morrow," I said.

"No," he said, "everything will never be all right while he's alive and I'm alive."

That didn't sound good to me, so I sat down by the bed and began to talk to him. We talked, I doing the most of it, until past daylight. We talked of her. "She's all right," he said at last, "I tell you she is. Even if she didn't like me and did him, it would be only natural. But she likes me—the best of her likes me better than him, and when she gets to know him all of her will like me. You'll see."

There were people who used to say Drislane was so innocent as to be a joke; but after that talk into that wintry dawn I had to salute him. He had just a little something on all of us who were so much more worldly-wise. It surely was a great gift he had—to see in every woman only the shining soul.

James B. Connolly

IV

No man could say where the word came from, no man could say that he had seen her himself; but the word was out that Oliver Sickles had boarded his vessel in the early morning with the red-haired girl of the Tidewater Cafe in tow.

Nobody on the *Sirius* ever intended to pass the word to Drislane, but no crew of a vessel can be whispering for hours without the one man they don't discuss the mysterious matter with wanting to guess what it is they are trying to keep from him. Drislane guessed.

I had brought him to the *Sirius* in a carriage just before she sailed. Captain Norman had told him to keep to his bunk until the *Sirius* tied up to the dock in Boston if he wished, but Drislane did not wish. He came on deck, still bandaged and battered, on the first morning out, to stand his watch. A word blown across the deck, when he was thought to be still in his bunk below, halted him in his walk aft. He turned and stared at the man who was speaking, whereupon followed such a sudden and foolish twist to the conversation that he might just as well have been told.

Throughout his trick at the wheel Drislane said nothing, but every moment the compass could spare his eyes saw them roaming across to where the *Orion*, like ourselves, was plugging through the short green seas for home. When his watch was done he borrowed my glasses, climbed by painful relays to the masthead and trained them on the *Orion*. After he came down and had gone below, I went aloft and spent the rest of the morning trying to see what it was that Drislane may have seen on the deck of Oliver Sickles's vessel.

Was it a woman's head showing above the cabin

companionway? or was it a man passenger Oliver Sickles had taken aboard at the last minute? If a man, he surely was no seagoer; for in the two hours that I watched he never once stepped out on deck. He leaned dejectedly, or it might be patiently, but, either way, motionless as a stanchion against the companion casing, his soft flapping hat and the shoulders of a loose coat showing just above the woodwork. Man or woman, the face was pointed steadily toward the *Sirius*.

Our captain said it was a passenger of some kind. It had to be, he said, because during the morning he had kept an eye on the *Orion's* deck and accounted for every man of her crew, which numbered exactly the same as his own; even for the cook, who had shown himself on deck to heave a bucket of galley refuse over the rail. It could not be an extra hand shipped for the trip, because no hand would be allowed to stand on the cabin stairs.

And did he think it was a man or a woman? The shoulders in the loose coat looked wide enough to be a man's. And I looked at him and he at me. So was Drislane's Rose big enough for a man, but we said no more of that then— Drislane had just come on deck and was making his way aft. Again he borrowed my glasses, went aloft, and trained them on the *Orion*. From time to time he looked down to the man at the wheel, as if to hint to him to get a little nearer the *Orion*, but the man at the wheel had already got a quiet word from the captain. We were to leeward. "Keep off—keep off—off—off—!" Captain Norman was saying in a low voice to the helmsman. "Don't let her get any nearer, leastwise while he's aloft with the glasses."

It looked as if we would have to wait to get to Boston to settle the question. Meantime, if Drislane would only try to forget everything of shore matters, he might be getting great comfort of a run like this. If he were himself, he would by

James B. Connolly

now, being half in the way of a poet and half hoping some day to be an artist, be drawing little water-colors and writing little rhymes of these two big schooners racing home together.

'Twould have been well worth his paint and paper. The *Orion* and the *Sirius* were two of the best in their class and more trimly modelled than most. What the *Orion* looked like we must have looked like, and she was something I used to spend whole watches on deck just looking at. She carried an open rail amidships, and her white-painted stanchions, carved to hour-glass form, with the white-painted flat hand-rail atop, stood clearly, sharply, beautifully out above her black lower sides and the pale-green seas.

Not that either of us had much lower planking to show, for four thousand five hundred tons of coal had brought us pretty well down to our scuppers. Too deep-loaded for our best looks, some would say; but I don't know—with all her jibs and all whole sail to her five lower spars, we must have looked pretty good, the pair of us, plugging along together through the curling rollers. We had set no topsails or staysails, because they would not have stayed on, blowing as it was a good half-gale.

It could have been blowing twice a gale and nothing happened to either of us. Probably no stiffer class of vessels sails the seas than the big coasters of our side of the North Atlantic. Give them plenty of ballast and there is no capsizing them. We surely had plenty of ballast in us now, and took cheerfully all the hard westerly had to give us, and foamed along. Foamed? We wallowed—like a couple of sailing submarines almost. In that wind and sea, with all that loose water sloshing around her deck, there was no careless standing around of course; but with rubber boots to your hips, a good oil-slicker to your back, and yourself lashed to something solid up to wind'ard, it was a great place for a man to let the wind blow away three months of coal-dust from his eyelids; and what the wind couldn't blow away the sea would surely wash out.

That loose water flopping around her deck—that was no harm. "Tarpaulin her hatches, clamp 'em down, and let her roll!"—that had been Captain Norman's word coming out of Hampton Roads. And "Batten her down and let her plug into it!" had come roaring across to us at almost the same moment from the deck of the *Orion*. And no more than into the open Atlantic than we were plugging into it. The sea came mounting up over our low lee-rails—up, up our swash-swept decks, clear across us sometimes, when for a moment a doubtful helmsman would let her ship an extra cargo. But, again, no harm in that. Let 'em slosh and let 'em roll—we were standing up, the pair of us, like two brick houses. And the rest didn't matter. And so almost forgetting Drislane's trouble in the strain of the race, we batted our way through the winter seas on which the sun was dancing—batted and slatted, plugged and slugged our way beside the *Orion* for the New England coast.

Two vessels may be built alike and rigged alike, but that doesn't mean they will sail alike. The *Orion*, in the judgment of seafaring folk, was a shade faster reaching and running than the *Sirius*. At any rate, the *Orion* proved to us that she was faster off the wind than we were by rounding Cape Cod before us. To there it had been a good passage. No collier loaded to her scuppers is ever going to break any sailing records, but hard driving had brought the pair of us along at a good clip. So far, fine; but it was to be a beat to windward for the rest of the way. West-north-west is the course from Cape Cod to Boston, and west-north-west was where the wind was coming from when it hit us on the nose as we rounded the Cape.

The *Orion* might outrun us, the *Sirius*, but to windward there was no difference except in their masters; and there we had the best of it. Norman Sickles could get more out of a vessel than his cousin when the going was bad. Oliver used to claw around deck like a sore-headed bear, and every now and then go below and have a drink for himself when things weren't breaking right. Norman took things more quietly, and so taking them wasn't too busy to grab every little chance that bobbed up.

The *Orion* stood off on one tack, we on the other, and by and by we lost her below the horizon; but standing in, after some hours found her again; and finding her, were pleased to see that we had made up something on her. We filled away once more, and by and by stood back to her. We were making distance fast. Had we held on we would have crossed her wake almost under her stern on that tack. On our next tack we would be crossing her bow, and it would then be on past the lightship in the lead, and the race over; for neither of us was going to tack up the channel, deep-loaded, against a tide which would soon be ebbing. Up at the harbor entrance two tugs had already seen that and were racing out to pick us up.

To more quickly get in tow of the tug nearest us, which was coming hooked up for us, our captain put the *Sirius* about earlier than he had originally intended. As we tacked, so did the *Orion*. We stood in toward the harbor. The *Orion* stood in toward the harbor. We were surely going to pass close to each other—very close. Altogether too close.

I didn't like the looks of things. Being a passenger, I had a mind free for other things than navigation. "In case of doubt who gives way—the *Orion* or the *Sirius*?" I asked Captain Norman. "Why, she does," he said, surprised. "It has to be her—not us. Both of us close-hauled, but we being starboard tack have the right of way. He'll have to come about and give us the road."

"But suppose, captain, he will not give way?"

"What! not give way! That'd be foolish. He c'n go bulling his way on shore all he pleases, but out here he'll only get what's due him. He'll have to give way."

So Norman Sickles said, but he wasn't the man to lose his vessel or risk men's lives. The *Orion* was holding on. She was going to force us. When Norman Sickles saw that, he motioned with his arm for the man at our wheel to keep off. But the *Sirius* wasn't keeping off. Norman Sickles turned and yelled: "Keep her off—off—off, I say!" starting aft, at the same time, to take the wheel himself.

He was too late. They seemed drawn together. We took a shoot. The *Orion* took a shoot. "Damned if she didn't get away from him!" I remember hearing one of our fellows jerk out, but I remember also I was left wondering whether he meant our vessel or the *Orion*.

They rushed together and g-g-h-h! Talk of a smash! Forty-five hundred tons of coal, nine-tenths of it below the water-line, and a breeze of wind! Either one would have sunk a battle-ship. It shook the spars out of the *Orion*. Her after-mast came down, the next one came down, the others were swaying. "The boat—the boat!" her crew yelled, but taking another look up at those wabbling masts, they waited to launch no boat. With few words but much action, they went over her side, one after the other, and began to claw out for the *Sirius*, on which—she was sinking too—our crew had a big quarter-boat ready to launch.

While the two vessels were still locked in collision I had seen Drislane come running from aft and leap into the *Orion*.

I lost sight of him then, because with our captain I had jumped below into our cabin, he to save his ship's papers and I to save my firm's. We were on deck in time to get into our boat, and help pick up the crew of the *Orion* in the water.

Looking for Drislane then, I saw him and Captain Oliver Sickles at each other's throats in the stern of the *Orion*. There wasn't much left of her above water then. And on her deck it was a mess of fallen spars, with her foremast the only stick left, and that—unsupported by backstays and the wind still pressing against the big sail—that was wabbling. Even as we looked it came down—lower and top parts—with a smash which snapped the topmast off and sent it twisting and gyrating to where, after a bound or two, it rolled down and pinned to the deck the two battling men in the stern. With it came a tangled mess of halyards and stays.

We had picked up all of the *Orion's* crew from the water and were now hurrying to get to the two men on the *Orion*, which was fast settling, when a red-haired girl came running from the cabin companionway. Almost as if she had been waiting in ambush, she rushed over to the fallen spar, untangled the halyards from the legs of one of the furthest men, and after an effort lifted the end of the spar so that he could scramble free. She needed to be strong to do that; but she was strong. If she had held the spar up only an instant longer, the other man might have wiggled free too. But she let it drop back. The man she had freed she picked up and carried to the quarter-rail, where she waited for us in the boat. He made an effort as if to get back to the man left under the spar, but she would not let him. "Tain't no crime, Honey," I heard her say as we got to them. She went overboard as she said it, and we had to hurry to get her. "I know him a heap better than you-all, Honey—let him rest where he done fall to."

She couldn't swim, but we got them in time. She didn't mind us in the least. "He done tol' me, Honey, you was dyin' abo'd yo' ship 'n' o' coase I goes on down to see. It sure did look like yo' own ship, Honey"—she was saying to him before we had them both fairly in the boat. It was Drislane she had, his head cuddled on her knees till the tug came and got us.

We weren't in time to get to the man she had left behind. The last we saw of him was his head sticking out like a turtle's from under the fallen spar as the *Orion* went under.

* * * * *

We were all in Boston by Christmas Eve; that is, all of course but Oliver Sickles—and nobody gibed at his memory for that. He had his good reason.

The tug rushed the two crews up the harbor to our dock, where I left them while I went to get carriages and warm clothes and so on. When I came back Drislane and his Rose were gone and no word behind them. But the day after Christmas he came to the office early to get his semiannual check and cash it. I wasn't there, but he left word for me that he and Rose were married, and he was going to take my advice and go home to his people. The office force said that with him was a girl of glorious Titian hair and super-physique, who smiled wonderfully on him.

Captain Norman married the girl he should have married in the first place. And so all the good people came happy out of it; all except our firm. Nine thousand tons at two dollars per ton—there was eighteen thousand dollars' worth of freights that we never collected.

* * * * *

James B. Connolly

So there's the *Orion* and *Sirius* thing, only, in telling it at the Sailor's Haven the other night, our old stevedore didn't say anything of Rose's part in it. He probably didn't see what that had to do with it. However, he said enough to convince the lecturer, who was a pretty fair-minded kind, that perhaps he would have to reconstruct his views about sailors' superstitions.

And perhaps there is something in it; but it's a poor case won't stand hearing both sides of the evidence. "Hoodoo ships!" It's a fascinating phrase, but—Oliver Sickles it was who held the wheel of the *Orion*, and it was Drislane to the wheel of the *Sirius*, when they came together.

LEARY OF THE "LIGONIER"

It was a gloomy house, set in the shadow of a rocky bluff, and made more gloomy within by the close-drawn curtains. Since the news had come of the loss of John Lowe's son, no man in all Placentia Bay could say he had seen those curtains raised; and, so ran the gossip, John Lowe being what John Lowe was, a long time again before those curtains would be raised.

John Lowe sat reading his black-typed, double-columned page by the table, and over by the stove John Lowe's second wife sat rocking herself.

John Lowe's daughter came in, removed her shawl, and took a chair on the other side of the stove. Her stepmother spoke a word; but no word of greeting did her father offer until his chapter was finished, and then he no more than half turned, while his harsh voice asked: "Has he come into the bay yet?"

"He has. Tim Lacy, that shipped wi' him out o' here, was to Shepperd's to-day—and he'll be to Shepperd's to-night, Tim says."

"Tim Lacy. Another o' his kin. And what would be bringin' him to Shepperd's to-night?"

"It will be a dance to-night."

"Oh, the dancin'! No fear but you'll know o' the dancin'. An' he'll be there, the drinkin', murderin'—"

"It's no' right, father, to be speakin' like that o' a man you never set eyes on."

"An' how come it you know him, girl? Where was it you had truck wi' him? Where?"

"I never had truck wi' him. But I see him. Who could help seein' him—he was in an' out o' Shepperd's his last time in."

"Well, take care you see him no more. An'—" A step outside the door caused John Lowe to pause.

"Ah-h—" John Lowe almost smiled.

His wife glanced at the clock. "It will be the trader," she explained.

"Aye, an' now we'll ha' the news—now we'll ha' the news."

A knock followed the step, and, following the knock, the door opened and in stepped the expected trader. No wild daredevil, no sail carrier this, but a smooth, passionless man of business. And he got right down to business.

"By dawn, John Lowe, there'll be two hundred men of the bay drawn up on Half-Tide Beach. And an hour later the *Ligonier* and all's in her will be lyin' on the bottom of the bay—or so"—he glanced doubtfully at the girl—"or so we planned it. Will you be there, John Lowe?"

"He'll no' be there, Mr. Lackford." Mrs. Lowe half rose from her chair.

John Lowe glared at her. "And since when is it for you to say I'll not be there?"

"I'm your lawful wife, John Lowe. And who is this man would tell you what to do? You read your Bible night and morn, John Lowe, and you tell me and you tell Bess we should read it, too, and all the bay knows it. An' how can you preach to us as you do an' join in this deed? 'Righteous shall be all my days,' say you, an' you think o' joinin' a band that will sink an' destroy—yes, an' mayhap kill in the morning. This American has as much right to what herrin' his men can ketch as anybody else."

John Lowe turned to the trader. "She's right, Mr. Lackford, she's right."

"You'll not be with us?"

"I can't."

"After all you said! Well, there will be enough without you." He was still addressing John Lowe, but it was on the woman his eyes were bent. "Only let me carry back the word you'll not be against us."

"No, no—I'll not be against you."

"That's enough. Good night."

"Good night."

The door closed. They listened to the crunching of the trader's boot-heels on the pebbly beach outside.

"They'll be killing, mayhaps, in the morning, and it's well for you to be clear of it, John Lowe."

"But he lost my son."

"It was a natural death for a fisherman, John Lowe, to be lost that way."

"But what reason to love him for it?"

"What reason ha' ye to hate him till you know more of him?"

Silence reigned again in the kitchen; silence until John Lowe set aside his book and made for the stairs. With his foot on the bottom step he paused and sighed. "Even after three months it's no' easy to bear. But you're right, wife, it's no' right what some of them be up to."

"No, it's no' right. An' he's not the man Lackford an' the others would ha' you believe, John."

He looked long at his wife. "No? No doubt no—but no stop to it now. If there was a way to slip a word and not be known for it; but there's no way. Come to bed, woman. But"—the girl was standing up—"where be you off to?"

The girl looked to her stepmother; and the stepmother answered for her.

"It's o'er-early for bed yet—she's goin' for an hour to Shepperd's, John. Go on, Bess, but don't stay too long."

The girl snatched her shawl and hurried out.

"And is't so you manage her, woman?"

"Let be, man, let be. She's no child to be managed—your way o' managin'. Why shouldn't she have her little pleasure? What's one here for? Prayers an' psalms, prayers an' psalms—"

"An' do you rail against the prayin'?"

"Not me. Prayin's for good, no doubt; but all of us hasn't the sin so black that it needs prayin' night an' day to burn it out."

He glared at her. "An' you're waitin' up for her?"

"I am."

"Some night you'll wait o'er-long, woman."

"No, no. She's young, is Bess, and a bit soft. But no bad—no, no, no bad in Bess. She's all we ha' left now, John—lay a light hand to her."

II

Up to old man Shepperd's the dance was on, and Bess Lowe was there; and not long before the American captain blew through the door; and no dreary passage of time before he spied Bess.

"Why, Bess, God bless you, how are you? And you ain't forgot? And do I get a dance this evenin' or no? Tell me, do I, now? Ay, that's you—hard-hearted as ever. Eyes to light a vessel to port, but never a soft look in 'em."

"My eyes, Captain Leary?"

"Ay, your eyes, Bess. Eyes, Bess, that the likes of never looked across the bay before—eyes that flash out from the dark like twin shore-lights when a man's been weeks to sea."

"Oh, Captain Leary!" breathed Bess; and presently took to sighing, and from sighing to smiling, and all at once burst out into such laughter that the whole company took notice; whereat a huge, surly man in a corner went into the back room.

"Gi' me one drink and I'll smash him into bits," the big man said to Lackford, the trader, who was standing guard in the back room over the little jug which Shepperd kept handy for his guests.

"What, now? No. Not now, please, not now. There'll be plenty of chances for fighting in the morning. The crowd is only waiting for daylight to make a move. They want you. Come on now, do, and get a good night's sleep so's to be feeling good in the morning. Come on now. And you'll have two hundred men at your back in the morning, remember;

and remember, too, that after you've put the American out of the way all the girls in the bay'll fall to your hand."

The big man was diverted, and passed out with Lackford, meantime that Leary, with an arm half around the girl's waist, was pleading: "The next dance for me, hah, Bess?"

"Ay, captain—who could deny you?" and they went at it.

'Twas a shuffling across the floor, a whirling of buxom partners by husky men, who never omitted to mark the measure with the thump of boot-heels that jumped the dust from cellar to roof. Shouting, stamping, joking, smiling, with quick breathing—such joy entirely it was, with Tim Lacy, oilskinned and jack-booted, leading the swing across the floor. Yes, and back again, although on him, even as on Leary, old Shepperd looked with disapproving eye.

"A wonder, Tim Lacy, you wouldn't leave your gear on your vessel," he snorted.

"Sure, an' I'm on my way to the vessel now, an' she'll be leavin' the bay for the States in the mornin'."

"You think she will," amended Shepperd, from behind the musician, who was his own strong-lunged daughter Sue.

On a chair atop of a fish-box in one corner was balanced Sue, a native genius, who puffed most industriously into a musical instrument made of a sheet of tissue-paper wrapped around a fine-tooth comb.

Tim Lacy, though he never let on, caught the sly remark. Less guileless than he looked was Lacy, a little man, forever lighting his pipe. He struck another match now, and between puffs delivered a belated message. So many years senior was

Lacy to his skipper that he used to talk to him like a father.

"You know, as you said yourself, we was to hurry, Sammie—and do come now, Sammie"—*puff*—"and hurry on"—*puff*—"to Half-Tide Beach"—*puff*—"and there we'll take the dory for the vessel. Ah-h, there she's goin'. No, drat her, she's out again! Hurry on, boy. We oughtn't be standin' here all night. The crew'll be waitin' for us wi' the vessel at Caplin Cove. A special word they left for you, Sammie. They says if you was here"—here Tim stepped close and whispered—"as how I was to tell you they're feared for trouble."

He peered over the flame of the last-lit match at his skipper.

"'Tell him, Tim,' they says to me, 'that if we're to get the last o' the herrin' aboard that they're afeard it'll have to be an early start.' I misdoubt"—*puff*—"they have a notion of how there was goin' to be trouble. So come on; do, boy."

"One more, Tim; one more dance before we break up. A crime to go out on a cold night like this and not have a farewell dance. Come on, Bess; what d'y' say? There's the girl!"

Tim was gone, but back and forth Sam and Bess sidled and stamped, and many another minute passed with Sam still whirling his able-bodied partner, pacing her across and back again, lifting her off her feet, and swinging her—one, two, three full circles off the floor. And Sam was the boy could do it, a hundred and seventy pounds though she weighed, and continued to whirl her after the last dance till they were out of the room and into the shadows of the porch, where he snatched her up and kissed her fair.

The girl's heart leaped out to him. Did ever such a man make landing in the bay before? And surely he must think the world of her? Tenderness for him overwhelmed her; and out under the stars she whispered the words of warning in his ear.

"What's it, Bess? You're not foolin'? The trader to the head of them?"

"Ay, an' they'll be at Half-Tide Beach afore the sun rises—"

"D'y' mean, Bessie, d'y' mean—"

"I mean all that's bad they'll do to you, Sammie. I heard 'em my own self. 'What right has this American to come here and take the herrin' from our very doors? What right?' That's the way the trader talked to 'em in the back room afore you came in. 'In the old days I've seen men beat to death on the beach for less,' I heard 'em through the bulkhead. 'Ay, an' their vessels run up on the rocks somewhere,' he goes on. An' it's you, Sammie, they has in mind."

"And the crew to Caplin Cove, an' only me and Tim to stand by the vessel. The vessel and her full hold. But who'll get the word to them? If only there was some one, some one we could trust, Bess!"

"There is one that could do that, too, boy."

"Who? What! Yourself, Bess? Could you make where they are—Caplin Cove—alone, and by night—and tell 'em what's in the wind, so they'll be aboard in time, while I go and hurry after Tim Lacy to the vessel at Half-Tide Harbor? Could a woman like a man well enough to do that?"

"Well, women likes men sometimes, Sammie."

"God bless you, Bess, of course. And sometimes, too, a man

likes—But, Bess!" She lay swaying in the hollow of his arm. "Bessie!"—and oh, the nearness of him! "I don't want to fool you, girl—we *was* carryin' sail the night your brother Simon was lost. A livin' gale, and she buttin' into it with a whole mains'l—you won't hold that agin' me?"

"How could I, Sammie? A man that's a man at all is bound to carry sail at times. And fishermen, sail-carryin' or no sail-carryin', they comes and goes."

"Ay, girl, and sometimes goes quicker than they comes. Oh, Bess, the fine men I've been shipmates with! And now 'twould take a chart of all the banks 'tween Hatteras and Greenland to find out where the bones of the half of 'em lie."

"But do go now, Sammie." She snuggled closer to him. "Have a care now, for I'm lovin' you now, Sammie."

"Ay, you are. And I'm lovin' you, Bess. But your father, Bess; he'll put you out."

"Well, if he do—"

"If he do, Bess, you know who'll be waitin' for you."

"Ay, I do. An' I'll come to you, too, no fear, boy. But no matter about John Lowe now, boy, so you won't forget me, Sammie."

"Never a forget, Bessie."

"Then hold me again, Sammie, afore we part. And don't forget—never a man afore did I like like I likes you, Sammie."

* * * * *

And Bess had gone and delivered her message to Leary's crew at Caplin Cove. "Be all hands aboard afore dawn and have her ready to sail," was Bessie's message, and with that put off for home in her father's little sloop. There had been stars on her run over, bright, cheerful stars that made you overlook the frost in the air, but no stars now. But that was the way of the weather in the bay.

In the lee of Shingle Spit it was calm enough, and so, for all the boom of the sea outside, Bess had time for revery. A gran' figur' of a man, Sammie Leary. Strong he was. Ay, strong. An' not stern. Lord knows, there was enough of that to home. No, no, saft-like same as Sammie—that was the kind for a woman to love.

And Sammie now. Out under the shadow of the porch he had said: "You're the lass for me." Ay, he did. But so many talked like that and meant naught by it, but took your kiss and your heart wi' the kiss and sailed away, and you never again see 'em, mayhap. There was Jessie Mann, and—Oh, no matter them. Sammie was none o' their kind o' men. An' yet—there were those who said that one like Sammie never made a good husband. Sailed wi' too free a sheet, he did. An' yet, did ever a vessel get anywhere without a free sheet at times?

And, thinking of a free sheet, Bess gave the little sloop a foot or two more of main-sheet. And there she was going through the water faster for it. And she would need to go fast through the water if so be she was to get home this night. And if she didn't get home—but 'twas o'er-early to worry about what her father would say.

But was it all so true about a free sheet? Was it no' true that, holdin' a vessel's nose to the wind, she'd sail her course wi' never a foot o' leeway? 'Twas so her father maintained.

James B. Connolly

Always safest to be on the straight course, her father held. True enough, but wi' the wind ahead, what headway? None at all—while, if you let them run off a bit, when they did come back on the course they was farther on the road, arter all. Ay, so it was. And Sammie? What did the poor boy ever know of a home or a lovin' heart to guide him! Oh, ay, women should make allowances for men like Sammie. 'Twas the good heart in him.

Out beyond the end of the spit the little boat began to feel the pressure of the wind and the thump of the sea. She jumped so because there wasn't much ballast in her. An' there was the matter o' ballast now. A gran' thing in a vessel, a bit o' ballast—like religion in a body. Not all religion, like her father, for then 'twas like a vessel loaded down wi' ballast—took a gale o' wind to stir her, and a vessel o' that kind was no mortal use whatever—except mayhap for a lightship or something o' that kind.

The sea by now was coming inboard regularly, and Bess knew she should be carrying less sail; but it would mean a lot of time to reef the mainsail, and if she was to get on there was small time for reefing, 'specially as the wind was hauling to the east. A beat home now, as Captain Leary warned her, 'twould be. Surely she would never be home by daylight now. And colder now it was. Ay, it was. She drew the tarpaulin over her knees, and that helped to keep off the spray which, as it splashed up from her bows, was carried aft in sheets before every squall.

And those squalls were frequent. And little pellets of hail were thickening the air. And over the tarpaulin that covered her the ice was making. Sailin' by the wind, 'tis terrible cold. She was becoming drowsy—hard work to keep from falling asleep. Good enough for her—ay, good enough, her father would say—dancin' half the night and carryin' messages to strangers the other half.

The air softened and that was some relief; but in place of the awful cold—and still cold enough—was now the snow. And in that snow-storm, with the wind continually veering, she knew at last she must have run off her course; for the sound of the surf beating against the rocks came to her.

And what would that be? What now? Ay, Shark's Fin Ledge it must be. She must ha' sailed wi' too free a sheet, arter all. Ay, she must ha'. Time to come about now. But not so much sail on! Well, sail or no sail, it was time to come about. About she was comin'—ay—she was—no!—ay—

Over came the boom, and then high it skied, and then the wind took it and slit the sail from boom to gaff and off to leeward went the sloop.

Too much sheet that time, thought poor Bess, and could have cried at herself. And might have cried if she had nothing else to do. But no time now. Her little sloop was rolling and pitching in the seas, and drifting, always drifting; and in that snow there was no seeing how fast she was drifting in to the ledge; but fast enough, no doubt.

No use wailing over it. Bess took to bailing, and the work kept her from thinking overmuch of herself; only she couldn't help picturing her father with his Bible, and her stepmother waiting up for her. And Sammie? Never another dance or kiss from Sammie. And oh, the black disgrace of it if she was lost in the bay, when maybe they found her body ground to pieces on the ledge! There would be those who would say—what wouldn't they say—of her that couldn't hide her likin' for him up to the dance at Shepperd's?

James B. Connolly

III

The tail of the night found Leary striding over the hills. "Going to heave her herrin' overboard, are they? And she'll never clear for home, hah? She won't, eh?" And over the hills he ran. In and out, up and down, over the crests, and at last down the tangled slope across moss-grown rocks where lay the tide-tossed kelp, and onto the beach, where in the dawn he came suddenly on them.

A great shout went up when they were certain 'twas he; and down upon him presently they bore.

"Two hundred of 'em, maybe," calculated Leary, and looked wistfully toward where his vessel should have been laying to anchor. "If I weren't such a hand for skylarkin' she'd be lay-in' there now with Tim Lacy standin' by the old six-pounder, and she loaded to the muzzle with nails and one thing and another, ready to sweep the beach of 'em." And somewhat sadly he waited for the mob; and, waiting, wondered how Bess was making out, for the squalls were chasing each other off the hills, and out beyond the little harbor, all whitecapped, lay the open bay.

As a sea sweeps up and buries the lone rock under its surge, so did it seem to Leary that the mob must overwhelm him as he stood there alone on the beach. Annihilation! Their gestures and imprecations, as they drew near, implied nothing less. "Well, let it come!" and from his mind flew all but one clear idea. He would deal them all the damage he could before they overbore him; and if under their heels on the sand they strove to crush the life out of him, he would reach up and grasp as many as his arms would circle.

And then he heard the hail from behind him. He flashed a

look. Yes, there was the vessel, and it was Tim Lacy calling. She was coming into the wind. Her jibs were down by the run. Ay, and there was the rattling of her chain-anchor.

"Skipper, oh, skipper," came the hail again, and he heard the hoisting of a dory. To one hand was the mob which meant his destruction; to the other hand by the open water to the vessel if he could make it. He had farther to go than they, but they were mostly in oilskins, and he was a rarely active man. That he knew. Away he went over the little bowlders.

Diagonally he had to go. A straight parallel to the beach it was for them. Fast as he was, some of them would intercept his way to the incoming dory. Three, four, perhaps a dozen would be there before him.

A dozen it was, and one huge man and Lackford, with no oilskins to hamper them, were in the front; and because they were in front they felt the force of Leary's arm. It would have been joy to stop and battle with them all, but that wasn't saving the vessel. He caught one with one hand, and one with the other—and it was so easy and so satisfying!

But that wouldn't be making Bess happy by and by. There were two more that he could have reached, but those two he dodged. But two now between him, and he was for stopping to box with them—the battle fever was getting him—but a voice came to him: "Don't stop for them, skipper. Come on. We're here."

Leary turned and saw, and raced for the water's edge. A wide leap and he was in the dory. They tore after him, minding not the fallen bodies in their eagerness. Up to their waists in the water they rushed with yells of rage. Stones came flying after him. A few struck him, but they were too small to do damage.

From the dory Leary faced them again. "That's you—two hundred of you—you spawn of dogfish."

"Blast 'em, Sammie, don't talk to them. Out oars, Ned, and drive her! Here's the kind of talk for the likes of them!" and between his skipper's arm and body Tim Lacy from behind thrust an old-fashioned heavy dragoon pistol. "Only one shot in her, but make that one good; here y'are, Sammie."

Leary's fingers curled about the stock of it, and it felt pleasant to the touch. Yet for all that he thrust it back, but as he did so Tim's dory-mate tumbled down beside Leary in the dory. On the bottom of the dory the jagged rock was rolling even as the blood welled from his temple. And then came a report—another, and a third; and with the third a bullet whizzed close.

"Blast you all!" shrieked Leary, and with a leg either side of the fallen man's body he held the pistol waist-high. "Come on now! Come on now, I say! *You*, and *you*, and *you*, you white-livered—"

"After him—drag him out of the dory!"

"Ay, drag me out! Come you and drag me out!" And threatening variously with his pistol, Leary pointed directly at what seemed to be a new leader, a man with a revolver. "And let me tell you"—he pointed to the armed man— "whoever you are, you round-shouldered, glue-eyed squid you, whoever goes, you go first. Mind that—whatever happens, *you* go first. I've got *you*, you pop-eyed, slit-mouthed dogfish—and now shoot again."

The man with the revolver shrank back; but Leary's pistol was still trained on him, and farther and farther he shrank until he melted into the body of the crowd.

In the rear of the crowd were those who struggled to get nearer. "Why don't you go after him down there?" they yelled. "Or let us do it? One man against you all! Why don't you pull him out of the dory?"

"Ay, pull him out! Send him to hell!" roared another.

"Well, send me to hell," retorted Leary—"maybe I've got friends in hell, too!"

Back onto the beach receded the mob. Leary turned to his mate. "To the vessel, Tim—and drive her!"

By the time they reached the vessel's deck the injured man came to. A cup of coffee and five minutes by the fire and he was ready to turn to, but Leary turned him into a bunk instead. "We've men enough without you—a full crew. Lie down, boy, and go to sleep." Which he did.

"Now, fellows, make sail. Drive her. The trader an' that whole crowd, they'll be after us soon in their jacks. Come on—lively—there's thirty sail of 'em ready to round the point! An', Tim?"

"Ay, Sammie."

"Get out that old salutin' six-pounder and lash it for'ard o' the windlass. Lash her hard so she won't kick overboard when she's fired."

"Ay, Sammie," and Lacy hurried off.

"And now, up with the jibs. And then mains'l—we've lost a lot of time already. With her four lowers and those squalls shootin' off the high hills from the other side of the bay, she'll soon have wind enough. And we've got to be out of here before the snow sets in. A bad place here in thick weather. Drive her, fellows—drive her!"

They were swaying up the mainsail when Leary happened to look over his shoulder. With the wind of the frequently recurring squalls taking hold of the great sail, they had a hard task to get it up; but at last it was set; and then they trimmed in the main-sheet, while Leary ran forward to the howitzer.

"What you got to load it with, Tim?"

"There's black powder enough, Sammie."

"But we want to do something more than salute 'em, Tim."

"M-m—there's the soundin' leads, Sammie."

"Get 'em!" And Tim went and came back with a deep-sea lead which he rammed in after a hatful or so of powder.

When all was ready four inches of the lead stuck out of the muzzle.

"No matter; you'll do," Leary commented, and cast another look toward the open water of the bay where were now twenty-five or thirty small schooners rounding the headland.

Leary now contemplated the anchor chain of his vessel.

"I hate to lose you, 'specially like this, but—" And without further word he reduced the chain to one turn of the windlass. "And now let all hands tuck away under the rail, all but one man to go aloft and look out for a small white sloop." And he took the wheel, where he was needed, for the squalls, in full force, were now whistling battle-hymns from deck to truck.

The fleet of jacks were now to be seen coming on rapidly; but presently, the squall proving too strong for them, they all came fluttering up into the wind and began to shorten sail.

"No heaving-to for this one, eh, Tim?" yelled Leary; and putting his wheel up, and feeling the *Ligonier* beginning to pay off and the anchor to drag, he gave the word to slip the cable.

Through the hawse-hole the clanking chain tore swiftly, and away came the *Ligonier* like a wild thing. Leary patted the wheel and began to talk to her:

"Crazy to get away, aren't you? Been laying too long to anchor, yes. No wonder. And I'll not stint you now—take your fill of it, girl." Which she did, and with Leary giving her plenty of wheel, through the white swash she scooped a long, wet rail.

Tim Lacy now came aft. "There they are waitin' for us—an' the joke of it is, Sammie, we c'n go out the North Passage with a fair wind. They must 'a' forgot that I was born and brought up in this very bay."

"But we're not goin' out the North Passage, Tim."

"No?"

"No."

"But why? An' it's a beat up by them."

"Well, a beat it'll be. Go for'ard now."

"What'll he be at now?" muttered Tim.

But Leary knew. One eye he had for the approaching fleet and one to the ledge of rocks toward which the *Ligonier* was winging. "Some of 'em, by this time, think we're trying to run away. But they'll know better in a minute. And now do you, Tim, stand by that old cannon."

She was almost into the rocks then, holding in for the last foot of clear water; but not for too long did he allow her to run on. Just in time he tacked, and then it was about and away, for the fleet of native schooners, who, watching her closely and assured now of her course, spread out to intercept her. Expert seamen themselves, nowhere did they leave a space wide enough for a rowboat, let alone a ninety-ton fisherman, to slip through.

And they were armed. A shot rang out. Leary looked to see where the ball struck, but among the endless merging of whitecaps there was no discovering that. "Not that I care where it hit, blast ye—ye'll never stop me now—for—hide under the rail you, Tim, with the rest—I'm after some of you." And he headed the *Ligonier* straight for the windward jack, which now he could see was that of the trader Lackford, whose round-shouldered figure in the bow betrayed him.

"Out of my way!" roared Leary before he realized that he was too far away to be heard against the whistling squall. "But you'll hear me well enough soon," he muttered. "And, Tim, so long as you won't hide away, stand by that old fog-buster, and be sure to have the lanyard long enough to let you hide behind the forem'st, for there's no telling—the old antiquity might explode. I don't s'pose she's been shot off this ten years. When I give the word, now—but wait, wait yet!" For a flying moment he brought the *Ligonier's* head into the wind. "Now!"

Boom! It made more noise than a modern six-inch. They could see the long lead go skipping under the bow of the trader's jack.

"Heave to!" roared Leary, "or the next one goes aboard." No question but they could hear him now. "Heave her to, I say! Ay, that's right. Load the old lady again, Tim. And now"— his voice rose high again—"you'd better all heave to, and stand aside, for this one's bound out, and 'll come blessed handy to cuttin' in two whatever gets in her way."

And they luffed, twenty-odd sail of them, with six to eight men aboard each, and stood to attention while the *Ligonier*, with her crew's inquisitive, grinning faces poked above her rail, came tearing up and by.

"And now let be your batteries, Tim, and run the ensign to the peak." Which was done; and passed on in glory did the *Ligonier*, the old six-pounder adorning one rail, a swish of white foam burying the other, the colors aloft, and Sam Leary singing war-songs to the wheel. And perfectly happy would he have been only the snow was thickening and no Bess in sight. But maybe she had got safely home. Maybe. And just then came from aloft:

"There's a little white sloop—an' some one in it—at Shark's Fin Ledge a'most."

"Break out that gaff tops'l, fellows—and you, Tim, go aloft and point the way—and hurry, afore the snow comes."

"Point the way to what, Sammie?"

"For a little white sloop with a girl in it."

"Ho-oh—that's it, is it?"

James B. Connolly

IV

Bess had curled herself up and was falling asleep; and her last sleep it would have been but for the boom of a small gun and the hail of a familiar voice. She stood up. Again a hail. And through the curtain of white it came almost atop of her, the grandest schooner ever was! The long lines of her seemed familiar. Then a clearer glimpse. Ay, she'd know her anywhere—by the rust on her jumbo she would—the *Ligonier*. And then it swept on by—ay, sailing as a wild gull.

Out of sight it went in the snow-squall, but leaving a voice in its trail.

"Bessie! Bessie!" it called.

And now no schooner at all. Gone it was. And she remembered that that was the way of it—the beautiful picture afore they went at last. But soon again the sweep of the great white sails and the black body beneath. And the beautiful handling of her! "Seamen, them!" said Bess admiringly, and then alongside it came—beautiful, beautiful.

Then two arms scooped down and swept her over the rail of the lovely big American schooner. A strong arm and a voice. "Oh, Bessie! Bessie! and the big, warm, foolish heart of you!" said the voice, and the arms carried her below and wrapped her in blankets and poured hot coffee, mugs of it, down her throat, and laid her in a bunk, while he sat on the locker and looked—just looked at her.

"Ah-h, Sammie!" murmured Bess blissfully. "An' now you'll bring me home, Sammie?"

"Ay, home, Bess."

"Ah-h! An' my mother'll no ha' to cry for me, arter all. An' father, too, he'll ha' no cause to—Ah-h, God love you, Sammie."

* * * * *

By the light of the kerosene lamp in John Lowe's kitchen sat John Lowe reading his favorite volume, harrowing tales of religious persecution centuries agone. And Mrs. Lowe sat rocking herself by the stove. Every once in a while she would hide her head in her skirt, and, on withdrawing it, wipe her eyes.

Now and again she would sigh wearily. "Too harsh, too harsh we were on the lass. The blood runs warm at her age."

Whereat John Lowe would turn and look fixedly at her, open his lips as if to say something but, always without speaking, refix his attention on the fine black print before him.

A knock on the door and a tall man in oilskins and sea-boots entered. "I've come to say—" he began: but by then John Lowe was on his feet.

"Captain Leary is it?"

"Captain Leary it is."

"Then, I've this to say to you, Captain Leary—"

"Hush, John. Captain"—beside her husband Mrs. Lowe stood trembling—"Captain Leary, we've a little girl—an' the story's around the bay—"

Leary raised a hand. "I know, ma'am; I know. Your daughter, Mrs. Lowe, she's safe. Yes, John Lowe, safe—in every way safe. No thanks to me, but to herself. And she and me, we're going to be married. Yes, ma'am, married. Don't look so hard, man. You're thinkin' now, I know—you're thinkin' it's a poor pilot I'll be for her on life's course?"

"Ay, I'm thinkin' so, captain, and not afeard to say it—I fear no man. Ay, a poor compass."

"Compass? There—a fine word, compass. But the compass itself that 'most every one thinks is so true, John Lowe, we have to make allowances for it, don't we? And after we've made the allowances, it's as though it never pointed anywhere but true north, isn't it? There's only one circle on the ocean, John Lowe, where a compass don't veer, but every ship can't be always on that line. And even when you're sailin' that one circle, John Lowe, there's sometimes deviations. And me—no doubt I have my little variations and deviations."

"Ay, no doubt o' that," muttered John Lowe.

"Ay, like everything and everybody else, John Lowe. But at last I've got to where I think I know what little allowances to make. I think so. And after we've made our little allowances, and we c'n make 'em in advance same's if we took it from a chart, why—there's Sammie Leary as true as the next one."

Mrs. Lowe laid her hand on the American's arm. "And Bess, captain; where is she?"

"Outside, Mrs. Lowe, with Tim. And she's waiting."

"Waiting for what?"

"To be asked inside. Will I call her?"

"Call her, captain—call her."

"Yes, Mrs. Lowe, but—" Leary faced the man at the table.

"Oh, well"—John Lowe sighed. "No doubt you ha' the right o' it, captain. You're one who ha' sailed many courses, an' your navigation, 'tis possible, is better than mine. Call her, captain, call her."

Next morning, for all the bay to see, the curtains in John Lowe's house were raised high.

HOW THEY GOT THE "HATTIE RENNISH"

On the word being passed that Alec Corning was back from the West Coast, a few reminiscent friends went to hunt him up, and found him in the Anchorage, in a back room overlooking Duncan's wharf; and Alec was agreeable, over a social glass and a good cigar, to explain how it came he was back in Gloucester.

"If they'd only let us alone I'd 'a' got—and Archie Gillis too—good and rich."

"Rich, Alec? You rich?"

"Well, maybe not quite rich, for that, o' course, would call for saving, but certainly I'd had a roll to spend before I was done—if only they'd let us alone. But would they? Man, the meddlers they were!—the brass-buttoned, steam-winched buttinskis!"

"But if that is their business, Alec?"

"M-m—maybe. But Russians, English, Japs—yes, an' American cutters and gunboats before they were done—you ought to seen them!"

Alec paused, but only for a quick breath. "We had the finest little scheme of sealing till they took to hunting us. Up and down the length and breadth of the sealing-grounds they'd up and chase us whenever they'd get word of us—from the Japan coast back by way of the Aleutians—clear down, one time, a pair of 'em, till we had to put in behind Vancouver Island and hide the *Hattie* behind a lot o' screen boughs."

Alec paused; this time for a longer, an almost reflective, breath. "That being their business, p'r'aps they were all right; but ain't it a fine thing when a gang wants to go seal-hunting that a lot o' gover'ment people must specify where they can kill 'em, and when?—and they swimmin' the wide ocean as the Lord intended! And our little vessel—the *Hattie Rennish* when she used to go fresh halibutin' out o' here—remember her?"

There were several who heartily remembered the fast and able *Hattie*.

Presently, letting the elevated front legs of his chair drop to the floor, Alec rested one forearm on the table and went on to tell of how at last they got the *Hattie Rennish*.

"'Twas a Californian man named Trumbull bought the *Hattie* when she was fresh halibutin' out o' Gloucester. A good sort of a man, and 'twas him got me, with Archie Gillis for mate, to bring her 'round to Frisco."

"But the time I'm going to speak of, the *Hattie*—painted green she was, and called the *Pioneer*—was layin' into Seattle, when a chap comes aboard with a letter from Trumbull to me explaining that certain aspects of the sealing business 'd been taking on a serious look to him lately and he'd sold the *Hattie*, and the party who'd bought her, letter herewith, might want to do business with me."

"The looks of the new owner didn't warm me toward him in the start-off. Looks, of course, ain't everything, but when you don't know much about a man you got to go a lot by his looks. Yes, you sure have. And I'd seen him before, joy cruisin' on the Barbary Coast one night with a lot of drunken sailors—only he wasn't drunk. And I knew what he was— some Chinese blood in him, and the name o' being a slick one. But I didn't say anything about that. Gratu'tously telling a man you don't like him don't lay you up to wind'ard any. No. And we sat down and he explains what he wanted. There was a consignment of a few bales of hemp waiting up on the British Columbia coast, and would I run the *Hattie* over and slip back with 'em? And we'd have to leave right away."

"Well, I would—after a talk. And with Archie Gillis and a few hoboes that called themselves sailors, which I'd picked up in Jack Downing's place in Seattle, we put out. Archie was mate and to get two hundred dollars and me five hundred."

"It was a fine night, that night, and we put out into the sound and worked our way up through the islands, and the second morning later slips into a little cove behind some high hills with trees along the banks—in Georgia Strait. Twenty-four hours we lay there, and then we hears a steamer's wheel, but we don't see her; only a couple of hours later the owner comes for me in a big ship's quarter-boat, and we work the *Hattie* over to a little island where we find a lot of bales wrapped in burlap and hid in a cook's shack."

"'That all?' I asks my new owner—Durks his name."

"'Oh, yes—there's a couple o' Chinamen here. But let's see— where are they?' He looks around. 'They're not here— strolling in the woods somewhere. We'll take them along, too,' he says. 'You won't mind that, will you?'"

"Now there was nothing in the contract about Chinamen, and I didn't like the notion of him working 'em aboard in that way, but I said all right and soon as dark came we'd roll 'em aboard and put out."

"Well, the boss and I sits down to lunch in the cook-house, and by and by, with nothing to do but wait for dark, we stroll around the island. Now I'm no wizard in anything, but I always did have a good ear. And no harm at all, a good ear, when you got to do most of your own watching out. Before we'd gone far I knew somebody was trailing me and the new owner. I could hear steps behind us an' dead twigs snapping and somebody shoving aside branches, and once, when we stopped for a talk on the edge of a clearing, I knew I heard somebody breathing just behind the bushes which was hanging over the logs we were sitting on.

"Now I knew that this Durks wasn't very popular in the quarters where he did business, and 's I wasn't aching to have any Chinese tong man hit me over the head with any hatchet by mistake in a shaded wood, I just naturally fell out of step and lost him, and being some trailer myself, I took to trailing whoever it was 'd been trailing me and Durks, and by and by I come up behind him, and when I do I grip him where he won't make too much noise nor do me too much harm till I let him. He wasn't a very big chap, nor any too strong, and I sets him down on the nearest old tree trunk and—'What is it?' I asks.

"He looks at me and shakes his head and says, 'No sabby,' and I looks at him and I shakes my head and says: 'Oh, yes, you do, Johnnie Sing. I wasn't wearing any whiskers when I used to meet you in Wall-Eye Bunsen's place. I've cultivated them for protective purposes only, to hide my face but not my intelligence—so you just overlook them and try and recollect Alec Corning. Now what d' y' say?'"

James B. Connolly

"'Halloo, Captain Corning!' he says; and, no pretending, he was glad to see me."

"'Whitely,' I says—'Bill Whitely when you say it out loud. What's your trouble, Johnnie?' And so you c'n all get it right, I ought to say first that Johnnie Sing was a sort of Americanized Chinaman, who the last time I'd seen him was inquiring if he couldn't become a real American some way. He'd been born in Lima on the West Coast, where there's a big colony o' Chinamen, and he was part Chinese, the rest of him Peruvian Indian. A Christian, too, he was; which I'm not putting up as being for or against him, except so you'll see he had as much right to be a Christian as anything else. His mother was Christian, and so it wasn't like as if he had turned against his own to get on in the world."

"Johnnie was a good sort, and he'd made a few dollars in the tea business, and so maybe ought to 'a' been happy. But he wasn't. There was an old Chinaman, and not too old either, who'd married a Finn woman came off a wrecked Norwegian bark. They ran a laundry together, and by'n'by they came on to Frisco and ran a laundry there. And Johnnie followed them. A good woman, and she died leaving a well-grown little girl, and by'n'by the old fellow he figures he's made enough and goes back to have a look at China. But no sooner there than he learns he won't live very long, and he writes Johnnie of it, or maybe it was the girl did, her and Johnnie having been always about three-quarters in love with each other. And Johnnie he cruises over to China, and the old fellow, savvying how things are, says all right, marry, and they get married, and he gives 'em his blessing and lays down and dies. A good old scout, Johnnie said, and I guess he was."

"Well, everything's fine, only Johnnie wants to come back and live in the United States, and the girl too. She was sixteen years old when she left California, and a woman's life in the United States looked a lot better to her than in this land of one-half her ancestors. So she and Johnnie takes a steamer to Vancouver, and they get there all right; but not till they got there did either of them happen to think that they were foreigners and barred as Chinese from coming into the United States. Which was a pity, they being pretty white and so strong for everything American. Anyway, Johnnie writes to Trumbull, my old boss, to see what he could do, and after ten days or so Durks happens along and bumps into Johnnie and is surprised as you please to see him, and Johnnie tells him his story, and Durks tells him not to worry about that—that he'd smuggle him and his wife across in a schooner he'd just bought. They would take a little coast steamer and meet her a few hours up the coast, and then across the sound to Seattle—'twould be the easiest thing ever you see."

"And there they were, Johnnie and his wife, and when he got that far in his story Johnnie stops and looks up at the sky most mournful-like. Springtime it was, mind you, and fine weather, with the sun shining and the waters of the inlet rolling up on the rocks gentle-like, and the first of the birds were up from the south and singing and chirping, and, I s'pose, nesting overhead—a bran'-new spring day in a piny grove on a pretty little island off the coast of British Columbia, when anybody should 'a' been happy, 'specially with a new young wife.

"'Well, what's wrong—what you so blue about?' I asks Johnnie when he'd got through squinting up the tree branches to the sky."

"And he tells me how after his wife was aboard the steamer which 'd brought 'em to this place she sees Durks and tells Johnnie how Durks came near kidnapping her one time—before she went back to China with her father. Her father and

James B. Connolly

Durks had a terrible row over it. Her father near killed Durks with a hatchet. And now here was Durks turning up in this accidental way; too accidental altogether—for Durks. He would steal her or something, and once he got her into San Francisco they could be swallowed up with her. Huh—a Chinese row, the police would say, and not bother too much. Not like stealing an American girl. 'And if he gives me over to the police, I am not an American citizen—out of the country I must go,' winds up Johnnie.

"Terrible downcast is Johnnie Sing, but I stands him on his feet and tells him to cheer up. Durks was head of the expedition, yes, and paying the bills, yes; but me, Alec Corning, was skipper of the *Hattie*. 'Go down and tell your little wife that everything'll be all right,' says I—'that Alec Corning'll be on the job. Where is she?'"

"'She is here,' he says, and whistles, and out from the brush steps a cute little girl dressed like a man, and with a hard hat to make her look all the more like a man. Johnnie lifted the little hat, and under it she has a lot of yellow-ash hair coiled up where a reg'lar Chinaman 'd have only a black pigtail."

"'Don't let on to Durks either of you ever saw me in your life,' I advises 'em, 'and when it's time to go aboard the vessel you go.'"

"And they went aboard with what Durks says was bales of hemp; and we put out that night in open water, and next day threading inside passages so far as we could. Another night and another morning found us in Puget Sound, and there on a little neck of land on the American shore we hoisted our load of hemp onto a little, rough-made wooden pier. A narrow-gauge track ran up from the pier, and standing on the track was a hand flat car."

"'Now,' says Durks, 'I will pay off" these men, so they won't be hanging around and possibly talking too much before we get clear.' And he did— ten dollars to the hands and fifteen to the cook, and a silver dollar all around for car-fare. And they went ashore, he telling them where they would find a little branch station about a mile up the road to take them to Seattle. And so we got through with them.

"He himself goes ashore after they're out the way, and stays an hour or so, and when he's back, 'How about paying off me and my mate now?' I asks."

"'You take the schooner to a little place west of here and then I'll pay you both off,' he answers."

"'And how about landing those two passengers?' I asks."

"'No, no, don't land them here,' he says. 'Somebody might see them and pounce on us for landing them. Keep them aboard for a while—to the next anchorage.'"

"And we put out late in the morning then, and, there being no wind, 'twas in the middle of the afternoon before we came to anchor in a little harbor about five miles from where we landed the cargo. And we'd hardly been there when an American gunboat comes to anchor just off our hiding-place, and Archie and me we looks at each other, but don't say anything."

"And Durks? He's terribly surprised at the sight of the gunboat—terribly. By and by he stops walking the deck and says to me: 'I have a plan, captain. I will go aboard that gunboat and find out what they want here. If they think there is anything wrong about us, I will invite them to come aboard and look us over. What do you say to that?'"

James B. Connolly

"I didn't say anything to it, but 'What will become of me and my wife—I paid you five hundred dollars for us?' pipes up Johnnie Sing."

"'Why'—and Durks smiles—'that is easy. You can hide—oh, where now? Why, of course, in the lazaretto. And your wife in a locker somewhere that Captain Corning will pick out for her. They will not look far, even if they shall suspect us—they will think we would have fifty or a hundred aboard or none at all. So they will not look into every corner. If you both hide away somewhere everything will be all right.'"

"Johnnie is uneasy, but I nods my head to him on the sly, and he says all right and goes below with his wife. And making sure they are below, Durks turns to me and hands over five hundred to me, and to Archie two hundred dollars. And he shows us another five hundred and says: 'And this will be for you two to divide as you please when I get Johnnie Sing away from the ship and the girl is left behind. What do you say?'"

"And I looks over at the five hundred and says, 'It looks pretty good'; and Archie he looks at me and at the extra money and says, 'It looks pretty good'; and Durks laughs and says, 'It will feel pretty good, too; but better put that money out of sight, hadn't you, captain—and you too, Mr. Gillis?' and goes off in the big quarter-boat—the only boat we had aboard, by the way."

"No sooner was he gone than up pops Johnnie Sing out of the cabin companionway. 'Captain,' he says, 'must I hide away?'"

"Can you swim?"

"A little bit."

"'A little bit? Not enough. And your wife?'"

"From over his shoulder she shook her head."

"'Then you can't swim ashore, can you? You got to stay aboard, that's plain. Well, you and your wife go with Mr. Gillis, who'll stow you in a place he knows under the forec's'le floor. Neither o' you bein' too tall or too fat, you c'n stow away in this place without smotherin' for an hour or two. We've used it before. Go by way of the cabin and through the hold below decks, so if anybody's got a glass on us from the gunboat they won't see you.'"

"And they went, she crawling behind him like a little mouse. And Archie tucked 'em away and comes on deck, looking at his money as he comes—two one-hundred-dollar bills. 'Tuck it out o' sight!' Archie was sayin'—'tuck it out o' sight, hah?' And the more he looks the more doubtful he becomes, and I looks at mine, and I get a magnifyin' glass from my dunnage to have a closer look, and sure enough it's the phony kind of money men like Durks used sometimes to pass off on unsuspecting Chinks on that coast. 'Johnnie Sing tips me off about it just now,' explains Archie to me.

"And while we're swearing at Durks for that, back he comes with a young officer and four armed sailors. The officer looks at me and says: 'You have contraband Chinamen aboard here?'"

"Well, that got me. I looks at him, and then, thinking of the phony money, I looks at Durks. And I don't answer."

"'We shall have to search the ship,' says the officer."

"'Sure,' I says, 'search away.'"

"And they went and dropped straight into the cabin and made for the lazaretto, Durks waiting and whistling to himself on deck. Pretty soon the officer comes up and reports nobody in the lazaretto. Durks goes up in the air. 'Where is he?' he says to me."

"He? Who?"

"Johnnie Sing."

"'What you talkin' about?' I asks, and at the same time Archie carelessly hauls out a hundred-dollar bill and lights a cigarette with it. And Durks suddenly changes, and with the officer's permission steps with me into the cabin. And the first thing he does is to count out seven hundred dollars good money and hand it to me. 'I took that other from the wrong pile,' he says, and smiles, but not as if he expects to be believed. And he holds out another five hundred—good money—and says, 'Where are they?' And I looks wise and says, 'Suppose that Chink gave me a thousand to get 'em clear?' 'A thousand? Well, here—here's a thousand when you turn him over to me. Where are they?'"

"And I whispered, so the lockers themselves couldn't hear me: 'They swam ashore and are hid away. To-morrow morning I give them the signal and they'll come back aboard.'"

"'Then,' says Durks, 'you can get his five hundred and my thousand. Will that satisfy you?'"

"And I said I'd think it over, and we went on deck, where Durks told the officer there might be a way to get hold of the contraband Chinamen yet. And the officer eyes us both and finally says: 'You'd better both come with me to the ship and make it clear to the captain. He is now up the Sound, but will be aboard in the morning. And we went, leaving Archie to look after the vessel."

"We went aboard the gunboat, not exactly under guard, but just so's to be sure we'd be there when we were wanted. It was now getting on toward six o'clock, and the first thing meal call blew, and up steps an old shipmate, Ed Gurney, and invites me down to the chief petty officers' mess for supper."

"Ed and me we'd been snapper-fishing together in the Gulf o' Mexico, on the Campeche Bank, in one of those little short bowsprit schooners out o' Pensacola, and now he was high-line marksman of the ship, wore extra marks on his sleeve and got extra money, and all that kind o' stuff, for his shooting. Well, Ed always could tell an oil-tanker from a banana steamer as far as any man in the Gulf, and we talked of those days during supper, and after we'd had a good smoke we walked the deck together, talking of one thing and another, and before I got through I told him all about the scrape I was in.

"'The grab-all snake!' says Ed. 'And what you goin' to do, Alec?'"

"'My name is Bill,' I answers; 'Bill Whitely if there's anybody likely to be in hearing. But I tell you, Ed,' I says, 'I don't like the notion o' little Johnnie Sing and his wife getting caught— or separated.'"

"We were looking over the side then, where to the boom was tied a string of small boats, our big quarter-boat to the end."

"'What do you know about this fellow Durks, Ed?' I said, after a time."

"'Nothing,' he said, 'except that he's under suspicion of smuggling opium for a long time. They say he's money-mad and woman-mad, and always was.'"

"So I've heard. And what's his game here with me?"

"'It's going around the ship that you ran away with his schooner and smuggled a Chink aboard unbeknownst, but that he's going to forgive you if you hand over the Chinaman and so put him right with the Gover'ment. He didn't say anything about any woman.'"

"'He's one fine gentleman,' I says. And, by 'n' by: 'Suppose you saw somebody was trying to slip the *Hattie*—the *Pioneer*—out by you in the dark, what would happen?'"

"'Happen?' says Ed. 'A lot o' things. And quick. It'd be up with a lot of three-inch ammunition, and some high-rating gun pointer, who's as likely to be me as anybody else, would probably have to use you for a little target practice.'"

"'And you c'n lay 'em pretty close aboard, can't you, Ed— strings o' bull's-eyes at six and eight and ten thousand yards—hah?'"

"'I have landed 'em as close as that,' says Ed."

"'But an old shipmate, Ed?' I says."

"Now, Alec—"

"'Bill—Bill Whitely,' I says."

"'Well, Bill Whitely, then, though you'd better let me call you Alec. I think I'd shoot a bit wider thinking of Alec Corning than anybody named Bill Whitely. If you don't leave me any other way out of it, I'd maybe keep scraping the paint off you as long as I could.'"

"'Your idea bein' to do the right thing by the Gover'ment in the end, Ed?'"

"'That's it,' says Ed."

"'Well, Ed,' I says, 'if you should happen to see such a thing as a moving picture of the *Hattie* stealin' out to sea, and it's up to you to bring her to, say at five or six or eight thousand yards, just scrape the paint with the first two or three, will you, by way o' telling me how it's you, Ed?'"

"'All right,' says Ed."

"'And we shook hands over that. 'And maybe the Gover'ment won't be losing anything at that,' I says."

"After a time Ed Gurney left me to go on the night watch, and I was standing by the rail, figuring how I was going to get back to the *Hattie*, when Durks comes looking for me."

"'Of course,' says Durks, 'you had no idea of it, but I organized this expedition as much to get Johnnie Sing out of the way and separate him from his wife as to smuggle in the cargo of hemp.'"

"'The duty on hemp,' I interrupts, 'must be very high, Mr. Durks.'"

"'What? It is—yes,' he says."

"'And how much *is* the duty on hemp?' I asks."

"And he don't know. 'Hemp, humph!' I says, 'how much is

the duty on—?' and I stops."

"'On what?' he says."

"'On whatever's in those bales?' I answers."

"'Why, what is the duty?' he asks."

"Maybe there's no duty—maybe it's against the law to bring it in, no matter what the duty,' I answers."

"And he sees I know too much, and from out of a pocket inside his vest he draws a package of money and lets me look to see how much, and he says: 'Five hundred now and five hundred when you turn over to me Johnnie Sing— separate from his wife.'"

"'If I could get back on the schooner,' I says, like I was studying it out, 'back on her to-night, I'd guarantee I'd have Johnnie Sing aboard her in the morning.'"

"'But how can you get off this ship?' he says."

"'Easy enough,' I says. 'Nobody here cares whether I stay aboard or get away, and nobody's watching me too close. You ask the executive officer's permission to go down aboard your quarter-boat, swinging from the boom there, by way of seeing it's all right, and you get into it and look it over, and the last thing you do before leaving it you unfasten the painter and let her go adrift. And in the morning, when you see the *Hattie*, Johnnie Sing and his wife will be aboard— on her deck in plain sight. And then you come and get 'em. But you'll have to come and get 'em yourself—and give me five hundred dollars now on account—good money, mind.' And he does—good money.

"And while he's going down over the boom ladder to one side I'm climbing down a side ladder on the other, and soon standing on the last rung, just above the water-line, and waiting. And pretty soon I see the shadow of our quarter-boat drifting past her stern, and as I do I slips overboard and strikes out for her, quiet and mostly under water, because I had my clothes on."

"I get aboard the quarter-boat and I let her drift till maybe I am a quarter of a mile away, and then I out oars and heads her in for where I can see the *Hattie's* riding light. I comes alongside. Archie's shape looms up over the rail. 'Hi-i!' he yells, 'keep off!' 'It's all right, Archie,' I says, and he reaches down and takes the painter. 'What's doing?' he says."

"Where's Johnnie Sing and his wife?"

"She's asleep in the cabin and he's awake watching her. What you going to do?"

"'You tell Johnnie here's his five hundred passage money back, will you, Archie? And then we'll make ready to skip out of here.'"

"'Skip out? Not enough wind,' says Archie."

"'Not now,' I says, 'but there will be.'"

"'I hope so,' says Archie, and calls Johnnie and tells him, and I gives him his money which he didn't want to take but had to and we slip her chain cable but left her riding light on a buoy in case the gunboat watch were having an eye on her. 'And now,' I says, 'to that lighter where those bales of hemp are.'"

"'Hadn't we better put straight for the open sound and head to sea,' says Archie, 'while it's dark? What do we want with a lot o' hemp?' growls Archie."

"'We'll go after the hemp, all the same, Archie,' I says."

"It took us three hours from our anchorage to make the lighter, where the hemp was, and that made it midnight. We let the schooner drift a couple of hundred yards off the little pier, and Archie and me paddled ashore in our quarter-boat with a spare lantern."

"There was the lighter, but no bales of hemp. Up on the pier, about two hundred yards, we see a streak of light. We crept up to that, and through a pane of glass high up—me standing on Archie's shoulders to get a look through—was four men playing cards, with money and a bottle of whiskey and a kerosene lamp on the table. We looked around. On the narrow-gauge railroad track we found the little flat hand-car, and on that, under a tarpaulin, were the bales of hemp."

"We crept around to the door of the shack. By feeling we saw it opened out; so the two of us felt around for big-sized stones, a hundred pounds apiece, or so, and them we piled in front of the door, fifteen or twenty of 'em, very softly, and then I whispers to Archie to hustle the flat car along to the pier."

"And he did, but in getting started the car wheels grinded a little, and somebody inside yells, 'What's that!' and again, 'Listen!' and then I could hear one of 'em jumping up and cursing and swearing: 'What started her?' Next thing somebody rattled the door-latch and pushed. And pushed again. And then—bam! his whole weight against the door. The top part springs out, but the bottom half sticks."

"Then there was a quiet, and then somebody said something

quick, and I could hear 'em all jumping up and yelling out, and they came piling bang-up for the door and slammed against it, but the big stones held 'em. Then they stopped, and one of 'em says: 'We're locked in all right.' 'Yes,' I calls out, 'and you'd better stay locked in, for the first man, and the second man, and the third man comes out the door he gets his. And now, men,' I calls out, 'keep that door covered and cut loose if it's knocked open.' And then I hurried after Archie's lantern, which I see is now to the pier."

"It didn't take us more than a couple o' minutes to pitch those little bales off that car, tote 'em across the lighter and drop 'em into our quarter-boat. Then we rowed out to our vessel and threw them over the rail and let 'em lay there amidships till we could get a chance to rip 'em open and see what we got."

"It was then two o'clock, and 's by this time the breeze'd made a bit, I was hoping we'd slip by the gunboat before daylight. And we did—almost; but not far enough by. Before the sun was fair up they saw us and puts after us. It took her a few minutes to get under way and steam up on her, and then she came a-belting. Twelve knots she was probably steaming, but by now the breeze was strong enough for the *Hattie* to hold her own, but not to draw away. And soon the breeze comes stronger, and we begin to lengthen and draw away from the gunboat. And it breezed up more, and the *Hattie*, balloon and stays'l on now, and taking it over her quarter, was beginning to show the stuff in her.

"She was lifting her forefoot and kicking her way through like she knew what we wanted. We were walking away from the gunboat, and I was wondering why she didn't reach out for us with one of her long five-inch lads. But I see why pretty soon. In the clearing light a point of land shows up ahead of us, making out maybe a couple of miles to the windward of our course. We couldn't turn out, for here was the main shore and there was the gunboat. 'And a pity, too,' I says to Archie, 'with enough opium aboard to keep us many a year.'"

"Archie'd 'most forgot the bales. 'Cut 'em open,' I says to him, and he did, and out they come—six or eight pound tins they looked—dozens of 'em. And Archie, looking at the bright shiny tins, said, 'What a pity!' again, and we both said what a pity it was, too, for Johnnie Sing and his wife. 'But don't you worry about 'em,' I says; 'Nor you about your wife,' I says to Johnnie, who was looking heart-broken, with his arm around her."

"All the time we were hopping on toward the point, and if 'twas anything but a steamer with guns was chasing us we'd 'a' squeezed by, and, once by, it was good night to the gunboat or anything like her in that breeze. It looked that way even as it was, till a shell goes skipping across the water ahead of us. In half a minute there came another one astern. There wasn't any sea on this time—inshore this and the water smooth, and the two shells had a fine chance to show how they could pile up little hills of water and then go skipping across the surface, making quarter circles to the right. I had hopes, a few hopes yet. For the wind was still there, and the *Hattie* she had everything on her, and she was pirooting 'tween earth and sky like a picnic swing. And looking out in terror was Johnnie Sing's little wife, and I was saying to her: 'She's all right—she'll stay up, never fear.'"

"'Oh, she'll stay up,' says Archie, 'if one of them shells don't come aboard,' and we both eying a flash o' flame that just then came out the side of the gunboat."

"'They're only fourteen-pounders,' I says."

"'Is that all?' says Archie. 'Only fourteen pounds o' nitroglycerine, or cordite, or dynamite, or guncotton, or whatever 'tis they packs into 'em! Only fourteen pounds!— and fourteen ounces is enough to send the *Hattie* to the clouds and eternal glory if ever it comes aboard,' and just then one came right under her forefoot and another under her counter. And I looks back to the gunboat. She's less than a mile away now, and I takes the glasses and has a peek, and I imagines I sees a tall, rangy lad standing beside a long, slim, steel-shiny, needle-lookin' gun, and I says to myself: 'Eddie boy, you miss us about twice more and Alec Corning'll be buying you more than one drink next time we meet,' for I knew the end was near. Ahead of me I see a passage making an island of the last half mile o' that point o' land, and it looked like water enough in the passage to let the *Hattie* through.

"I calls out to Archie and tells him to heave the tins of opium into the quarter-boat, and he did, and 'Now get into her,' I says, 'and pull for the beach.' And they did, me staying aboard the *Hattie* to luff her for them to get away. And then I cut the stays'l free and gave the *Hattie* her wheel again, and when she was going full-tilt I jibed her over, and she had everything on, and it was blowing blue devils, and only one thing you'd think could happen after that long main-boom went swinging across her deck—over the side had to go her spars. But they didn't. A twenty-two-inch forem'st she carried, a great stick, and when she was away again and going straight for the passage I says to myself: 'You'll have to hurry, Ed Gurney, or I'll be beating you to it!' For after all, when you're put to it, Durks or no Durks, there's only one thing to do—try and save your vessel.

"The *Hattie* rushes straight for the passage, and I thought maybe she'd make it, when whing! whing! whing! you'd think somebody was trying to cut his initials in the water around her. One after the other, like somebody having fun with her, and then wr-r-t! I felt her shiver, and then she seemed to shake herself, and then straight into the air her bowsprit seemed to rise and point to the morning sky, and from out of her waist came flame and smoke. Straight on and up the bowsprit went, and down! and plump! her after-part went! and flying junks of one thing and another filled the air, and some smoke, and then in the sea around the small parts that'd blown up began to fall. But I wasn't watching them. I was watching the for'ard half of her as it went pitching up, the bowsprit making a quarter circle in the air, and then plunk! down and under. The great little *Hattie* was gone. By that time I was in the water reaching out for the quarter-boat.

"'Too bad,' says Archie, 'too bad!' when I was safe in her. 'Too bad!' he says, and stops rowing. 'Pull, you sentimental loafer; pull for the beach!' I yells at him."

"And he did, and we all did—all but Johnnie's wife—and landed, and ran up and hid in the brush up top of the cliff, and lay on our stomachs watching the gunboat come stealing in and put off a steam-barge and grab our quarter-boat with all the opium in it. And we could hear Ed Gurney whoop when he held a tin of it aloft. 'Man, tons of it, tons of it!' Archie swore he could hear Ed yelling, and we guessed that would square him for those few wide shots. And then they headed back and went aboard the gunboat, and pretty soon she steamed off."

"'Vessel and opium both gone—I wonder how Durks is feeling now,' says Archie; 'and we with his—but how much is it altogether, Alec?' And that reminded me, and I says to Archie, 'Where'd you leave your two hundred dollars?' and he stops and swears. He'd left it under his mattress in the cabin of the *Hattie*. And I'd left my five hundred hanging up in my coat in the cabin of the *Hattie*, and there she was in ten fathom of water. I broke the news to Archie."

"Archie said he'd be damned. Then: 'How'll we get out of here? For we gotta go east after this, Alec.'"

"And Johnnie Sing, listening, takes the five hundred I'd given him and hands it to me. I don't want to take it, and he says, 'Plenty more—see,' and with his jackknife begins opening the wadding of his coat, and out come bills and bills and bills. All his property, twenty-odd thousand dollars, was sewed up there in big bills. And when 'twas all out he offers it to us, telling us to help ourselves. And Archie and me said no, the five hundred would do us to pay our way back to Gloucester here, and meals on the way, o' course. And Johnnie, by our advice, he comes east, too, with his little wife, and stepped off in New York; and that's where we left him."

"A fine little team, Johnnie and his wife. And the *Hattie*? If there's any of you never seen her, then you ought to when she was alive. A great little vessel, the *Hattie Rennish*!"

KILLORIN'S CARIBBEAN DAYS

Revolutions? These days? In those South American countries? Sh-h, boy, sh-h—you don't know. In th' old gunboat days in the Caribbeans we never called it a good week 'nless we suppressed three or four. And at that I think we used to miss some.

Believe me, son, those were the days when they knew how to revolutionize. You'd turn in of a night with the Blues or the Reds or Greens, in, and have breakfast maybe in the mornin' with the Purples or the Violets and brass bands celebratin' the vict'ry in the Palace square.

And the first thing every new party did when they got in was to start up the Bureau of Printin' 'nd Engravin' and roll off a few billion dollars of gover'ment money. In Guadalquique the money for all parties was the same, except each party used to rubber-stamp its name across the face. An old navy yeoman hit the beach there one time named Tommie Anderson and he was made chief of the Bureau o' Printin' 'nd Engravin' by the Greens because he could make a rubber hand-stamp while they waited. Some traitor who didn't get his 'd absconded with the 'ficial one, Tommie said.

Of course that kind o' work tends to debilitate the best kind o' money. In Almatara, which was one o' the best little revolutionary countries ever I struck, you could see nigger boot-blacks shootin' crap for two or three thousand dollars a throw of a holiday in the market square. It used to cost a thousand dollars for a shine—that's a first-class shine for a foreigner, I mean. The natives didn't have to pay that much.

Yes sir, son, a great old cruisin'-ground in the old days, the Caribbeans, and fine times there, believe me. In the old *Hiawatha* we'd be layin' in to Kingston, or Havana, or Matanzas, or some port along there, with big liberty parties ashore every day, when word 'd come from Washington tellin' us there was hell to pay over to Guadalquique, or Almatara, or somewhere else, and for us to beat it over there and sit on 'em before they got going.

The *Hiawatha* she was a good old gunboat ratin' four fourteen and two six-pounders, and, bein' the handiest thing in the fleet, 'twas always her they detailed for those little revolutionary jobs, and aboard her we got so, after a while, we didn't mind the report of a new revolution any more 'n you'd mind the ringin' of the cash-register in a barroom up here. Sometimes you'd see the skipper showin' signs of impatience, rumplin' his hair and rubbin' his chin and maybe cussin' a little; but he always ended by hurryin' a patrol party ashore, and we'd beat up the grog-shops 'n' the dance-halls and the park benches and hustle everybody aboard, and the chief engineer he'd rouse out a couple of extra stokers, and up steam and away we'd go.

Foolish things—revolutions? Maybe. But people who say no good can come out o' revolutions, they don't know. I got rank an' fortune out of a revolution one time. Yes, sir, me, Killorin, bosun's mate, second class, U.S.N. and on my first Caribbean cruise it was, and—but I'll get to the rest of it. When I was drafted to the *Hiawatha* on the Caribbean station I had what you might call only a virgin notion of revolutions.

My first enlistment was 'most run out, and I was looking to be put aboard some home-bound ship, but I was still on the *Hiawatha* when she was told to jog along over to Tangarine, a bustling young republic which was beginnin' to make a name for itself in the revolutionary way.

Whatever they were doin' we were to stop it. That was the Monroe Doctrine, the officers said. And so we put over there, but we didn't stop it. It was all over, with the Reds in an' printin' new money and postage-stamps and makin' a bluff to collect customs fine as could be when we got there.

There was nothin' to keep us there, but it was a fruitful-lookin' country and the skipper he thought he might 's well get a little fresh grub for his mess, and he sends me ashore to do the buyin'. And I goes. And the first grocery store I come to I says to the man behind the counter: "How much for a ham?" And he says, quick and brisk, "Four thousand dollars," and I was most stunned, but I manages to slap a five-dollar gold piece down on the counter and I says, quick and brisk too: "In God's name gimme a bite out of it!" An' I had to hire two coolies to wheel the change back to the ship.

Well, the money values of that Tangarine place had me mesmerized, and when my time ran out a few weeks later I settles up with the paymaster and stands by to go over the side with my bag. The skipper he says: "Killorin, I'll be over here by'n'by and take you off. And you'll be glad to come, I'll wager." And I says, "Thank you, sir, but this is the dolsee far nanity country for me. With the number o' gold pieces I got in my pants pocket I oughter be able to pass the rest o' my days here," and with my big ticket and my bag I hit the beach in Tangarine, intendin' to go straight to the palace and get chummy with the new President first thing.

But I never got so far as the palace. Not that time. About a quarter-mile up from the beach was a joyous-lookin' hotel with shaded verandas all 'round and a banana grove in the yard, and on a second look a *cantina* shinin' with mirrors and glasses and colored bottles on the ground floor, and on another look spacious-lookin' suites o' rooms such as were befittin' to *senors* of wealth and leisure on the floor above. And over these premises I cast one sailor-like view, and through the for'ard gangway of that glass-mounted *cantina* I hove my clothes-bag and myself followed after. There was also a roulette wheel, which didn't hurt the looks of the place either.

I felt so right to home that I anchored right there—oh, three or four or five or six days; maybe it was two weeks; but anyway—all that don't matter—when I steadied down so's to reason like the man o' sense my skipper always used to say I was at bottom, I was down on the beach and it was early in the mornin', and I was watchin' a lemon-colored sun trying to rise out of the smooth Caribbean sea, and I was wonderin' where it was I'd mislaid my clothes-bag. I could account for everythin' but my clothes-bag. But that don't matter either now. I never saw it again.

And while I sat there, not feelin' just like a high-score gun-captain after target-practice, I hears a light step behind me, and pretty soon I could feel an eye looking me over, and by'n'by a voice said: "A ver-ry fine good morning, sir."

"Is it?" I says, and I looks up to see who the cheerful party is. And there was a good-lookin', well-dressed, young, dark-complected chap, with a little bamboo cane which he kept stickin' into the sand.

And he looks at me again and says, plainly pleased and yet a little sad, too: "The Blues are in." And I says: "That so? Since when?" And he says: "Since last nigh-it. You did not hear, the revoloo-shee-onn?"

And I says: "I didn't—I must 'a' been takin' a nap." But I guessed it was a good thing; leastways they couldn't be any worse than the Reds—or was it the Yellow chaps were in last?

"No Yellow in Tangarine," he says.

"Ha, ha!" I says—"an authority."

"No Yellow—Blues and Reds only. And as for the Reds, bah! But the Blues, good—ver-ry good," and he pulls the cane out of the sand, lunges at the air, comes to a present, and says: "I salute you, sir." And I said: "And I al-so salute you, senor." And he says: "Americano?" And I said: "You betcher." And he said: "Of course. Ver-ry good. I have been one time in your country. I have studied the langooage there, yes. Ver-ry fine, ver-ry fine. All American people ver-ry fine. All heroes. Yes, yes, I think so. I have read it also in your books. But par-don, sir, what is it you do now?"

And I said I wasn't doing anything except makin' up my mind whether I'd go back to the navy or not, and if I did, how I'd get back.

"Ah-h, man-o'-war-man. I have thought so. You sail ship— navigate, yes?" And I said I didn't know about navigatin', but I could sail a ship if I had to."

"I have thought so," he says. "Listen, please. While you— compose, is it not?—your brains, should you not wish to engage in privateerin'? It is ver-ry good wonderful opportune time now for that, while the Blues are in control and the Reds who are on the ocean know not of it."

"H'm, we kind o' lost the privateerin' habit in our country. How do you do it these days?" I says.

"Oh-h, sir, ver-ry sim-ple, ver-ry. My friend he is in the Blue cabinet. A fine man, yes. He shall make for me all the privateerin' documents I shall require. It is necessary only to request respectfully of him. Then we shall engage a small ship and you shall navigate her, and when we shall perceive other ships, the same who shall display the Red flag, we shall display suddenly a Blue flag on our ship and capture them."

"And loot 'em?"

"Par-don, sir," says he, "but what is that lootem?"

"Why, whatever's in the ships we capture. Don't we get everythin' we c'n find in 'em?"

"Oh, sir, of a surely, abso-lutely. It is the article of war. But"—he holds up a finger warnin'like—"as commander of the expedition I shall reserve to myself one article of any kind which shall be captured. One chest, one table, even"— he looked at me to see if I got this part—"even one prisoner, if I shall so desire."

"Well, that's all right, too," I said; "for I s'pose you're payin' for the outfittin' o' this expedition?" And he says he was. "Then it's a go," I says; "for I don't see but I might 's well be privateerin' an' pickin' up a little loose loot as lyin' around on the beach wonderin' where my eats are comin' from f'r the next few weeks."

So he brings me around and shows me a little brigantine, he'd chartered, and with three dusky lads for a crew and some grub and two big chests on her quarter-deck we sail out. And the first thing I says when we were clear o' the harbor was: "What's them chests for?" And he opens up one of 'em and says: "Behold, senor, your uniform!"

And I looks and there's five gold stripes on the sleeve of the coat to begin with. And draws it all out, pants and all, and I see it's an admiral's special full-dress uniform!

"For me?" I says.

"Certain-ly," he says. "You, senor, shall be an admiral. Why not?"

"Well," I says, "I don' know why not either, only it's some rank to start with. But what'll you be?" And at that he opens up the other chest and hauls out another uniform and holds it up f'r me to look at, and, pointin' to the insignia, he asks: "What rank shall such be?"

It was a general's uniform, and I tells him so.

"So?" he says. Then bowing to me: "Then I, senor, if you do not object, shall be a gen'ral."

"Sure—why not, senor?" I says. "And there's cert'nly some class to the quarter-deck o' this brigantine. Let's get into 'em." And we got into 'em, an' gorgeous, oh, gorgeous, they were. An' rememberin' the market price o' hams when I was buyin' hams, I figured they must 'a' cost ten or fifteen million dollars apiece. And I hadn't been an hour in mine—solid gold almost, and a gold-mounted shappo and a gold belt and a dazzlin' sword—before I begins to appreciate what it was to be an admiral and to respect every admiral ever I'd sailed under—except maybe two or three—for bein' good enough to look at me at all while they were standing round deck in their uniforms. An' f'r the next hour I kept that crew hoppin' from one end of the brigantine to the other, just to see 'em hop when I gives an order with my admiral's uniform on.

But after I got so I could take off my shappo and draw my sword and look down at myself without swellin' up, I says to the gen'ral, "What d'y'say, senor gen'ral, to a little action?" and points to a lad quarterin' down the wind toward us with a Red flag up. "It's plain," I says, "he don't know the Blues is in. What d'y'say if we shake him up same as a real privateer—send a hot shot across his forefoot and make him haul his wind?"

"No, no," and the gen'ral shakes his head.

And soon there came another fellow inbound and with a Red flag up, but again the gen'ral said, "Paysheeons, paysheeons, senor admiral," and raises one hand to restrain my impulsive motions.

And four or five more passed, all flyin' the Red flag. But no word from the gen'ral until toward the middle of the afternoon—and a hot afternoon it was. The gen'ral, with the glasses to his eyes, bounces into the air. "Ah-h!" and again, "Ah-h!" and points to her. "Now the fair prize-a, the rich prize-a!" he says, and draws deep breaths, and cinches up on his belt, and runs his fingers between his red and green and yellow gold-mounted collar and his neck, and runs below and takes a last look at himself in the mirror, and comes runnin' up on deck and calls out: "Senor admiral, you shall prepare the ship for combat!"

"Ay, ay, gen'ral!" I says and takes out my bosun's whistle, which I'd never turned in of a night without hangin' it 'round my neck, and which I now lifts from the breast of my gold-mounted coat, and pipes all hands to battle quarters. But the crew, except the one to the wheel, was under the rail, asleep, and so I had to enforce my pipin' with the flat of my sword.

It'd been quicker to kick 'em, but, it bein' a hot day, I'd left off my shoes. And when they come awake I orders 'em to fly the battle-flag, which the gen'ral brings up from the bottom of his uniform chest, a fine large bright-blue thing, with stars and horned moons on it.

And then I makes ready a little old muzzle-loadin' gun, which was lashed in the waist, but pointin' over the port side, which happened to be the wrong side when we wanted to fire a shot across the enemy's bow. So we had to tack ship, which took about ten minutes, my crew not bein' A. B.'s. But when we did fire, the noise and the splash of water the ball threw up was war enough for the enemy. She was about a 100-ton tradin' schooner, and she came into the wind.

"Haul down your flag!" hollers the gen'ral in the Tangarine language, and one of their crew was goin' to haul it down, only for a stout little chap who came runnin' up out of her cabin and put his glasses on the gen'ral, and then rushes over and grabs the signal halyards from the man who was goin' to lower 'em, and hits him a clip in the neck at the same time— a scrappy chap he looked.

"He is there—it is heemself," says the gen'ral, excitedly. But to me, very courteous, he said: "Senor admiral, shall you manoeuvre the ship to approach the enemy, if you please?"

"Ay, ay, sir!" I says cheerily, and puts the brigantine alongside, and the pair of us, in our gorgeous uniforms, we leaps aboard.

"Surrender!" orders the gen'ral in a commandin' voice, but the scrappy little man he wouldn't. He yelled somethin' at his crew, and they got behind him. And there were four of them against me an' the gen'ral, for our brigantine started to drift away soon as we left her, and our spiggity crew couldn't get her alongside again.

There we were, us two heroes, marooned on the enemy's deck, in the most magnificent uniforms, but not another blessed thing to fight with except a couple o' gold-plated swords. But the little captain and his crew had only what loose things they could grab in a hurry—oars, deck-swabs, marlin-spikes, and one thing or another; but with them, without wastin' any flourishes, they came at me an' the gen'ral, and we draws our swords.

"What d' y' say, will we have at 'em, gen'ral?" I says.

"As you say, senor admiral, have at 'em!" answers the gen'ral, and we haves at 'em.

But I soon begin to see we wasn't havin' at 'em in any great shape. Our swords had two backs but no edge. It was like hittin' 'em with barrel-staves. Fine grand echoes, but the echoes wasn't knockin' 'em down. And the gold-mounted uniforms were in the way, too—in my way, anyway. My gold-mounted collar was gettin' so tight after I'd warmed up to the work that I 'most choked.

"Have at 'em!" the gen'ral cried again, "but have great care for the old gentleman."

I was just goin' to welt the little captain a good one when I heard that. "Not hurt him!" I says. "A hell of a battle this where we have to play fav'rites among th' enemy. And why won't I hurt him, senor gen'ral, an' him the best scrapper o'the lot?"

"You must not. No, no! He is the father of the lady."

"So that's it? And where's the fair lady?" I asks.

James B. Connolly

"I know not. I trust she is on this ship, but I know not. But have at 'em, as you say, senor admiral, once more, and possibly we shall discover."

"All right, but let's have at 'em right," I says, and down on the deck I throws my grand sword, and with it the very fine scabbard which I'd been holdin' with one hand to keep from givin' myself the leg. And I sheds the gold-embroidered coat on top of it. I kept wearin' the gold-mounted shappo because the sun was hot, but the rest of me was stripped to the waist. And I felt better, and then I says: "Come on, gen'ral, unhook that golden armor and be free an' easy in y'ur motions like me."

"No, no, senor admiral. I shall wear my uniform, even though it is to die in it," he answers back.

"All right, senor gen'ral," I says, "have your own way. It's the privilege of your rank, but for me a little looser motions and a heavier armament," and I picks up what looks like a baseball bat, but a little longer and a little thicker and a good deal heavier than any baseball bat. A capstan-bar it was. And if y'ever handled one you know what a great little persuader a capstan-bar is. I could tell you a hundred stories o' capstan-bars. Many a good fight used to be settled in th' old sailin'-ship days with a capstan-bar.

And with my capstan-bar I haves at 'em right. Soon I had two of the enemy backed up to the forehatch, and before their worryin' eyes I flourishes my capstan-bar. "Now then," I says, "it's go below for you two or a pair of cracked skulls—which?" And they went below, the pair of them together like divin' seals, into what I see, when I takes a peek, was mostly a cargo of pineapples and cocoanuts in bulk. I could hear 'em bouncin' around among 'em after they struck.

And now, being well warmed up to my work and my head

bustin' with strategy, I takes the little captain in the rear and was about to lay him low, when the gen'ral hollers: "Senor admiral, you for-get—spare him!" So I spares him, but I whales the other last one a couple in a soft spot and chases him, till he took a high dive too into the forehold; and I could also hear him rattlin' and bouncin' around after he struck the cocoanuts or the pineapples, whichever it was. Then I goes for the little captain again, only now I picks him up and holds him while the gen'ral ties his arms, and then, first clampin' down the forehatches on the captured crew, we lowers him into the cabin whilst we take a look around.

It was me for loot, the gen'ral for the fair lady. But not a thing could I find, and him no fair lady. In the hold, topside, between decks, everywhere; but nothin' besides cocoanuts and other fruit and some hogsheads o' rum. The rum was an encouragin' item, but not what you'd call loot. So we came back to the cabin and untied the captain, who begins at once to go rollin' cigarettes and shootin' green eyes at the pair of us. The gen'ral takes a seat opposite him and argues beseechin'ly, but not one soft look from the little man.

The gen'ral, discouraged, turns to me. "Senor admiral, what do you say for him? Is it not a hard heart? I love his daughter, but he—"

"She no lofe you!" snaps the little man.

"Ah-h, but how can you say that truly?" says the gen'ral, and turns to me and says: "Is it not just, senor admiral, that I should have one opportuni-ty to see her?"

By this time I'd filled a little jug with some rum, and there was lemons and brown sugar and a little ice, and I thought 'twas kind o' rough on him, and so I says: "Yes, I think y'oughter, 'specially while you got that uniform on. But where is she?"

"Ah-h, that is it, where is she? On this ship I have thought, but evident-ly not so."

"Maybe she's here at that, hidden somewhere," I says, "and if she is, believe me, gen'ral, I'll find her," and leavin' a lemon swizzle to cool I begins to search the schooner again. And this time I takes a good look into the little captain's stateroom. I didn't find the fair lady, but packed cutely away under the old fellow's bunk was about a cord o' money! Nothing less than a thousand-dollar bill, but five and ten-thousand dollar bills mostly, and all new. Lord knows how much there was there, but I hauled a bushel or so of it out on the cabin floor by way of a sample. And the little man never stirred when he saw it; and as for the gen'ral, "Bah!" he said—"Red moneys!"

I was thinkin' I'd done a fine stroke, and that made me feel kind o' put out. "I'll find that girl if she's on the ship," I says then, and I steps over to a corner of the cabin where there'd been a fresh boarding-up of the bulkhead.

I gazes steady at it. And I could almost feel the little man's eyes borin' into my back! And I whirls around quick; there he was—paying no attention to the gen'ral, but starin' at me. And to myself I says: "If losin' all that money in his room don't jar him, it must be somethin' good behind that bulkhead for him to worry over." And with that in my mind I looks again at the old fellow, and now I know what it is, and the old man knew I knew, and into his eyes came such a look that I stopped dead. You mustn't forget that I was a big, loose, rangy 180-pounder, and standin' there—I can see it now; I didn't then—but me standin' there, with the heat of warm exercise and three West Indian rum swizzles oozing out of me on that tropic afternoon, I c'n see now I wasn't any winged angel to look at.

But I had no notion of that then, only that I was beginnin' to like the little captain; and with that new feelin' I spoke to the gen'ral. "Here," I says, "let's step on deck for a minute." And we went up, leaving the old fellow below with his hands tied while we were gone. And up on deck I says, quick and sharp: "Look here, mate, what's this about you and the old chap's daughter? Is it all straight?"

"Straight?" repeats the gen'ral, puzzled like. "Straight? Ah-h—listen, my friend," and he pours out on me what I wasn't huntin' for—his autobie-ography. It was her father who had kept them apart so. Her father, he did not love his—the gen'ral's—father. An old family quarrel, yes. Oh, for a long time back. Politics. He was of the Reds, her father, and his own father of the Blues. Her uncle he had been vice-president of the Red republic. It was true. But why should he and the beautiful daughter suffer for a quarrel which was so old, and the girl and himself all that were left of both families? Why? And I scratched my head and said I couldn't see why either.

And love her! Before he got through I could hear whole poems in the little wavelets lappin' under our run, and in the evenin' breeze which was kissin' my cheek. And the smell of oranges and pineapples and molasses and good West India rum coming up from the main hold—'twas the breath of roses—only I stopped to hope the captured crew in the forehold wasn't drinkin' up all the rum in their end of the ship—and to this side and that the lights of passin' ships were showin' and the voices of men and women floatin' over the water, darky voices mostly, and some were chorusin', chorusin' a shanty air which I'd last heard from a crowd of Georgia darkies loadin' a lumber schooner, a four-masted lumber schooner, through a great square hole in her bow from a railroad dock on the Savannah River—one time, that was, my ship put into Savannah and I got to know a girl lived in the Yamacraw there, and on Sunday afternoons we used to walk up and sit on the lumber piles on that same railroad wharf and watch the yellow river flowing by and dream o' things that never did happen an' never could—not for her and me. And now, aboard the little Caribbean trader, the moon was beginnin' to poke over our starboard rail and the first little white stars were peekin' out over the foretopsail, and the gen'ral was still talking. And when he'd done he laid his hand on my shoulder and said: "Straight, my brave American friend? As straight as a tall palm-tree. And all this"—he pulls on the end of a couple of cords on his gold-mounted coat—"I thought it would look well in her eyes." And he stops.

"But you are of the North," he says after a little while; "you think that foolish, possibly?"

"We do," I says. "We unanimously do," and as I said it I got to thinkin' of how when I was a boy I used to walk on my hands, and stand on my head, and throw flip-flaps, or stop to knock the head off some passin' kid—if I was able—anythin' so a red-ginghamed, pop-eyed little girl sittin' on the door-step across the street would take notice. "We do those things when we are boys," says I aloud.

"Ah-h! So you think—" says the gen'ral. "Ver-ry good," and starts to throw off his uniform.

"No, no," I says. "Keep that on. It becomes you. And, besides, I don't know's I'm so sure we ought all to grow up. And come below—come!" I thought I heard the old fellow's voice below and I jumped down, and there he was, the little captain, hurryin' away from the bulkhead.

And now I examines the bulkhead carefully, and I goes up on deck and resumes my full admiral's coat and buckles on the fine gold-mounted belt and sword and sets my shappo just a little to one side. I was wishin' I had my shoes, but they were on the brigantine and she was a quarter-mile away and still driftin'. And back in the cabin again, I picks up the hammer and draws from the bulkhead plankin' half a dozen nails, and in two minutes it's done, and out under the lights o' the cabin lamp steps—O, the prettiest, slimmest little dark-eyed girl, just a match for the gen'ral. But the first thing she sees is me, Killorin. "Ah-h—" she says, in a long sigh with her mouth a little open, and I tosses the hammer and nails into a corner and straightens up and takes a full breath; and let me tell you, son, in those days the worst-lookin' flatfoot ever climbed over a gunboat's side wasn't me, Killorin, bosun's mate, second-class—or was I first-class then? No matter; I was in a full-dress admiral's uniform then, and from me cocked hat to me bare toes I was some class. I knew I was—even without my shoes. And when again she looks at me and when again she sighs, "Ah-h—" with her little red lips apart, I says to myself: "Killorin, son, you're makin' one big hit." And just then her eyes looked past me and again she said, "Ah-h—" and down among my lower ribs somewhere dropped my quick-firm' heart, and "Killorin," I whispers to myself, "she loves you—not." For that last ah-h—and sigh-h for the gen'ral was seven times deeper and longer than the one she hove up at sight of me.

And while they were gazin' rapturous at each other the little captain's eyes met mine. And with a memory o' the last time I'd been up before a summary court-martial, I takes charge of the case. And "Sir," I says, "it appears to me like I'd have to be judge here. You, sir, are a prisoner o' war. And, to be more explicit, all aboard here are prisoners o' war. But no gentleman, and I say gentleman advisedly, is goin' to include a woman in the loot without her own consent, even if her

James B. Connolly

father did hide her away and deny the same, which is against all articles o' war, besides bein' most disrespectful of service regulations. But in consideration of your previous good conduct we will not mention that now."

I turns to the gen'ral. "You, senor gen'ral, do you believe me an honest man?" And without even lookin' at me he says, "Pff—a foolish queschee-own, senor admiral. I have known you are honest from the mo-ment I have seen you spendin' your money foolishly at the hotel. And brave—as all American sailormen are brave."

"Tis well," I says. "And you"—I turned to the little captain— "you, I fear me, sir, will have to take my honesty for granted. Now I'll be the judge. Do you"—I faces the gen'ral again— "agree? 'Cause if you don't you an' me'll have to hop up on deck and fight it out."

The gen'ral was still lookin' up at the little captain's daughter. "Silence gives consent," I says. "And now," I says, "it's the young lady will say the word. Attend me, senorita. This young man here, but two moments agone, up on deck declared to me, while below the blue Caribbean the sun like a fine ripe orange was sinkin', and likewise the Southern Cross was shinin', lopsided, like a blessin' in the southwest over toward where the hills o' South America would 'a' been if we could 'a' seen 'em—to me, on this occasion, this young man declared he loved you. This young man—attend me, and not him, fair lady, please—and a gallant young man he is—I never knew a gallanter on such short notice—this young man on the occasion aforementioned declared to me that he loves you and wants you to wife. What have you to say to this charge? Do you love him or do you not? Take your time in answerin'."

And I stood to one side. She was still lookin' at the gen'ral and him at her. Just once she looked at her father and once at me—and I winked by way of encouragement—and she looked at her gen'ral again, and looked and looked, till all at once the gen'ral just nachally stepped across the cabin floor and took her in his arms.

"Look here, boy," I says, stern-like, "ain't that kind o' rushin' things? Have you a steady job—outside o' privateerin'?"

"I do not work. I have money," he says over her shoulder.

"Real money? Or this kind?" and I points to the bales of new bills in the little captain's room.

"I have gold in the bank and much sugar plantations."

"Then, orer pro nobis, she is yours," I says, and waves my arms beneficent-like over the pair of them. "And you and me," I says to the old man, "as I don't see how we c'n help it, what d'ye say if we two call the war off and have a few lemon swizzles with ice in 'em?"

And I draws a jug o' Santiago rum, and there was lemons an' sugar and a little ice, and we foregathers like a couple of old shipmates after a foreign cruise. And when, in the mornin', from out of the smooth Caribbean Sea the rosy sun came swimmin' we was right there, joyous as a liberty party on pay-day, to greet it. And the gen'ral and the senorita also saluted the goddess o' the mornin', and after breakfast we all went ashore, and that night I danced a taranteller at the weddin'. And, believe me, there's class to a good taranteller dancer.

And likewise that night, with the silver moon risin' like a goddess o' wisdom above the smooth Caribbean, and me and the little captain mixin' lemon swizzles on the veranda of the gen'ral's plantation *hacienda*, the little captain says to me: "I love you as one son. You shall be captain of my ship." And as a sort of weddin' legacy he bequeathes to me all the money was in the schooner when the gen'ral and me captured her.

And next mornin' I took up my quarters on the schooner, with the crews of the schooner and the brigantine for body-servants. And I had one good time. There was a basket there—a basket about the size of a good-sized wash-basket—and every mornin' I'd shovel a lot of money into that. Oh, I don' know how much, maybe two or three or four or five or six hundred thousand dollars, and I'd say to the cook, or maybe one of the deck force: "Here you, Fernando, go on up now an' hurry back." And they weren't bad traders at all. In a couple of hours they'd come hustling back with the full o' the basket o' chickens, eggs, butter, cheese, bologny, and fruit—everything a man 'd want for breakfast—in place o' the money. Fifty thousand dollars a day apiece I paid the crew, and good and plenty for them—a lot o' lazy loafers. It used to take three of 'em to buckle me into my uniform of a hot mornin'.

I never knew how much money was in that pile, but three or four, or maybe five or six hundred million dollars. And maybe I didn't live on the fat o' the land with it, for eight weeks! It would 'a' lasted longer only it was the divil tryin' to be thrifty with my admiral's uniform on, and then one mornin' the *Hiawatha* came to port, and with what I had left—forty or fifty million, or whatever it was—I gave a farewell party that night at the hotel where the banana grove was in the yard. I wore my admiral's uniform for the last time that night, and maybe that made 'em charge me a little more, but no matter that. In the mornin' I didn't have hardly enough to tip the waiters, three or four hundred thousand dollars, maybe, but—whatever it was, I tips 'em with it, and goes down to the beach to where the little, old, homely *Hiawatha* was laying to anchor, and 'twas eight o'clock and the bugler was sounding colors and it made me feel homesick, and I waves my hand back to the town, and "Fare thee well, O Tangarine-a," I says, "Tangarine-a, fare thee well." Secretary o' the navy I could 'a' been, I know, but back aboard the old *Hiawatha* I goes. And damn glad, you betcher, I was to be there.

But an admiral of the Blue I was once, with a hogshead of nothin' less than thousand-dollar bills; and I helped to make two young people happy. And no one c'n take that from me. And so I say when people say there's no good in revolutions you refer 'em to me, Killorin, bosun's mate, U.S.N.-I'll tell 'em.

THE BATTLE-CRUISE OF THE "SVEND FOYN"

At this time I had drifted down South America way, and was master of a combination whaling and sealing steamer sailing out of Punta 'renas for the firm of Amundsen & Co.

Punta Arenas, if you don't happen to know, is at the tip end of Patagonia, in the Magellan Straits. It is now a highly respectable place under the Chilean flag, but there was a time it wasn't. All kinds of human wreckage used to drift onto the west coast of South America in those days, and when the Chilean Government couldn't take care of them any other way they would ship them down through the straits to Punta 'renas. At the time I was there most of the bad ones had been run out, but every now and then a few of the old crew would pop up and worry people into thinking Punta 'renas must still be a hard place, which it wasn't.

Mr. Amundsen lived in a big house up on the plaza where the bandstand was, with a fine open-air veranda in front and a glassed-in conservatory on the side, and aft of the house a garden with a waterfall modelled after something he had left behind him in Norway. He designed the waterfall himself, and over the grandpiano in the front room looking out on the plaza was an oil-painting of it—a whale of a painting, done by a stranded Scandinavian who told Mr. Amundsen he'd seen that identical waterfall in Norway many a time, which perhaps he had.

We didn't like Mr. Amundsen any the less because of his collection of old sagas which he used to spin out for hours on end. Whoppers, some of them were, but we, his whaling and sealing captains, we'd sit there and never let on, eating thin Norwegian bread and goats' cheese and dried chips of ptarmigan, with Trondhjem beer, and none of us but would have sat longer any time, so that after he got through there was a chance to hear his daughter Hilda play the grandpiano—and sing, maybe, while she played. And I tell you, the thought of that fine old Norwegian and Hilda after months of banging around to the west'ard of Cape Horn in a little whaling steamer—it was surely like coming home to be home-bound then.

Norwegian songs were they, and I, American-born, and only half Scandinavian by blood, was probably the one man coming to Amundsen's who didn't know every word of them by heart. But not much of the sentiment of them I missed at that, because in other days I'd cruised off Norway, too, and knew the places the songs told about—the high-running fjords and the little white lighthouses; the fish drying on the rocks and the night sun floating just above the edge of the gray sea; and, again, the long black night of winter and the dead piled up to wait till they could be buried when the snow went in the spring.

But shore time in Punta 'renas was holiday time. Wet days, hard days at sea have their time, too; and Mr. Amundsen and Hilda and Punta 'renas were a long way behind me. I was whaling and sealing in the South Pacific, and had been doing pretty well, but nothing record-breaking till one day I picked up a lot of ambergris.

Now I could have stocked a million dollars in a regular way

James B. Connolly

and nobody pay any great attention; but the tale of that find went through half the South Pacific. A dozen whaling and sealing masters boarded me in one month to see if it was so, and after I'd told them the story of it about forty-five times, I began to see myself telling it to old Amundsen and Hilda in the big front room looking out on the plaza, her father and I having a late supper of flat bread and the goats' cheese and the dried ptarmigan chips, with Trondhjem beer, and Hilda playing softly on the piano with an eye and an ear maybe sidewise now and again to me.

And now we were truly homeward bound in old Magellan Straits, with the hills back of Punta 'renas in sight from our masthead, when we spied a Norwegian bark with a deckload of lumber ashore on the spit of Pouvenir Bay, which is on the southerly—the Terra del Fuego—shore of the straits. Her ensign was upside down in her rigging, and I headed in to see if we could help her out. I thought it was queer no one showed up aboard her to answer when I hailed, but no matter—I moored my steamer just inside the spit and put off with half a dozen men in a boat and went aboard.

Nobody on her deck, nobody in her below for-'ard. I went aft and dropped into her cabin, my men behind me, and we were peeking here and there to see what it was could be wrong, when slap! on goes the cabin hatch over our heads. Then we hear the padlock slipped on and the lock sprung. We are prisoners, without even a peek at who it was did it.

We heard them going off. Without waiting any longer, I began slashing away with my pocket-knife, the only knife among us, and by and by I had cut our way through the cabin door; but that took a lot of time. From the bark's deck, when we were clear, there was nothing in sight except our own steamer to anchor in the bay beyond the spit. The boat we had come in was gone.

Well, we weren't worrying about the boat, only we had to take the time to lash together twenty or thirty pine planks and some scantling from the bark's deckload of lumber and raft ourselves around the spit and into the little bay to get to our steamer. Everything about her looked all right, except that none of the crew were in sight when we paddled alongside. I hurried over the rail to see what was the matter. It didn't take long to see. The hatches were off her hold and our sealskins and our ambergris gone from below. A fortune it was, gone—s-st!—like that.

Looking further, we found the rest of the crew nicely locked up in the fo'c's'le. They didn't know what happened, except that some men had come rowing in from the direction of the lumber bark in our boat, and one of them had sung out in English and another in Norwegian that they were the crew of the bark, with a message from me.

My crew, of course, said: "Come aboard." But no sooner aboard than the strangers out with revolvers, back my men into the fo'c's'le, and lock them in. That was all they knew about that, except they heard the noise of the hurrying of our cargo out of the hold, and then the sound of a steamer making fast alongside and of shifting our cargo to her deck and of her moving away. And then all quiet till we came back.

Well, whoever did it must have had us timed pretty well. They must have had a gang hid in the lumber bark and a steamer hid somewhere in the straits near by waiting for us. It looked as if there was nothing for us to do but take our loss and keep on for Punta 'renas, but first I went to the masthead and had a look out.

Opposite Pouvenir Bay the Straits of Magellan are at their widest. From the crow's-nest there was a good stretch of sea

James B. Connolly

to look at. To the west'ard was a touch of smoke, which might be the steamer which looted us; surely she didn't go to the east'ard, for there it was open water with nothing in sight. To the northward, toward Patagonia, of course, she would not go, because Punta 'renas was there. But I had a look that way, and as I looked I could see what looked like an open boat heading our way; and I wondered who she would be and what she would be after in a place like Terra del Fuego.

They came skipping on at a great clip for an open boat. They were running her to a long main-sheet, but keeping a tight hand on the sheet.

As they drew nearer I see she was white-painted, and pretty soon I see she was too big to be anything but a navy sailing cutter, and soon again I made out that they were a crew of American naval officers and bluejackets.

They went out of their way some to sweep under the stern of the bark, and I noticed they all took a look up at her and back at her, wondering, as I thought, how she came to go ashore. They held on for the inside of the bay and ran straight up onto a little reach of pebbly beach; and no sooner grounded than most of them went tearing across the spit with rifles and shotguns. I see what they were now—it was a hunting party.

Without wasting a second they began to blaze away at the wild ducks as they came swooping down from the west. In that country the wild game don't know what a man looks like, and as it was late in the afternoon, with the ducks coming back for the night from the west'ard, the shooting was good. Swooping along the shore they came, across the mouth of the bay, flock after flock so close-set and low-lying that they didn't need guns. They could have sat on the beach and hove up stones or drift-wood and killed 'em as they went kiting by, sixty miles or more an hour to the east'ard.

After twenty minutes or so they must have thought that kind of shooting was too easy, for part of them went off into the brush and the others came back to the spit of beach and, with some kindlings from their boat and some drift-wood and brush, started a fire. It was a north wind, and I could smell the ducks cooking and the coffee making, and I couldn't hold off any longer. I rowed myself over in our second boat. The senior line officer of the party, a lieutenant, invited me to join them, which I did, and pretty soon I was eating broiled duck and drinking real American coffee, with bacon and eggs, and forgetting my troubles.

After supper we sat around and talked, and they told me what had happened to the lumber bark. She had been lured inshore by false lights the night before and boarded by a gang under Red Dick, who had cleaned her out of stores and what money they had, and had driven the crew off in the morning after beating up most of them by way of diverting himself. Then the bark's captain and his crew rowed across the Straits of Punta Arenas in their quarter-boat, looking for satisfaction. Nobody there could do anything for them, because nothing less than a war-ship could have overcome Red Dick, and there was no Chilean war-ship nearer than Valparaiso, and that was six days' steaming away.

"But how did that lumber captain know it was Red Dick?" I asked at this point.

"He didn't know," answered the officer who'd been talking. "But when he described him everybody in Punta Arenas said it was Red Dick. But aren't you an American?"

I said I was and told them my experience, and they all said what a pity my ship wasn't under the American flag so they could put it up to their captain and be sure he would send a party after Red Dick. And they would all like nothing better

James B. Connolly

than to join that party, and an easy matter all 'round, as their ship was to be hanging around the straits for another week.

By this time the others of the party, who'd gone into the brush for wild geese, were coming back. They didn't get any geese, because geese, wild geese, anyway, aren't near so foolish as a lot of people think. They were hungry and sat right down to supper.

Among them, as I looked, was one I knew for Peter Lawson, an old shipmate. A warrant officer I saw he was now, but when I knew him he was a chief carpenter's mate on the old *Missalama*. We kept eying each other, and by and by he remembered, and we stood up and shook hands across the fire. In half a minute we were talking of old days in the navy.

By this time it was late day, with the sun going down below the hills on the other side of Pouvenir Bay. I remember it went down red as the heart of the fire we were sitting by. Through the little thin whiffs of the smoke of the fire it looked like that—all hot color and no flame. Nothing to that, of course, only pictures like that do start your brain to going. The little bay was there at our feet and the wide straits off to our elbow, and the water of that bay was smooth green where it shoaled on the pebbly spit; but the straits, as far as we could see them, were one long roll of tossing ridges and scooping hollows, and they were all black except where the williwaws, cutting across the tide, would whip the ridges to a marble white.

I saw the sun set red through the thin blue smoke of the fire, and almost in line with the sun and the smoke was the stranded bark with her deckload of lumber. A little farther off was my own little *Svend Foyn*. It was coming on dark by then and I could see them making ready the anchor light on the *Svend Foyn*. And it was coming colder, too, for the broad, warm north wind had changed to a thin little icy wind from the south.

And now the fiery-red reflection of the sun was gone from above the hills across the bay, and when that went all warmth went with it. Everybody drew nearer to the fire except the two apprentice boys, who were cleaning up the mess gear in water made hot at a little fire of their own. One of them was singing to himself little jiggly, ragtime songs while he wiped the dishes:

"Oh-h, ahm gwine down to Macon town
Ter buy mah 'Liza Jane a gown—
Ah feel so happy 'n' ah don' know why,
Mah bai-bie, mah hon-ie!"

Every time he stacked up a few plates he would stop to roll a few more cake-walk steps.

"I wish I was feeling as good as you!" I said to myself while I watched him.

And, watching him, I got to thinking of Hilda in the big front room in what was home for me—and of having to tell her what a failure my cruise had been. It did set me to thinking.

All at once it came to me, and "I've got it!" I said, not knowing I said it out loud until I saw that everybody around the fire was looking at me; and at last Peter said, "What's it you got?"

And I told them what I had in mind, and they all thought it was a great scheme—if I could carry it out. And the lieutenant in charge of the party said: "And we'll help you; but not to-night—the first thing in the morning after a good night's sleep."

We had a good sleep that night, sleeping till sunrise on the pebbly beach with the mainsail of the sailing cutter for a tent over us. And in the morning the first thing after breakfast I pulled the lumber bark off the beach and moored her in the bay. That was so she wouldn't break up and go to pieces the first gale of wind came along; and, as after that service I figured her owners wouldn't call it stealing, I helped myself to a few thousand feet of lumber off her deck, and we all set to work to make the *Svend Foyn* over into what her builder back in Norway certainly never intended her for.

First, we built up her topsides to make a superstructure, and then added the other things a first-class battle-ship ought to have. The *Svend Foyn* had two masts and one smoke-stack. The two masts were all right. We had only to set fighting-tops around them, but she would be a poor class of a battle-ship with only one smoke-stack. So we gave her two more. We painted her lower sides white and her topsides yellow-brown, and for turrets we had one to each end with what was intended for 12-inch gun muzzles sticking out of them. And we allowed the ends of what looked like twelve 7-inch black boys to peek through the sides of what we called her gun-deck. Two of those 7-inch muzzles were real muzzles, that is, black-tarred wood like the others, but they were hollow so we could train a bomb-lance whaling-gun through them, one to each side. When we got that far they said I would have to name her, and I called her the *Cape Horn*, and there being no flag that any of us had ever heard of for Terra del Fuego, we made one for her out of three pieces of green, red, and purple cloth, and broke it out to her main-peak.

And when that little round-bowed, fat-sterned whaler waddled out of Pouvenir Bay that afternoon there wasn't a thing that one lieutenant, one ensign, one doctor, a warrant carpenter, and sixteen enlisted men of the United States Navy could see she was shy of, except a wireless outfit, and we soon fixed that by stringing a stretch of old wire between her masts, with half a dozen old barrel hoops for a wireless plant, and for fear there was anybody of Red Dick's party who knew battle-ships only from pictures, I had the stokers keep feeding her fires with whale-oil. After that, with the clouds of smoke belching out of her, I felt sure nobody could doubt us—especially at a distance.

We gave three whistles and dipped the ensign to our navy friends, and for the rest of that day and night, and all next day and night, we steamed through the straits toward the Pacific. And on the second morning we turned north and ran in among the islands off the Chilean coast; and pretty soon we ran into the place I was bound for—a bottle-shaped passage with a narrow inlet to each end and the shadow of the Andes Mountains darkening all. And, laying to moorings there, was a cargo steamer of perhaps fifteen hundred tons. Even if she wasn't too big a steamer to be loafing there, I knew her of old. Red Dick was handy. I took a look around to the north'ard, and at the other end of the passage and jam in to the high rocks was a whaling steamer about our own tonnage. I also knew her of old.

I might as well say now that Red Dick and I weren't strangers. We used to be sort of friends, but not since the day we walked up the long timber pier in Punta 'renas together and met Hilda with her father. She was straight from school in Norway then, and 'twas the first time we'd seen her. We looked out together on the wonderful straits, and 'twas me she walked home with.

But that was a year back, and it was other business now. I had now to make an impression, and right away, to back up our battle-ship looks. So we cut loose and gave them, port and starboard, one after the other, twenty-one whaling bombs in good, regulation style. They made a terrible racket against the Andes Mountains, which come down here to the water's edge.

And Red Dick's gang must have thought we were some awful power, for there was soon great doings on the deck of the whaling steamer. Smoke began to come out of her, and pretty soon she began to move; but when we bore down, with a great white wave ahead of us and rolls of smoke over us, they quit. Two boats dropped over her side and headed for a bit of beach, and twenty men scurried off and lost themselves in holes between the rocks. We shot a few bombs over their heads just to let them know we were a rich nation with ammunition to spare. The echoes coming back sounded like a battle-fleet saluting port in foreign waters.

We boarded Red Dick's steamer, and there were our sealskins and ambergris. There were also four or five thousand other fine sealskins which weren't ours, but which we took along, knowing they weren't Red Dick's. And with Red Dick's steamer in charge of six of my crew behind us, we started back the way we came. In steaming past the cargo steamer we counted four long glasses levelled at us.

The first likely place we came to we hauled to and shifted Red Dick's cargo to the *Svend Foyn*. By this time, with the ambergris back and five thousand extra sealskins below, all hands were willing to take a moderate chance on almost anything. We swung away for the straits, but not making great headway. The little old *Svend Foyn* was never any wonder for steaming. At her best she could do perhaps ten miles an hour. Now, with all her battle-ship topgear and with the wind ahead, she was doing perhaps six.

It began to breeze up, but nothing for us to worry over until we saw a steamer's smoke coming up astern. We were then clear of the coast islands and into the straits, with wind and sea fighting each other.

I had another good look at the steamer coming up astern, and took my prize crew off Red Dick's whaler and turned her adrift. I hated to. Not alone the prize money, but to see a good ship go to loss any time is bad. I did it in hopes that the cargo steamer coming upon us would stop to get her, and while they were getting her—what with the gale and the dark coming—we would be able to slip away. But they didn't stop. Perhaps the little whaler was too close in to the cliffs for the big steamer to have a chance in the tide that was running. They let her pile up against the cliffs, and came on and ranged up abreast of us. Red Dick was on her bridge. She came so close to us that I could almost have jumped aboard. It was blowing pretty hard at the time, but she was making easy weather of it—a good sea-boat. We weren't. The williwaws, which are what they call the hard squalls off the high hills down there, were having a great time with out battle-ship topsides. She was something of a roller on her own account at any time, the *Svend Foyn*, but now she rolled her wooden turrets under and every once in a while her bridge.

Red Dick leaned over the bridge rail and laughed. He looked the *Svend Foyn's* top gear over and laughed again. "Blank shells and wooden guns!" he called out. "Fine! Any more left?"

"Oh," I said, "not all blanks and not all wooden, and a few left—yes."

"So?" he says, and gives an order. A man pulls a tarpaulin off a long needle-gun amidships. "Got anything like that in your battery?" he calls out.

I looked it over as if I was interested. At the same time I

James B. Connolly

made a sign to my mate behind me. I'd long before this loaded my two whaling bomb-lance guns, but this time I put in them the lances, which were of steel, weighed eighty pounds, and were four and a half feet long—not a bad little projectile at all.

"What's it for?" I called out, pointing to his needle-gun.

"What's it for?" he mimics. "What d'y' think it's for?"

I shake my head. "I could never guess."

"Well, you will soon. You know me?"

"I do. And you know me?"

"I know you, and I'll take no chances with you. I'm going to heave you a line and take you in tow."

"I don't remember flying any signals for a tow."

"No? Well, I think you'd be better off for a tow. Take my line."

"We don't want your line."

"Take my line or I'll blow a few holes in you, and while you're on your way to the bottom of the straits—all hands of you—I'll ram you to make sure."

"You're foolish to sink us," I says, "till you take off the ambergris and the sealskins."

He began to get mad. "Take my line or take a shell from this gun. Which is it?" he yells.

His gun was trained on our midship topsides. I couldn't see where he was going to sink us, leastwise not with one shot, so, "Come aboard with your shell!" I called out, and he did. I didn't look to see what damage the shell did in passing, but it went clear through our pine topsides one side and out the other.

I'd already passed the word to my mate, and wh-r-oo! went the four-and-a-half-foot bomb-lance from the inside of one of our make-believe seven-inch rifles. The lance tore through just above the water-line of Red Dick's steamer. The bomb exploded inside her hull. Through the hold the sea rushed, and from her deck below came whoops of surprise.

I rolled the little fat *Svend Foyn* around. She near capsized in turning, especially as Red Dick let me have two more from his needle-gun while we were coming around. One of them burst inside, but didn't kill anybody. Around came the *Svend Foyn*.

"Her water-line!" I yelled, and we let her have it. And again we gave it to her. They both went home.

Red Dick quit laughing. He ran down from the bridge and out of sight below. Pretty soon, through her sides, as we hear him and his gang yelling, came the ends of blankets and mattresses, to keep the sea out of the holes we'd made.

And while they are at that we give them another. And that settled it. Five minutes before, I had an idea we might have to go to the bottom—s-sst! like that. And now Red Dick and his cargo steamer were belting through the tide rips toward the Terra del Fuego shore, to find a bay, I suppose, and a bit of a beach to haul up and patch things. And I couldn't help thinking as he went that he'd lost a desperate reputation about as easy as any ever I heard of; but I might as well also say now that I'd been shipmates with Red Dick, and I always did believe he was a good deal of a bluff. But my crew didn't think that. There was great rejoicing among them, and I let them rejoice so long as they didn't stop setting things to rights.

We were shook up some—our bridge loosened up, our wireless hoops hanging droopy, our two fake smoke-stacks lying over on their sides, and the for'ard turret with some dents in it; but bow first, and in peace and quiet, we steamed on. And we were still steaming in peace and quiet when we made Punta Arenas.

And, steaming in, I thought I might as well do it in style. Here we were, a victorious battle-ship entering a foreign port, and so I hoisted our international code—spelling it out that we were the *Cape Horn* of the Terra del Fuegan navy, and asking permission to anchor. The captain of the American battle-ship was standing on his bridge as we steamed down the line, with a man in our chains heaving the lead, my mate on the fore-bridge and myself on the after-bridge, a quartermaster to the wheel, and the second mate spying, busy as could be, through a long glass; and not alone the captain, but the nine hundred and odd officers and men of the American battle-ship roared in review of us. The other ships in port didn't know what to make of it no way.

We came around and dropped our young anchor, splash! and saluted the port—twenty-one guns from our bomb-lance things.

Our lieutenant of the hunting party seemed to be officer of the deck on the real battle-ship. "How'd you come out?" he hails.

"We met the enemy and their loot is ours," I answers.

"Captain Fenton presents his compliments and would like to have you come aboard," he hails.

And I went aboard, sitting in the stern-sheets of my second boat, with the red, green, and purple flag trailing astern and eight men to the oars. And they gave me two bosun's pipes with four side-boys and two long ruffles from the drums as I came over the side, and in the captain's cabin I told him what the officers of the hunting party couldn't tell him already. And he thought it the best story he'd heard in a long time.

I thought it was a pretty good story myself, and told it again to Mr. Amundsen on the same long pier where I had first met him with Hilda, and he said the blood of the old vikings must be in my veins, and uncorked four solid hours of the old sagas, finishing up in the big front room with fiat bread and goats' cheese and dried ptarmigan chips and Trondhjem beer.

By and by I got a chance to tell it to Hilda—that and a little more while I was telling it. The band, a fine band, too, was playing their Sunday-night concert out in the plaza. I remember how the music made pictures in my brain while I talked, though I never could remember what they played.

However, that's no matter. Hilda says I told the story right that night. And I've told it many a time since—to her and the children when I'm home from sea. They are good children, who believe everything that is told them—even the sagas of their grandfather.

THE LAST PASSENGER

Meade was having his coffee in the smoking-room. Major Crupp came in and took a seat beside him.

A watchful steward hurried over. "Coffee, sir?"

"Please."

"Cigarette, Major?" asked Meade.

"I will—thanks."

Lavis came in. Both men passed the greetings of the evening with him, and then Meade, at least, forgot that he existed. Only interesting people were of value to Meade, and he had early in the passage appraised Lavis—one of those negligible persons whose habit was to hover near some group of notables and look at them or listen to them, and, if encouraged, join in the conversation, or, if invited, take a hand in a game of cards.

"Seen Cadogan since dinner, Major?" asked Meade.

"He's patrolling the deck right now."

"With the beautiful lady?"

"Nope—alone."

"Thank God! And where is she?"

"Oh, she's nicely enthroned, thank you, in an angle of the loungeroom with that sixty-millionaire coal baron, Drissler."

"It's bath-tubs, and he's only got twenty millions."

"The poor beggar! Well, Meade, if ever she gets within shelling distance of his little twenty millions they'll melt like a dobey house in the rain."

"No doubt of that, I guess. And yet—and yet up to late this afternoon, at least, she appeared to be delighting in the presence of Cadogan."

"She surely did. But"—Major Crupp eyed Meade quizzically —"what are you worrying about?"

"I'm afraid she hasn't really shook him. I know too much about her. The twenty millions would be nice to draw upon, but her one unquenchable passion is man, and in build, looks, age, and temperament Cadogan is just one rich prize. But how do you account for Cadogan? He's certainly bright enough in other matters."

Crupp projected three smoke rings across the table at Meade. "I was stationed in the wilds of the Philippines one time. The native women where I was were unwashed, bow-legged, black creatures about four feet high. After three years of it I returned home in a government transport. I landed in San Francisco. At first I thought it was a dream."

"Thought what was a dream, Major?"

"The women going by. I posted myself on the corner of two streets, and there I stood transfixed, except every ten minutes or so, when I'd run into the hotel bar behind me and have another drink. And I'd come out again, and I'd take another look at those big, beautiful, upstanding creatures floating by, hosts and hosts of 'em, and I'd whisper to myself: 'Cruppie, you're dead. You've been boloed on outpost and gone to heaven, and you don't know it.' And googoo-eyed I kept staring at 'em, investing every last one of 'em with a double halo, till a long, splayfooted, thin-necked hombre in a policeman's uniform came along and says: 'Here, you, I've been pipin' you off for about four hours now. About time you moved on, ain't it?' Lord, and not one of 'em that couldn't have married me on the spot, I held 'em in such respect."

"Thick, wasn't he?"

"I thought so—then. But I wonder if Caddie would think we were thick, too, if we told him to move on? He's just back, remember, from two years in the jungle, and her eyes haven't changed color and her hair still shines like a new gold shoulder-knot at dress parade. She is still beautiful—and clever."

"Clever? She's surely that; but he's only a boy, Major."

"M-m—twenty-six!"

"What's twenty-six? He's still a dreaming boy. I'd like to say what I really thought of her."

"Don't. They'd be having a squad of stewards in here to police the place after you got through."

"Why don't you give him a hint?"

"Huh! No, no, Mister Meade—I'm still young and fair. You break it to him. Who knows, your age may save you from being projected through the nearest embrasure!" Crupp crushed the smoking end of his cigarette against the ash-tray. "I'll have to run along now."

"Back soon?"

"After I've said good night to two or three dear old ladies in the loungeroom before they go below."

"And two or three dear young ladies who won't be going below."

"Don't be saucy, Meade. You look out of uniform when you try to be saucy. Exactness as to fact and luminosity of language—that's you, if you please."

"Bring Vogel on your way back."

"If I can detach him from his beloved maps. Forty millions in railroads he's got now. And colored maps of 'em he's got. He gloats over 'em— gloats, every night before he turns in."

"Hurry him up, anyway. And drive Cadogan in. I'll get him going on a few adventures, and make him forget his beautiful lady."

* * * * *

Lavis had been sitting on the transom. He always seemed to be sitting on the transom—a long, lean, huddled-up figure in the corner, looking out with half-closed eyes on the life of the smoking-room.

Cadogan came in. Meade revolved the chair next to him at

the table, so that Cadogan had only to fall into it. Cadogan abstractedly nodded his thanks. Catching sight of Lavis, he nodded and smiled.

With eyes staring absently into space Cadogan was drumming on the table with his fingers.

"Sounds like some tom-tom march you're trying to play," interrupted Meade, and proffered a cigar. Cadogan shook his head.

"No?" Meade dropped his cigar placidly back into its case. "But listen here, Cadogan. As a writer and newspaper man, my main business in life is to discover people who know more than other people about some particular thing, and then get it out of them. What about this ocean-liner travelling of to-day—is it perfectly safe?"

"The safest mode of travel ever devised—or should be."

"But lives are lost?"

"Surely. And probably will be. But they should not be—not on the high sea—except in a collision, and then probably one ship or the other is to blame. Even inshore, if they keep their lead and foghorn going, and steam up to kick her off, nothing will happen either, unless"—he shrugged his shoulders—"they've gone foolish or something else on the bridge."

Meade questioned further. And Cadogan answered briefly, abstractedly, until—Meade growing more cunning and subtle—he was led into citing one experience after another from out of his own life in proof of this or that side of an argument.

Cadogan had begun in short, snappy sentences, and in a

tense, rather high-keyed voice; but once warmed up he swung along in rounded, almost classic periods; and his voice deepened and softened and, as he became yet more absorbed in his subject, grew rhythmical, musical almost, the while his words took on added color and glow.

Once in full swing it was not difficult for Meade to get him to run on; and he ran on for an hour, and would have gone on indefinitely only, suddenly coming to himself and looking around, he discovered that half the room had gathered in a semicircle behind his chair. He flushed, cut his story short, and said no more. The crowd dispersed to their various seats.

Presently Meade observed: "How did you ever find time in your young life for the half of it? And how you do suggest things—possibilities that try a man's spirit even to contemplate!"

Cadogan did not respond; but from Lavis, the man on the transom, came: "And now you are suggesting the really great adventuring!"

Meade turned in surprise. "What is that?"

"Isn't it in the spirit we have the really great adventures?"

Meade studied him curiously. "You mean that the most thrilling adventures are those we only dream about, but which never happen?"

"I didn't mean exactly that, for they do happen. What I meant was that to try your body was nothing, but to try your soul—try it to the utmost—there would be something."

"To risk it or try it?" asked Meade.

"Oh, to try it only. To risk it, would not that be sinful?"

Cadogan's instinctive liking for Lavis had led him from the beginning of the voyage to take a keen interest in whatever he might do or say; but until to-night he had found him a most unobtrusive and taciturn man. He had a feeling that this man, who before to-night had barely said more than good morning and good night to him, understood him much better than did Meade, the professional observer, who was forever questioning him. The answer to Meade's last question stirred him particularly, because he felt that it was meant, not for Meade, but for himself.

Thinking of Meade, who was a famous author and journalist, Cadogan said hesitatingly and shyly: "I've often thought I'd like to be a writer." He meant that for Lavis, but it was Meade who took it to himself to ask him why.

"If I were a writer, I'd have hope right now of taking part in one of the greatest adventures that could befall a man."

"Where, Cadogan?"

"Right aboard this ship. How? Here we are tearing through the iceberg country trying to make a record. If ever we piled up head on to one of those icebergs, where would we be?"

"But it is a clear night. And the lookouts."

"Never mind the clear night—or the lookouts if they are not looking out."

"But this ship can't sink."

"No? But suppose she can sink, and that she is sinking. There are four thousand people aboard—and down she goes.

Wouldn't that be an experience?"

With meditative eyes directed down to the ashes at the end of his cigar, Meade mulled over the question. "A great adventure it surely would be," he at length emitted from behind a puff of smoke. "The right man, a great writer, for instance, if he could live through that, would make a world's epic of it."

Cadogan wondered what the man on the transom was thinking of. He put his next question directly to him. "There would be some great deaths in such an event, don't you think, sir?" His own eyes were glowing.

"Some great deaths, surely—and some horrible ones, doubtless, too."

"Oh, but men would die like gods at such a time!"

"No doubt—and like dogs also."

Meade did not relish losing control of the conversation to an undistinguished outsider. "Look here, Cadogan," he interjected; "could a man live through that—go down with the ship and survive?"

"He could survive the sinking—yes; but he would not live long—not in water near icebergs. The numbness soon creeps up to your heart, and then—"

"But how could a man do it and live?"

"Why, sir, do you insist that he should live?" It was Lavis who had spoken.

Meade's eyebrows rose above the tops of his horn glasses.

"Eh!" Cadogan, too, stared at Lavis.

"To live after it would be only to half complete the adventure. We began by speaking of an adventure in the spirit. To make a real, a great adventure of it, should not the man die?"

Meade now smiled with obvious tolerance. "But a man dead and buried in the depths of the sea!"

"That would only be his body, and we were speaking of an adventure of the spirit—of the soul. The man should experience every physical dread, every nervous fear, every emotional horror of those last few minutes, share the bitterness of the disillusionment inevitable when three or four thousand ordinary, every-day human beings are dying in despair, because, as they would judge it, dying so needlessly. To get the full measure of it, and to share also in the sweetness and resignation of great souls in the hour of death, would not his mortal body have to meet death, even as the others?"

Meade readjusted his horned spectacles. He would have to revise his notes of the man, that was plain. Forty, or forty-five possibly, he was. Tall and large-framed, but spare, thin-checked, and hollow-templed, with white streaks among the close-clipped, very black, and very thick hair which showed from under his cap. A worn-looking man, a student. M-m— he had him now—a teacher of the classics in some college, possibly a young women's college.

"To get back to our steamer and your extraordinary proposition," suggested Meade; "you say that the man should actually die?"

"Surely die. And he should face death even as our highly

vitalized young friend here faces life. Mr. Cadogan, coming back to us from perilous experiences, makes us share with him in every tremor, every dread, every thought he himself felt in his adventure. And how does he manage to do that? Isn't it because in the perilous moment his soul remains tranquil? If death comes, well and good—it cannot be helped; if not, then a glorious adventure. He meets danger with every faculty keyed up to the highest. Now, if a man would meet his death, as this steamer went down, in the same mood, would he not march into the shadows with a soul ennobled?"

"And then what?"

"Then? If we are heirs in spirit even as in body will God ever allow a great spirit to become extinct?"

Meade abandoned his young-ladies'-teacher supposition. He speared the man with another glance. "Pardon me, you are not a scientist?"

Lavis smiled—for the first time. "Do I talk like one?"

"You do not believe, then, in present-day scientific methods?"

"I believe in any constructive method, but"—he betrayed a shadow of impatience—"why limit our beliefs to what can be proved with a surgeon's knife?"

Meade thought he remembered that Roman Catholic priests were on special occasions allowed to travel without the outer garb of their calling; but would a priest talk so freely to a stranger? And yet—"You must have had a religious training at some time in your life?"

Lavis smiled again, but more slowly. "You are persistent, Mr. Meade."

"I beg your pardon. It is the journalist's interviewing habit. And I thought I recalled, also—"

Lavis seemed to be waiting for Meade to finish, but Meade, who suddenly realized to what he was leading, did not finish; and Lavis turned his head so as to look squarely at Cadogan. Through the half-closed, wistful eyes Cadogan caught a gleam that he again felt was an answer to Meade's unfinished question, and yet was again meant, not for Meade, but for himself.

"But to return," persisted Meade; "how is the world to benefit by your theory that God does not allow a great spirit to die?"

"Well, call it theory. After the mortal death of a man whose dying was a tremendous experience, there will be born again a great soul. And if the being in whom that soul is enshrined is but true to the best in himself, he will attain to the utterance of a great message, compel the world to listen to his message; and the world, having listened, will be for all time the better."

"I suppose"—Meade was by now not wholly free of self-consciousness—"a man should have had a training as a writer to best fit him for such an experience?"

"Writer, sculptor, painter, musician, lawgiver—anything, so that he possesses the germ, the potential power to make others see, hear, or feel things as he does."

"But who aboard this ship possesses such a gift?"

Lavis turned to Cadogan. "Here is the man."

"Who!" Cadogan bounded in his seat; and then, smiling at himself: "That's a good one—I took it seriously."

"Take it seriously, please."

Cadogan instantly sobered. "But I'm not aching to die. And the Lord never intended me for a martyr."

"Are you sure you know what the Lord intended you for? You have done great deeds in one way. You could do great deeds in another way. A great deed is never more than a great thought in action. You need but the great thought to give the great deed birth."

"But I never originated a great thought in my life."

"What man ever did? The seeds of great thoughts are born in us, which means that they come from God. But great deeds are man's. And if it should come to pass in your adventurous life that you go to a calamitous death, it may not be altogether a pity. If your heart remains pure as now, it surely would not be. You have every qualification, if you could but be born again."

"Why wouldn't you yourself be the man for such a thing?" It was Meade, eying the man from under contracted eyebrows, who put this question.

"Thanks!" Lavis's smile was almost perceptible.

"I did not mean—"

"No harm. It would require the creative genius. I am no longer creative."

"But you have an intellect."

"Meaning that I have a well-developed muscle in the brain? The man who lifts heavy weights in the circus has also a well-developed muscle in his arm, or back, or legs, but what does he teach us that is for the betterment of the race? But Mr. Cadogan here has the flaming soul. And the last passenger on this ship should be such as he, a strong man with the innocence of the child." He turned from the older to the younger man. "You are creative in thought, powerful, direct, tireless in action, Mr. Cadogan. Every new experience still comes to you with the dew of the morning on it. You should die hard, with your eyes open to the last. Nothing would escape you. And you would know what dying was, because for you to give up life would be a great renunciation."

Cadogan shook his head. "Even if all the rest of it were true, I have nothing in life to renounce."

"How can you know that? You would be renouncing a limitless capacity for enjoyment, if nothing more." Lavis rose to his feet. "I hope I haven't bored you too much? I think I will go out and get some fresh air." He bowed and smiled to Meade, smiled more warmly on Cadogan, wrapped his top-coat over his evening clothes, and went out on deck.

Meade saw that Cadogan was gazing thoughtfully on the seat which Lavis had vacated. "What do you make of him, Cadogan?"

Cadogan's face, when he swung his chair around, was flushed, his dark-blue eyes more glowing than usual. "I don't know, except that he had me thinking. He made me feel that he was reading my mind, and before he left I was saying to myself, 'When I grow older I'll be something like him,' only, of course, with less brains than he's got."

"You'll have brains enough, don't fear. He made me think of the head of a religious order who went wrong some years ago. But that was before I knew much of the inside of Continental affairs. A woman, as I recall it. However, he's gone—he made my head ache trying to follow him, and—but there is the major and Vogel passing the port-hole. I'll call them in and we'll have our little rubber."

* * * * *

They sat in to their little rubber, and while they played a passenger of importance was auctioning off the pool on the ship's run for the next day.

He stood on a table to see and be seen, a short, fat, bearded man who sometimes had to pause for breath. "Here she is, gentlemen, the largest ship of all time making marine history. What d'y' say, gentlemen? We all know what we did up to noon to-day. We did even better, impossible though it may seem, this afternoon. Now, what am I offered for the high field? Come now, gentlemen. By Tuesday morning, at ten o'clock, are we to be abreast of Sandy Hook or not? It will be a record run if we make it, but whether we are a few minutes late or early, every indication points to a grand day's run for to-morrow. Come, gentlemen, bid up!"

"What of the rumors of icebergs?" asked a voice.

"Pray do not joke, gentlemen. I beg of you, do not joke. Has any person here observed any notice of icebergs posted on the ship's board? I fancy not. To-day I myself put the question to the man whose word is law on this ship. Do I have to name him, gentlemen? No need, is there? No. 'Are we going to slow down?' was my question. 'On the contrary, we are going to go faster,' was the reply."

James B. Connolly

There was a laugh. "Seventy pounds!" was called.

"That's the spirit, gentlemen. Seventy pounds for the high field. The gentleman who shall be fortunate enough to win this pool will have something to brag about in future days. Come, now, how much for the high field? Seventy-five? Good! Gentlemen, I am offered—"

"What's the high field worth, Cadogan?" asked Vogel.

"All you want to bid, if nothing goes wrong. But with ship's officers spending more time with distinguished passengers than on the bridge, I wouldn't give a nickel for it."

"I won't bid, then."

The voice of the man on the table was increasing in volume. "Eighty-five pounds I am offered for the high field. It is not enough, not enough by far, gentlemen—eh! Eh, I say."

The ship heaved, not violently; gently rather, under them. There was an easy, slight roll to port, a dull, almost noiseless bumping, a slow, heavy resistance, as of a heavy object being forced over a stubbornly yielding surface.

To either side of him and in the mirrors Cadogan could see a dozen men peer inquiringly up over cards or books or glasses. Meade stared around the room. "What the devil's that?" he asked, and held a card high, with eyes directed to the nearest deck door.

There was a recoil of the ship, which slowly and gently, but surely and almost comically, to Cadogan's way of thinking, urged the stout waist of Meade against the edge of the table.

Cadogan waited his last turn to play, laid down his card, and scooped in the trick. "Forty on points, eight on honors, Major," he said, and set it down. "If nobody minds, I'll step out on deck and see what stopped her."

"Stopped! Is she stopped?" exclaimed Vogel.

"She is." Cadogan strolled out of the smoking-room. Three or four had preceded him; half a dozen, who had nothing else to do, strolled out after him.

In a few minutes those who had gone out were beginning to return. "Well, what do you know about that?" whooped the first one. "Hit a lump of ice! Lucky for the ice we didn't hit it fair, with this forty-five-thousand-tonner going along at twenty-five or six knots an hour like she is!"

Several laughed at that, and Major Crupp, who was patiently riffling the cards, called out to the last speaker: "Did you see Mr. Cadogan out there?"

"I saw him going toward the bow of the ship, Major," was the answer.

"Investigating, I suppose. Well, suppose we play dummy— what do you-all say?—till Caddie comes back. He's possessed of a demon for finding out things. Your deal, Mr. Vogel."

A steward stepped in from the deck. "Major Crupp, sir?"

"Yes."

"Mr. Cadogan told me to say not to wait till he came back, sir, but to go on with the game, sir."

Vogel picked up his cards. "How long will we be delayed, steward?"

"Oh, not more than an hour or two, they say, sir."

"H-m-m"—Vogel stared reflectively at the table—"I'll have to buy Cadogan a good smoke when he comes back. He saved me ninety or a hundred pounds on that high field."

They resumed play.

II

Lavis was pacing the wide promenade deck and sniffing the air as he paced. It was as if a breath of the north were on them, and yet—having reached the uncovered part of the deck astern he looked up to observe the steamer's smoke— the wind was not from the north.

Such passengers as were still making their rounds were doing so determinedly, in sweaters or top-coats. Without halting in their rapid walking they, too, at times drew short, sharp breaths through high-held nostrils. It surely was growing colder. But why? A group held up an officer who was smoking his pipe in the lee of the canvas forward to ask him why. He at once set them right about it. Why, surely it should be cool—on the North Atlantic, in April, and well on in the evening!

A couple that Lavis knew for bride and groom turned out to lean over the rail. He was pointing down by the ship's side. "Hardly a ripple on it—see!" he exclaimed. "Only for the bubbling up from underneath, none at all. Like an endless belt sliding by so smoothly, isn't it? And above—see, sweetheart—a clear sky."

"Ah-h, a beautiful night!" she murmured. "On such a night— " Lavis, as he turned the corner of the house, saw him snatch her close and kiss her.

In lounge and smoking rooms all was cosey, cheerful, lively company. Lavis in passing had only to glance into air-ports to be sure of that. It was card-playing and easy gossip in the one, and not infrequent drinks being brought to impatient men by alert, deferential, many-buttoned servants in the other. In the grill those who must have a special little bite before turning in were having it; and, this being a chilly sort of a night, there were those who were also having a warming drink, with the bite or without it.

It was growing late. The deck was now almost deserted. Lavis took a last look over the rail, a last gulp of the cooling air, and went into the loungeroom. Here he got from the steward paper and envelopes, sat down and wrote:

Now see that you make no attempt to lure him back.

There was no address, no signature. He sealed the envelope and went below to where, at the end of a passageway, he found a stewardess on watch. "Miss Huttle hasn't come down yet, Hannah?"

"No, sir, Mr. Lavis."

"No? Well, there is a party in Mr. Drissler's suite."

"Mr. Drissler, sir?"

"The wealthy man in the royal suite."

"Oh, yes, sir."

"Miss Huttle is there. You take this note to her there, and let me know that it has been delivered, please."

Lavis went to his room, got out a long, loose linen duster from his wardrobe, removed his top-coat, pulled the duster over his evening clothes, found an old cloth cap, and waited for the return of the stewardess.

She came presently. "I gave it to Miss Huttle, Mr. Lavis. Into her own hand, sir."

"Thank you, Hannah."

* * * * *

Lavis left his room and descended deep down into the ship, to where a man in dungarees, but with an officer's cap of authority, was perched on a horizontal grating poring over the speed register. Over his shoulder Lavis watched the numerals shift—seven, eight, nine, thirty. One, two—eight, nine, forty. Click, click, click, click—he watched them until the officer turned and saw him.

"Ho, I was beginning to think you'd given me the go-by for to-night." They shook hands.

"Isn't it the most beautiful mechanism ever made by the hand of man!" exclaimed the officer. "A watch is nothing to it. And what you see here cost more than twenty thousand watches—twenty thousand of 'em, and every danged watch in a gold case."

He drew out his own gun-metal stop-watch. "I'll time her now for a hundred revolutions."

He caught the time, set it down in a little notebook, and from it slowly but surely reckoned her speed. "Grand, grand!" he said softly. "Will you come along? Good!"

They descended and ascended many narrow iron ladders and made their way through many narrow, grimy passageways. Oilers, stokers, coal-passers, water-tenders straightened up to give them a greeting as they passed. In one boiler-room a stoker was scooping a dipper through the water-pail at his feet as they entered.

"Are we holding our own this watch, Mr. Linnell?" He held

James B. Connolly

the dipper respectfully in suspense for the answer.

"Holding it? Yes, and more."

"Hi, hi! an' that gang went off watch before us, Mr. Linnell—an' I fancy they rate themselves a competent watch—among themselves, sir—they threw it at us as how we'd do mighty well to hold our own." By this time his chief had passed on, but Lavis, lingering, saw the stoker gulp a mouthful of water, hold it a moment, and squirt it, *s-s-t!* contemptuously into a heap of hot ashes.

Linnell continued his rounds, sparing a nod here; a nod there, almost a full smile at times, and at times, too, a sharp snap of criticism. Lavis in his rear caught the pursuing comment. He was the kind, was the chief, to soon let you know where you stood. And right he was. And no one would begrudge him what he could make of the passage, if so be he could make a bit more of reputation out of it, for surely his heart was in his work. Never one to loaf, by all reports, but this time!—not a single watch without his full rounds below.

Lavis followed the engineer up a narrow iron ladder, and thence up a wide iron ladder, to where, from a heavily grated brass-railed platform, Linnell surveyed his engines.

He laid a hand on Lavis's shoulder and extended an eloquent arm. "Worth looking at, aren't they? The largest engines ever went into a ship, those engines you are looking at now, Mr. Lavis. It is something to have charge of the likes of them. Wait till I see some of my old mates!" His was a low, chuckling laugh. "I'll be having a word to say, they better believe, of ship's engines! Talking of their ten and twenty thousand tonners—ferry-boats, river ferry-boats, that's what I'll tell 'em they have alongside o' this one. And everything working beautifully"—he hesitated a moment—"leastwise in my division. An' why shouldn't it, Mr. Lavis, after four days and three nights now of never closing an eye for more than two hours together? But two nights and another day now, an' 'twill be all behind us. And something to put behind a man, that—a record-breakin' maiden passage of the greatest ship ever built. And—but I'm gassin' again. We'll be moving on."

Lavis followed Linnell to where a man in grimy blue dungarees was standing silent watch. Before him was a row of levers and beside him a dial on which were words in very black letters: FULL SPEED, HALF SPEED, and so on. To one side was a disk around which two colored arrows, one red and one green, were racing. A gong was at the man's ear. At his feet was a pit into which a great mass of highly polished steel was driving in and out, in and out, up and down ceaselessly.

Linnell studied the colored arrows as they sped around the disk. "Port engine a bit the best of it?" He had to speak into the man's ear to make himself heard.

The man in dungarees nodded. "A wee bit, sir."

"How's all else?"

"Couldn't be better, sir." He had to yell to make himself heard. "Are we holding our own, sir?"

"A full revolution better than any watch since we left port."

The man nodded as if he had been expecting it, but presently chuckled and swung one foot playfully toward the glittering gray cross-head as it went driving down into the pit. "A full revolution!" he echoed—"t-t-t"—and spat with obvious significance into the pit.

"T-t-t—" mimicked Linnell, and slapped him lightly on the shoulder before he turned to Lavis.

"Will you go farther or wait here?"

"I'll wait here, if you don't mind, and stand part of the watch with Andie."

"Very good! I'll pick you up later."

Lavis, standing beside Andie and gazing into the pit, pointed to the great cross-head driving by. "If that were to fly out and go through the bottom of the ship, Andie, would it sink her?"

Andie projected his lower lip. "It *might* sink her, sir, though it don't seem possible-like. But if it *did* sink her, 'twould be *about* the only way *to* sink her, sir."

Lavis let his eyes roam above and about him. Andie observed the direction of his gaze. "A wonderful sight, aren't it?" he commented. "What wi' so many polished rods an' shafts all whity-gray, an' all them many beams an' bars so beautiful green an' red-painted!"

Lavis, still interested in the wonderful machinery, felt the deck lifted the least bit under him. It was as if the ship had risen to a rolling head sea. He laid hold of a handy stanchion to steady himself, but he saw Andie, unsupported, go sliding easily, gently, irresistibly to the bulkhead behind them. Lavis saw Andie brace his legs, and then, remindful and resentful, bound back to his station and set a hand to each of two levers. The iron deck beneath them was still rolling easily; from beneath the deck came a chafing noise, a slow, heavy grinding.

Lavis saw that with hands to levers, eyes on indicator, and

ears to gong, the man in dungarees had become oblivious to all but the expected order from the bridge. It came after a time—the warning clang and the needle pointing to ASTERN SLOW.

Andie shifted his levers. Rods and shafts reversed. Andie, eyes set on the bridge dial, waited.

Lavis could hear Linnell's voice sharply hailing somebody in the boiler-room passage. Presently he saw him running by the bulkhead door; and then, from the far end of the passage, his voice cracking out like a whip: "Back, I say! Back, you dogs, back to your stations! I'll tell you when you're to go."

He came bounding in and past Lavis and Andie, up the narrow iron ladder, up the wider one above it. Again Lavis heard him: "You thought to forelay me, eh—and breed panic above? You misbegotten spawn, I'd kill you as I'd kill a cockroach—and every last one of you, if you force me. You dogs—go back!"

Cries and oaths, then the thud of a heavy weapon on bone and flesh, the falling of stumbling bodies on the iron grating above. A silence, and then Linnell's voice again, now more controlled: "You there, Wallace? Well, stay there. An' let not a single one of 'em pass without my orders. Shoot 'em down if you have to, but keep 'em below."

The ship was still backing. *Wh-r-r-i-ng!* went the gong. Stop! commanded the indicator. Andie shifted the levers. The tremendous machinery hung motionless.

All was quiet. Not a quiver from out of the great compartment. Through the grating over his head Lavis saw the figure of the chief hurriedly descending. He saw him turn, pause a moment at the head of the narrow ladder, and then come sliding down.

"Doing our best, some of 'em will get up above," he said quietly. "But we've enough left for a watch." He stepped to Andie's side, all the while with his eyes roaming over the machinery. "She answered her bells promptly, Andie?"

"To the stroke, sir."

"Good! Stay by her. Pass the word to me if aught goes wrong."

He was through the bulkhead door and into the passageway before he had completed the order.

Lavis saw Andie pout his lower lip, and with a "T-t-t—" shift his gaze to the pit. "The blind bats!" burst from him, and he spat into the pit. "See there, sir!" he called out to Lavis.

Lavis nodded. He had already noticed it. There was a foot or so of water in the pit.

"How the devil came it there?" Andie stooped and scooped a handful of it, tasted it, and held it up for Lavis to view. "Salt! *And* cold. T-t-t—" Andie let his breath whistle softly through his parted teeth.

The water was rising. By and by it was over the top of the pit and crawling across the shiny deck. Andie looked about for relief.

"I'll tell him," volunteered Lavis.

"Thank you, sir. An' you might say, sir, there must be somethin' wrong wi' the bulkhead doors. They aren't closed yet."

Lavis met Linnell returning in the passageway. "Buttons in place of eyes in their heads aloft!" he was muttering. "An' for all o' forty mechanics brought specially to set things right, they can't close the doors below."

Together they waded in to where Andie was now to his knees in water. "Let be your levers, Andie, an' take a spell o' rest for yourself," commanded Linnell.

Andie slowly relaxed his fingers, pulled a bunch of waste from his hip pocket, and wiped his hands.

"She's hard hit," said Linnell to Lavis, "though there's few know it yet. And won't in a hurry."

"Then I'd better be going above?"

"That's right, do. Will you be back this way again?"

Lavis let his hand rest lightly on Andie's head. "I'm not sure." He extended his hand to Linnell. "If I don't see you again, good-by."

"Good-by, Mr. Lavis." The engineer stepped closer and whispered: "If any honest chance offers to leave the ship, leave her."

* * * * *

Lavis found his way through the crew's quarters to the lowest sleeping deck of steerage. Here a few old people and some children, too discouraged, too indifferent, or too helpless, were clinging to their bunks. On the next deck he found a gathering in the open space surrounding a freight hatch. One whom he knew for a Polish woman, with her baby at her breast, was on the edge of the crowd, and, like most of the others, glancing up to see what was doing on the higher decks. The Polish woman was too concerned with her baby to see exactly what they were doing on that high deck where all the boats were, but another woman was telling her how it was.

Lavis stepped closer and listened. She was telling, the tall one, how there were many men running about excitedly—ship's men with only shirts above their trousers some, and others with coats buttoned up. And they were pulling and hauling and knocking away blocks. Such a clear night one could see them—see their forms—and hear, too, their blows and shouts. The woman with the baby nodded. Without looking up she could hear the blows. And now the electric light had come, resumed the tall one; she could see that many women had gathered there, and some were pushing forward and others pushing back, and now women—yes, and a man—were being put into a boat.

"And now the boat is lowered," resumed the tall one.

"I can hear them," said the young mother. "And now it is rowing away from the ship in the dark."

"And there is another," informed the tall one by and by.

"I can hear that, too, rowing away in the dark. And from the water—do you hear it, too, baby—such a lonesome cry in the darkness?"

At that moment Lavis spoke to her in her own language. The young mother greeted him warmly. "Ah-h, baby," she said, "here is the good gentleman who lives in the country where your father is waiting." She turned from the baby to ply Lavis with rapid questions in Polish.

What did that mean—the boats leaving the great ship? Surely it must be true what the men had said, the ship's men—that there was no danger? Surely it must be true that such a monster of a ship, it could not sink? Surely it could not! And yet why were all the rich ladies being sent away and the gates to the upper decks closed, so that the poor people in the steerage could not get out? Was it really true there was no danger? Surely those officers would not deceive poor, friendless people! And yet here the oily men, the greasy ones who worked deep down in the ship, rushing every moment from below! And saying nothing but low-spoken words to each other, and into their rooms and out again in no time, but with more and heavier clothes upon them! Did men dress more warmly to work where the engines and hot fires were?

"Wait. I will return," said Lavis to her, and stepped over to where two stewards were on guard over a gate. One, observing him, turned to the other and remarked, with vast negligence: "A silly lot, steerage, ain't they? Always airin' a growl about something or other, as if ship's rulin's was a-goin' to be changed for the likes o' them!"

"I would like to get to the upper deck," interrupted Lavis.

"*You* would like to get to the upper deck, would you? And who, may I ask, do you take yourself for, a-trying to speak like a toff?" The man turned his back to Lavis. "Swine!" he repeated to his mate.

Lavis glanced down at himself. He had overlooked the effect of the old linen duster and the old cap.

"When *he* gets to 'arbor, of course there will be tugboat visitors and customs officers arskin' for 'im, won't they?"

The other cast half an eye on Lavis. "When the clarss will

look down on the tops o' their heads and remark: 'What a mob of 'em there! How many of 'em did you cart along this time, Captain?' I fancy he'll have only to cock his ear up to hear 'em."

"Bloody foreigners, most of 'em."

Lavis returned to the Polish mother. "Come," he said. "There is another way out of here."

"Please, sir, the big, jolly Irisher—what is she saying?"

Lavis listened to the big, jolly Irish girl, who, however, was not now so jolly. Lavis had seen a thousand like her gathering kelp on the west Irish coast—tall, deep-bosomed, barefooted girls with black hair to the waist, and glorious dark eyes. She was standing on the covered hatch, and pointing at the moment to one of the ship's men who had passed.

"Wet to his knees. Where is it he should be getting wet to his knees? And another one. And where is it they are going? And is it we that has to stay here till that kind"—she pointed to the two stewards on guard at the steerage gate—"are pleased to let us out? Haven't we as much right to our lives as them that lives higher up? Five hundred of us here, women and childther, and which of them above cares whether we live or die?"

She pointed to a woman with her brood clinging to her hands and skirts. "Look at that poor woman with her five childther. And that poor little thing"—she indicated the Polish woman—"that has a husband waiting for herself and her baby in New York. And that other one, and that one, and that one. God in heaven, mothers with their children to their breasts, and not to be given a chance to live at all! If 'tis a mother I was, and a child to my breast, it's not images of men in uniforms would hinder me from saving my baby this night! And myself with my baby, if my baby was in need of me, an' I could."

The two ship's men on guard were gazing, not at the steerage, but up at the higher decks, when a dozen or more of the steerage women swept across the deck. "Grand work for strong men," the Irish girl cried, "preventin' poor women and childther from looking out for themselves. It's not even shadows of men ye are!" and with that bowled the near one over; and her companions, sweeping up behind her, bowled the other one over. The two stewards had a look up and a look down, and then, with an outraged look at each other, they flew after the disappearing steerage women.

"Come, now." Lavis took the Polish mother's hand.

"Sh-h!" she warned. "He is sleeping."

Lavis, nodding that he saw, helped her carefully to her feet, and led her through the now unguarded gate, and by way of several ladders, to that high deck where the boats were.

A boat was all but ready for lowering. The last woman had been crowded into it. The Polish woman removed her shawl and wrapped it around her baby. "Baby!" Lavis could hear her saying over and over again in Polish. "Oh, my baby! my baby boy!" but softly, so as not to waken him. She stepped into the circle of light which surrounded the boat and the ship's people. "Sa-ave beb-by," she said in English, and held shawl and baby up at the end of her outstretched arms.

A rough hand gripped her by the shoulder.

"Stand back! Stand back, you! You've no right here! Saloon

goes first, don't y' understand?"

She stepped back in discouragement.

The men, busy at the falls, had swung the boat clear and were about to lower away. "Now!" said Lavis sharply in her ear, and pointed to the boat.

"Ah-h," she murmured, and darted under the arms of the ship's men and thrust her baby into the bosom of the nearest woman in the life-boat. "Save beb-by!" she breathed, and darted back into the crowd.

"I meant yourself also," said Lavis reproachfully.

"No, no, no—they would take baby, but me—no." Her eyes followed the lowered boat.

III

When Cadogan went forward he wished to see something other than the loom of the low-lying, misty, white berg against the sky. He peered down over the bow. He bent low his ear to catch the purr of eddying waters.

He turned sharply on his heel, and went below—deep below.

* * * * *

When he reappeared he went straight to his stateroom. Here, in the cabin sleeping quarters below the promenade deck, nothing disturbing had happened. When such passengers as were about to turn in became aware of that slow lurch and easy stoppage, they had stepped out into the passageways, and asked each other what was the matter; which question was answered almost immediately by ship's people who came hurrying among them with reassuring words. "It's nothing, ladies and gentlemen. If you will go back to your rooms, ladies and gentlemen—it's nothing." And they had gone back to their rooms.

Cadogan turned on the light in his room, and hauled out his suit-case. He found a pad of paper, found also a fountain pen, shook the pen to make sure there was ink in it, let down the covering of the wash-basin for a desk, laid thereon a small photograph of a beautiful face and head *en profile*, and began to write. He set down "Dear," and paused. He smiled faintly, wrote "Helen" after it, and went unhesitatingly on:

This afternoon, over our tea, as I concluded one of my almost endless monologues, you may remember you said, "You'd better watch out or some day you will be having your last adventure." Well, I have had it. Not with this ship—no, no. My last adventure was a dream of you. I was on the dock, about to board a steamer for South America, when I saw you step out of your cab. And so I came aboard here. I am glad I came.

You brushed me in passing, as I stood beside the gangplank trying not to stare at you; but you did not know that—did you?—although for an instant I thought you did. It was the conceit of youth, that thought.

Cadogan held up his pen. The sound of hurrying feet from the passageway, the noise of fists pounding on doors, of high-pitched voices asking and answering questions, broke on his ears. He listened, stared at the air-port for a moment, and resumed his writing:

About this time a steward is pounding on your door and *hin*forming you that you are to go on deck and be ready to go into the boats. Nothing serious, he is probably saying. The poor man who tells you so, I am sure, does not suspect, but whoever told him to carry that message knew better. Perhaps it is just as well he does not suspect.

When the steamer stopped that time, it was because she struck on the submerged shelf of an iceberg. In three hours—or less—she will go down, and all who happen to be on board will go with her. They should be able to stow a thousand women and children in the boats, and these should be picked up soon after daylight, if the sea stays smooth and the weather clear. To-night's indications were clear weather and a calm sea for at least another day, so that will be all right.

You will be in one of the boats, and—safe. It would be like you not to want to go. If I hear that you do not, then some one will see that you do go. But I shall not be by you when you leave the ship, for I do not want you to read in my face that I know I am not to see you again—nor to bother you in any way. I shall be looking on as you leave, and what you said to-night will not then matter. As you go over the side my prayer will go with you.

There came a sharp knock on the door.

"Come!" he called. It was his own steward, who thrust his head past the door's edge. "Saloon passengers are to go on deck, Mr. Cadogan."

"Why?"

"I 'ave no idea, sir. Orders, sir. I was to hinform the saloon passengers as how they were to go on deck, and women and children into boats."

"All right. Thank you. And, Hames."

"Yes, sir?"

"You hunt up Miss Huttle's maid, and have her tell Miss Huttle to be sure to wrap up warm. Be sure she gets that right—to wrap up warm. Two sets of everything all round. Got that right?"

"Two sets—yes, sir."

"That's all, Hames."

"'K you, sir."

He resumed writing:

And so it has come to write the adieu which I would dread

to have to speak. Four days only have I known you, but a man may build his life anew in four days, and this last adventure of mine has been such as in my visionary boyhood days I used to mark out for myself in rosy dreams.

I have the little snapshot you gave me yesterday. I will have it with me to the end, and your face in it will be the last thing I kiss this side of eternity. And so good-by, dear heart, and don't worry for me. Who lives by the sword, et cetera. It had to come to some such ending, I suppose, though rather a joke, isn't it, to be lost on an ocean liner crossing the Atlantic in these days?

To-day with you I saw the sun go down 'twixt purple bars, and what is the little matter of dying to that? And it is a consolation to know you will not mourn me. Good night, dear heart, and may God have ever a tender eye on you.

He sealed the envelope, and very carefully addressed it: "Miss Helen Huttle," placed it in his inside coat-pocket, kissed the little photograph, and placed that also in his inside coat-pocket.

He gazed about to see what else. His top-coat lay where he had last thrown it—across the edge of the berth. He shook his head at it, and from his wardrobe took a heavy ulster, scanned it approvingly and put it on. He hauled his steamer trunk out from under his berth, and from a corner of it dragged a thick wallet. He ran his thumb along the edge of the bills within it. Large banknotes they were mostly. He stuck the wallet into his hip pocket. The handle of a magazine pistol peeped up at him. He took it up, laid it flat in the palm of his hand, shook his head, and tossed it back. He took one more look around the room, waved his hand to the walls, and stepped out into the passageway.

A hurrying steward almost bumped into him. It was Hames. "Miss Huttle was told, sir."

"Good! Now, something else. Later on Miss Huttle will be going into a boat. Before she goes, be sure you give her this letter. Not now—no. But up on deck, just before she goes."

"Yes, sir."

Cadogan sought the upper deck by way of the second-cabin quarters. On the wide staircase he overtook an old couple who, at sight of him, began talking volubly. She was a little old lady with a confiding smile, and he a bent and round-backed man with a long, forked beard.

"Vot you t'ink, Mr. Cadogan? He tell me I shell go in der boads."

"And why not, Mrs. Weiscopf?"

"Und vere shell he go?"

"A man of Mr. Weiscopf's age—they may let him go with you."

"I go in der boads?" The old man tried to straighten up. "I shell not go in der boads. I, mit childrun und grandchildrun, to go in der boads? It is der foolishness—all der foolishness —dose boads."

"Why, then, shell I go in der boads, Simon?"

"For mens I say der foolishness. All der womans go in der boads, Meenie."

"I shell not go in der boads mitout you, Simon."

"Go in the boat, and take him with you, if you can, Mrs. Weiscopf," whispered Cadogan, and hurried on.

He came onto the boat-deck in the rear of the saloon passengers already gathered there. The first boat was clear. An officer stood at the stern of it. "Women and children!" he was calling out, and there was a rush to fill it.

"I don't see many children," said a voice.

"Do you ever—in saloon?" retorted another.

Cadogan, recognizing the second voice as Meade's, and seeing that he was also in the rear of the crowd, stepped over beside him.

The boat was filled, and lowered in jumps and jerks. The passengers moved to the next boat. Half a dozen ship's men and an officer stood by.

"They're taking enough of the crew along," observed Meade.

"Not much gets by you," commented Cadogan.

"It's my business. I'll have to write a story about this later."

"Women and children!" called the officer.

The boat was filled, except for a space for ship's men and the officer in charge, who stepped quickly in. This boat went down likewise in jumps and jerks.

In the next boat two men passengers jumped in at the last moment. The officer in charge seemed not to see them. The crew said nothing.

"Must have friends at court," muttered Meade. "Though why anybody should choose the staying out all night, half frozen, in those boats I don't understand, do you? But look—there's the Major marshalling his battalions. Old ladies and young, pretty and otherwise—instinctively gallant, the Major," observed Meade.

"We'll remember your friends in New York, Major!" two of the younger ones chorussed.

"Be sure you do!" he retorted. "And pay your bet with a box of candy when you're back aboard in the morning. But take care you keep those rugs around your feet in the meantime." He waved them smilingly down the side of the ship, but he was not smiling when he had turned his back to the ship's side, and made his way into the crowd of passengers.

Cadogan shrank back of Meade. It was Miss Huttle who had stepped into the light, with Drissler in attendance. And not alone Drissler. She was fully dressed, with heavy furs in addition. Her smile was not less frequent, and apparently her tongue no less ready than usual, when she replied to the sallies of her escorts.

The blocks were knocked away clumsily, the falls over-hauled bunglingly for the next boat. Cadogan ached to jump in and show them how to do it.

"The worst of standing here, Meade"—Major Crupp had taken his position by the side of the journalist—"is that no matter how matters are handled, we can no more interfere than if we were children in steerage. And yet some of us, Cadogan here especially, could help out a lot."

"Why can't you jump in there and help?" inquired Meade.

"Discipline. A man whose trade calls above all things for discipline must be the last of all to interfere with it. There's an officer there foolishly displaying a revolver, frightening people needlessly. Some foolish woman—did you hear her?—just said: 'How brave!' Brave! When his boat is loaded he goes off with it."

"Well, he's welcome, Major. I wouldn't care to be out there all night. What do you say, Cadogan?"

Cadogan made no answer. He was not losing a finger's crook of Miss Huttle's actions; and yet he was listening to and studying Meade and Crupp, old Mrs. Weiscopf and her husband, the ship's officers and men, a steerage woman with her baby in a shawl—however she came to be there—everybody and everything within sight and hearing. He could not help it. If he were one of a file of prisoners to be taken out and shot, his last curiosity would be to know what everybody was saying and doing—the executioners, the executed, himself, the spectators.

He noted the parting of bride and groom, and wondered what that groom would have given to go with her into the boat. He was taking note of the women who went reluctantly from the sides of their men-folk, and those who could hardly be held back until their turn came. He studied the faces of the men who by some mysterious dispensation were allowed to go into the boats. Some, as they stepped under the cluster of electric lights, betrayed to him that they knew. Some one in authority had told them, or, like himself, they had found out for themselves.

It was then that he saw Lavis. A woman with a baby in the shawl had, with a sublime gesture, abandoned her baby to a woman already in the boat, so that it might be saved. Lavis was standing behind her when she did it, and as she lost herself in the crowd, Lavis had looked after her with such an expression of pity that Cadogan's attention was attracted anew to him.

When Lavis turned to the circle of light again, his eyes met Cadogan's. "And you, too, know," thought Cadogan. Lavis came over to him.

"I was wishing I could give that poor woman this big coat of mine," began Cadogan; "it might make things a little less miserable for her."

Lavis's eyes thanked him. "I will find her and give it to her." Cadogan took it off. "I will see you again," said Lavis, and, went off with the coat.

Cadogan turned in time to see—and it thrilled him—old Mrs. Weiscopf refusing to go when her turn came. She pointed to the old man. "No, no," was the impatient answer from the officer. "But he iss so old," she pleaded again. She was roughly told to hurry up and get into the boat or stay behind. She marched back to her old husband, and gripped him tightly by the arm. The boat left without her.

Cadogan saw these things, and a hundred others, without ever losing sight of Miss Huttle. On the other side of the ship he knew that a gang of ship's men were fighting for the possession of a boat for themselves. He could hear them— half-smothered murmurs, cries, blows. He thought of going to his room, and getting his automatic pistol, and jumping in among them. But what good would it do? was his next thought. It would be only to substitute one set of dead men for another; and, doing it, he would lose sight of her.

At last she walked over to where the boat was ready to lower. Before she stepped in she cast a long look above the heads of the crowd. The thought that she might be looking for him set Cadogan to trembling. She was pale. He drew farther back into the shadows. He saw her face peering out again from the crowded hats, toques, and hoods of the close-packed women as the boat was lowered.

She appeared to be still searching for some one in the crowd as the boat disappeared below the deck rail. Cadogan forced his way to the rail to watch it. It was rolled from side to side, bumped against the ship's side, swung in and out as it descended. While yet some distance above the water, it stuck. Cadogan could just make it out. The falls had fouled. With a jerk the stern dropped several feet on the run, and the boat hung again in air, now with bow up and stern down. There were screams and shouts. Cadogan was at the rail, ready to leap, when the bow unexpectedly dropped. The boat was level again. It was in the water and floating. She was safe away.

Cadogan remained by the rail, tracing the course of the little boat on the sea. When he could no longer see the shadow of it, nor hear the voices from it, he still stayed, pursuing in his imagination her course and position out there on the waters.

When he faced inboard, all the boats were away, and Meade and Crupp were no longer on deck. He guessed they had gone into the smoking-room.

IV

Many other passengers had returned to the smoking-room by the time Cadogan got there. Meade, Crupp, and Vogel were already seated at the corner table. Cadogan sat down with them.

From the farther corner of the room came a strident voice. "They were all of them foolish to go at all, that's what I say. They will be out there all night, and in the morning we will be laughing at them when they return aboard. See here. Please see here."

The speaker opened and held up an illustrated advertising booklet. No one in the room could fail to see it. "Thirty-eight water-tight compartments. See, there it is. Non-sinkable. Non-sinkable—that's the word. See for yourself, whoever cares. But there's people who fancy they know more about ships than the men who make a trade of building 'em." He stared around the room to see who would gainsay him. Nobody seemed to care to.

Crupp turned around to see who it was. "It's that chap was auctioning off the ship's pool an hour or two ago," explained Vogel. "He never stops."

Major Crupp's questioning eyes roamed from Cadogan to the assertive man at the farther corner and back to Cadogan. "What d'you make of him, Cadogan?"

Cadogan shrugged his shoulders. "It is faith like his that builds empires. And stupidity like his that loses them."

The man with the booklet had not abated the fervor of his reading announcements; but those who were listening were

James B. Connolly

listening without comment. Thus far no one in the room had spoken aloud of danger except the man with the booklet. The effect of his loud insistence was to increase the unvoiced uneasiness.

A steward, with a face into which a white frost seemed to have bitten, burst into the smoking-room, revolved rapidly once in the middle of the room, and vanished through the door by which he came.

Everybody turned toward the door through which he disappeared, and then every head seemed to turn toward every other. The voice of the man with the booklet was lowered. Presently he ceased reading.

One man stood up and went silently out. The door closed behind him. Another stood up. One, two, three men followed him to the door. Several got up together. Another group was on its way when suddenly there was a rush for the door. The man with the booklet, whiskered, fat, and red-necked, stared down at his printed page in amaze. He gulped, blinked, heaved himself up, and lumbered after the others. Only the four gathered around the corner table remained in the smoking-room.

Crupp, with his thumbs hooked into his trousers pockets, was staring down between his knees. On Crupp's left was Vogel, the millionaire of the railroads. He was a tall, slope-shouldered man of fifty-five, bald at the top of his head. His forehead sloped back from speculative eyes. "Hi, wake up there, Major!" he bawled, most unexpectedly. "That steward who came running in that time, you'd think he thought the ship was going down. What d'y' imagine he wanted, Major?"

Crupp raised his head and stared abstractedly at Vogel. "Huh," repeated Vogel, "what was he after, Major?"

"Lord knows"—Crupp suddenly smiled—"perhaps it was a tip."

On the table was a siphon of soda and some empty glasses. Crupp selected one that had not been used, and, carefully gauging, poured about an inch of soda into the glass. "The ship going down, Mr. Vogel? Heroes then we'd have to be"—he glanced at each in turn over the rim of his glass—"whether we liked it or not, wouldn't we? What did you learn that time you went forward, Cadogan?"

Cadogan also helped himself to some soda-water, rolled it around in his mouth, swallowed it, and set down his glass. As if he had not heard Crupp, he drew out his cigar-case and offered it to the soldier.

Crupp nodded his thanks, took a cigar, bit off the end, and, without looking away from Cadogan, lit up. Vogel took one, but as if by way of courtesy only, for he indicated no desire to light it. Meade, waving Cadogan away, lit a cigarette of his own rolling. "Shortening my life smoking cigars," he explained.

The door opened. It was Lavis. With a pause and a bow, as if to ask their permission, he took the corner seat on the transom. Cadogan, waiting until he saw Lavis seated, tendered him the cigar-case. Lavis shook his head.

"If you're afraid it's my last—" suggested Cadogan.

"It's years since I've smoked."

"That saves me, for it *is* my last." With the word Cadogan threw the empty cigar-case on the table.

Meade picked up the case, a gun-metal one, with Cadogan's

monogram in thin, flat silver letters on the side. "You throw that down, Cadogan, as if you wanted to give it away."

"Did it look that way?" Cadogan took it from Meade's extended hand. "I've carried that a good many years." He stood up as he finished speaking, to reach for some matches from the next table. After lighting up he remained standing.

"Clear, settled weather, and a smooth sea." He was gazing reflectively through the weather air-port as he spoke.

"Cadogan"—Meade was speaking—"give us some more of your adventures."

Cadogan drew out his watch, also of gun-metal. "And I've carried that a good many years, too." He spoke as if to himself. He looked at the face. "No, it's too late, Mr. Meade. It's too late to begin now."

"It's never too late. Just think, in your short life you have lived more volumes than I have written. You know more, ten times more, about real life than I do, and I'm sixty. I wonder"—he fanned the smoke from him—"would you mind dying after all you've been through?"

Cadogan was still standing. He set his left foot on the seat of his chair, his left elbow on his knee, and his chin in the heel of his left hand. By extending two long, supple left fingers he could hold his cigar while he blew rings of smoke toward the air-port. He blew them now—once, twice, three times. "I don't know any healthy men who are eager to die, do you?" he said, half smiling, presently.

"Meaning you don't want to go yourself?"

"Just that. And yet, if I had to go, any time now, I don't see where I could have any kick coming. Somewhere, sometime, it had to come. And yet I was wondering, only to-night, queerly enough—" Between the first two fingers and thumb of his right hand he was somersaulting the gun-metal cigar-case against the table-top. *Tap—tap—tap*—one end, then the other—*tap—tap—tap*—it went.

While Cadogan paused Meade was making mental notes of him. How wide and powerful the shoulders loomed, how trim the waist, the grace of the long white fingers, the smooth curves of the strong face, all brown below the eyes and all white above! "What a fight you could put up!" thought Meade. "And what a pity if anything should happen to you before you should have had your chance!"

Cadogan ceased somersaulting the cigar-case. "Wouldn't it be queer, now, I was thinking—here I've drawn lots with Death a hundred times—a few more or less—and then to think of him coming along and grabbing a fellow off the deck of an ocean liner!"

"That *would* be a joke," commented Meade.

"Wouldn't it?" Cadogan carefully knocked his cigar-ashes onto the tray. His eyes and Crupp's met.

With his eyes now focussed on the ash-tray, Cadogan continued: "If I have left anybody worrying, or guessing, I can tell him where there is a collapsible life-boat which will be safe in smooth water."

"There are women still aboard," said Crupp.

"Eh, what's that?" Meade sat straight up.

"Yes"—Cadogan's response was directed to Crupp—"there

are many women aboard. But when that life-boat is launched, there is going to be a grand fight to see who will get on it. A half-dozen armed men could hold it for themselves, but not for anybody else—women or men. What do you say, Major? Would you be for that kind of a fight in the event of her sinking?"

Crupp shook his head firmly. "I'd better shoot myself—or any other army or navy officer—than be saved where a ship-load of women went down."

"What do you say, Mr. Vogel?"

Vogel smiled uneasily. "You gentlemen of the sword and pen, how you do try our nerve at times! But in my circle neither do men honor the craven. With many women still aboard, would I get into a boat and leave the ship? Why, no."

"Do you mean, Cadogan"—all was silence when Meade spoke up—"do you mean there is a possibility that this ship will founder?"

Cadogan nodded—twice—slowly.

"But for God's sake, when?"

"See"—he pointed to the deck at their feet—"the slant. Her bow is settling now."

No one spoke, and only Meade moved, and he to interlock his fingers and, pressing his hands together, to rest them on the edge of the table, and lower, for a moment, his head.

Only Cadogan seemed to remember that Lavis was on the transom seat. During all the time that he was speaking and acting, Cadogan knew that Lavis had never ceased to study him.

Cadogan addressed him directly. "The raft?" asked Cadogan. Lavis shook his head indifferently.

The soldier dropped the butt of his cigar straight down between his knees. Meade laid the ends of his fingers on the edge of the table, and stared at his nails.

Vogel sat a little higher in his chair. "Well, there's one thing. For three generations now our family have pursued a constructive policy. My son is almost of age. I hope he will not forget his responsibilities."

Major Crupp stood up. "Shall we go outside?"

Vogel stood up promptly. Meade got more slowly to his feet. "It doesn't seem real," he said to Cadogan; "so quiet! Do men die so easily?" Without waiting to hear the answer he walked after Crupp and Vogel.

Lavis had not moved from his transom seat. Cadogan walked half-way to the door and returned. "You set me thinking to-night, Mr. Lavis, but I see now that it is you the Eternal Verities should select to go down into the depths."

"No, no! Never immortality for me. I had my chance. I threw it away. I was dedicated to a sacred calling, Mr. Cadogan. I had almost achieved the heights, when I—fell. I sinned not only in body, but in spirit. To sin in body is to scorch the soul; but to sin in spirit is to consume the soul. Mine is but ashes. Yours is still a burning flame. And—but there is somebody at the door, I think, who wishes to speak to you."

It was a man in a steward's uniform. As Cadogan reached the door, the man retreated to the shadows of the deck. Cadogan followed. It was Hames, with a square envelope in his hand. "Miss Huttle, Mr. Cadogan," he whispered, "said I was to give you this. When there was nobody about, she said, sir. I've been trying ever since, sir, to find you alone."

Cadogan stepped to the light of a smoking-room air-port, held the sheet close up to the glass, and read:

It was all a mistake after dinner to-night. I will explain when next we meet—if ever we do meet. But you must see that we do meet. You must. The passengers do not know, even you may not know, but it is true—the ship is going to sink. I am frightened—dreadful thoughts—if you were only near!

You must save yourself. You can, if you will. You can do the impossible. You have done it before in play. Do it to-night for the woman who loves you.

I know you will never go into the boats, but after they are gone, when you can no longer help another, I ask you to save yourself—save yourself not for yourself, but for me.

A woman who loves—remember you said it yourself— hers is the call that no man has the choice of refusing. A woman who loves you and whose love is all for you, will be calling calling, calling, as you read this, from out on the dark sea.

Come, come, come, O Beloved, to me at the last. If you do not come, I shall believe always that you did not care. But I know you will come to me.

HELEN.

Cadogan stared at the sea about him, at the sky above him.

He rubbed his forehead. "'Come, come, oh, come!'" he murmured. He drove his clinched fist against the air-port.

"I'll come! I'll come!"

"Mr. Cadogan?" It was the steward.

"What is it?"

"There's queer talk going about between decks, sir. There will be desp'rate work doing to-night, if what they say is true, sir. I've a family in Southampton, sir, and I always tried to do my duty, sir."

"I never knew a better steward, Hames. Listen."

"'K you, sir. Yes, sir?"

"On the boat deck for'ard, port side—get that right now."

"Port side for'ard, sir. Yes, sir. Believe me, sir, I won't forget such directions as you are pleased to give, sir."

"There's a collapsible life-boat there under a tarpaulin. Somebody is saving that for the finish—for a favored few."

"I believe you, sir."

"Stand by it, and when they launch it jump on."

"But they will have spanners and wrenches, and such weapons, sir."

"They surely will. In the steamer trunk in my room you will find a magazine pistol."

"Yes, sir. 'K you, sir."

"But you must hurt nobody, mind, except those who try to hurt you."

"I'll promise, sir. An' I'll remember also I 'ave a missus an' three kiddies in Southampton, sir."

"And don't forget you have them, either."

"No, sir. 'K you, sir. But I never 'andled a magazine one. Any complications, sir?"

"Not many. You find the trigger, curl your finger around it, put the muzzle to the man's head who means you harm, and, if he persists, pull the trigger. It's very simple."

"Quite so, sir."

"Good luck to you. And don't forget—you keep pressing the trigger as long as you want to keep shooting. And—how old are the kiddies?"

"Five, and three, and the baby, one. A grand little chap, the baby, sir."

"Is he now? Isn't that fine!" Cadogan drew from his hip-pocket the wallet with the packet of bills. "Put this in the bank—for the kiddies and missus."

"It's a hawful kindness to 'em, sir."

"All right. Good luck to you."

"Good luck to you, I s'y, sir." He vanished.

V

From his seat on the transom, Lavis had caught sight of the face of Cadogan as he read the sheet of paper held up to the air-port. His chin came down on his chest, remained there a moment, and then he stood up and slowly went out on deck, by way of the door opposite to that which Cadogan had taken.

The passengers were gathering thickly on the top deck. There was now no restriction, ship's people having ceased their supervision, and many steerage passengers were crowding up to join first and second class on the higher decks.

"In the last death plunge," mused Lavis, "steerage may go first, if so be it pleases them."

He made out a couple standing hand in hand like children. He knew them, the couple from second cabin, and of the faith of the prophets of old.

"For why should I go in der boads, Simon?" the woman was saying. "No, no, mein husband. Fifty yahres together we hafe been now. Together we shell go now also."

"Surely God will welcome thee," murmured Lavis, and touched their clasped hands in passing.

He halted. A young man was staring out on the wide sea. Lavis remembered the bride and groom who had been so rapturously gazing out on the sea together before the collision. This was the groom, and he was speaking to another young man who was treading the deck restlessly, four paces one way, four paces back. "They said there was a lantern in the boat she was put in. I think I see it—a small light."

"Do you?"—the restless one halted—"I don't. How long were you married?"

"Four months."

"Oh-h! We were only ten weeks." With short, quick steps he resumed his striding.

Lavis leaned beside the young man at the rail. "I think I see the light you were looking for—there." He pointed.

"Yes, yes—that's it. See here!" He turned to address the pacing man. "Why, he's gone!" He peered into Lavis's face. "There were ten of us, you see, with our wives, returning from our wedding trips. We were going to have a supper together when we reached New York."

"But you are not afraid?"

"I am. And I wish I could have gone in the boat too. But look there!" He pointed to the hundreds of steerage passengers who were still crowded together three decks below. "What chance did they give those women to-night? what chance do they ever get? And my old mother came over steerage. And she is still alive. And she would stand me up before her and she'd say—I know how she would say it: 'Dannie, boy, do you tell me you came away from a sinking ship, and women and children behind you?'"

"But you are not sorry?"

"God, man, no! But only the night before last my wife all at once came close to me and said: 'Dannie, we're going to have a little baby.' And nothing more for a long time, me holding her. And then she whispers: 'And I hope he'll be a boy, and grow up to be a man like you, Dannie,' she said.

"And God help me! Already I had him grown up and was taking him out to see the Giants play."

"God help us all!" said Lavis; and gripped the other's hand swiftly, and passed on to the lowest open deck, where, by way of the long gangway, he might reach the after end of the ship. Already the deck was taking on a more noticeable forward slant. He saw a man lashing together some chairs. He paused long enough to see that it was Cadogan, but, without discovering himself, he passed on to where an isolated man in dungarees leaned with folded arms across the rail.

It was Andie, with his chin resting on his arms, and his face turned toward the placid sea. Once he lifted his head to gaze up at the sky.

Lavis touched him on the arm. "How did you leave Mr. Linnell, Andie?"

Andie unfolded his arms and faced around. "Eh? Oh! How do you do, sir? He comes to me, Mr. Lavis—an' 'twas somethin' beyond the fear o' death was in his eyes—an' he says: 'Andie, your work's done. 'Twas her death-blow they give her, an' she'll not live much longer now. Go above you now, Andie,' he says, 'and I'll stay here.' 'If you don't mind, I'll stay with you, sir,' I says. 'Don't be foolish, Andie,' he says. 'There's small reputation goes with eight pounds in the month. There's none will be lookin' in the papers to see did you desert your post, but there's many will be sayin' what a grand fool you was you didn't go when you could.'"

"'I know you mean that, sir, for the wharf-rats that ships an' shirks for one voyage, and stays drunk ashore for three more,' I says. 'I've no call to leave this ship while one passenger is aboard of her. An' more, Mister Linnell, many an' many's the watch I've stood under you, an', 'less you forbids it, I'll stand this last watch wi' you. Only, if you won't forbid me, sir, I'll go up on deck at the last, an' have a look at God's own sky before she goes.'"

"And what did he say to that, Andie?"

"He said naught to that, sir, excep' to shake hands wi' me. I was that embarrassed wi' the grup o' the hand he gave, I takes out my pipe an' baccy from the locker where the sea wasn't yet reached to, an' I cuts myself a pipeful an' lights up. An' he says, smilin'-like: 'Andie, is it the same old Buccaneer brand you're smokin'?' An' I says: 'The same, sir.' 'Well,' says he, 'I've always maintained it was the most outrageousest-smellin' baccy ever was brought into an engine-room. An' I won't change my opinion now, but if you will spare me a pipeful I'll risk my health to ha' a smoke wi' you now, Andie.'"

"An' while we was smokin', sir, man to man like he says: 'Andie, did ever you get it into your head you'd like to be marryin'?' And I answers, 'I did, sir,' an' I told him o' the Brighton lass I'd once courted, unobtrusive-like, between voyages, goin' on two year, and I would 'a' been most pleased to marry her, till of an evenin' we was sittin' out by the end o' the long pier, wi' the little waves from the Channel cooing among the pilin's where the long skelps o' sea-grass was clingin' to 'em under the planks at our feet. She was a doctor's wife's maid. An' I axed her, an' she says: 'The marster, an' my missus, too, says when ye're gettin' your twelve pound in the month, Andie, I'm to marry you.'"

"'Wherever will I be findin' twelve pound in the month?' I says. 'Your danged old doctor himsel' is collectin' but little more nor that of his bills in the month, him wi' his red herrin' an' oatmeal porridge for breakfast every mornin' of his life!' I says. She'd told me herself o' the red herrin'. An' I left her clickin' her fancy high heels together under her penny chair, an' I'd paid tuppence each for the two of us at the gate comin' in. 'But you wasn't ever thinkin' o' gettin' marrit yourself, Mr. Linnell?' I says.

"'Maybe you noticed a large photograph, Andie, above my desk whenever you come to my room?' he asks. I said as how I did. 'And you had no suspicions?' he says. 'Well, sir,' I says, 'I did make suspicion it wasn't altogether by way of exercisin' o' your muscles you dusted the gold frame of it so frequent.'"

"'I was only waitin',' he says, 'till I'd made a bit more reputation, and only to-night it was, me makin' my rounds, that I was thinkin' at last I had made it.' And he stop there, an' lets his pipe go out the while he looks down at his beautiful engines, an' then he has the loan of another match of me, an' he says: 'Andie, but it does seem hard that your life an' mine must be smashed through the misbehavior of others.' An' I thought myself it was, without meanin' to cast blame, sir, on others."

"An' we finished our pipeful together, an' he stands up an' says, 'Good luck to you, Andie, lad,' and I knew he was wishful to be alone. An' so, 'Good luck to you, Mister Linnell,' I says, an' we gave each other another long grup o' the hand. I was wantin' to tell him he was the best chief ever I worked under, but he wasn't ever the kind, you see, sir, to be praisin' to his face. An' at the top of the ladder I looks down, an' there he was wi' his arms folded across the shiny brass railin', an' he lookin' down, aweary-like, at his engines."

Lavis took Andie's hand. "A good man, Andie. And a good man yourself, Andie. Good-by, and God bless you!"

"Thank you, sir. Good-by, sir. And the same to you." Andie turned to the rail and with folded arms set his face to the impassive sea.

Lavis passed on to where from a tarpaulined hatch a Catholic priest was saying a litany, while around him a body of kneeling men and women were responding. He had donned his cassock, and a shining silver crucifix was on his breast, and his biretta at his feet. His voice was even and unhurried, his features composed.

"Lamb of God, Who takest away the sins of the world—"

"*Spare us, O Lord!*" came the response.

"Lamb of God, Who takest away the sins of the world—"

"*Graciously hear us, O Lord!*"

"Lamb of God, Who takest away the sins of the world—"

"*Have mercy on us!*"

"Pray for us, O Holy Mother of God—"

"*That we may be made worthy of the promises of Christ!*"

The priest rose from his knees. "And bear in mind, my children, that no matter what sin you may have committed, God will forgive you. No one born into this world of sin but has sinned at some time, so do not despair. Offer up your prayers, your heart, to God. He will hear you. He could save us, any one of us, or every one of us even now, if he so willed. If he does not, it is because it is better so. But merely to be saved in the body—what is that? A passing moment here, but the next world—for eternity. It is your soul, not your body, which is to live in eternity. Prepare your soul for that. And now our time is growing short, compose your minds and your hearts, and all kneel and say with me an act of contrition: O my God—"

"*O my God*—" came from them like a chanted hymn.

"I am most heartily sorry for all my sins—"

"*I am most heartily sorry for all my sins*—"

Lavis knelt and prayed also. When he rose from his knees it was to go to the side of the Polish woman, who was also kneeling at the edge of the crowd. He found her weeping.

"Why do you weep? Do you fear death so very much?"

"I weep for my baby."

"But your baby is safe—out there in the boat. They will bring him to his father, who will be there waiting on the dock in New York."

"Yes, yes; but who will be there to give him the breast when he wakes?"

"Who will give—Father in heaven! Come—come with me." Lavis helped her to her feet.

VI

Cadogan looked into the smoking-room. Lavis was gone. He hesitated, wheeled quickly, returned to the deck, sought the nearest gangway, and rapidly descended four decks. He traversed one passageway, another, and entered what looked like a carpenter's shop, where, he knew, was a thick-topped wooden table with its legs held by small angle-irons to the wooden planking over the steel-deck floor.

Cadogan crawled under the table, hunched his shoulders, straightened his legs, and had the table up by the roots. He stepped out from under it, grasped it across the beam, raised it high, brought two of the legs down against the deck, once, twice; reversed the ends and brought the other two legs down to the deck, once, twice. The legs were gone.

He set the table top on his head. A man stood in the doorway. Cadogan motioned him out of the way. "Where yuh goin' with that?" snarled the man. Cadogan set the end of his plank against the man's chest, walked straight ahead, and stepped over the man's body. In the passageway some one seized his table from behind. Cadogan let go entirely, wheeled sharply, caught the man by the collar and trousers, smashed him against the bulkhead, and, as the other dropped his hold of the table top, threw him a dozen feet down the passage. The man, rising to his feet, ran the other way. Cadogan picked up his plank and resumed his way.

At a place where a boat-falls dropped past the ship's rail Cadogan laid down his burden. This was on the lowest open deck, where not many people would be coming to bother him; but, to reduce the chance of loss, he set his table top up on edge in the shadow of the rail, while he went off for an armful of steamer chairs.

He needed lashings for his chairs. A transverse passageway opened on to the deck near by. Staterooms opened off either side of the passage. The door of the nearest room was locked. "Bright people," he muttered, "who didn't intend anybody should steal anything while they were gone!" He set one foot under the door-knob, rested his back against the bulkhead across the narrow aisle, and straightened his leg. The lock gave way; the door swung open. "When they return I hope you won't miss the fine bed sheets," he murmured, and swished them—one, two—from the berths, with the blankets and one pillow. He slit the hemmed edges of the sheets and tore them into strips lengthwise. With these strips he lashed his chairs compactly together. The chairs in turn he lashed to the heavy plank.

Cadogan had taken off dinner coat, waistcoat, collar, tie, and linen shirt to work more freely. Now he looked about for the coat. All the while he had been working he was not unaware that forms of men had flitted by him, and that more than one had stopped as if curious to know what he was at. He knew that more than one of these were now prowling within leaping distance and that from them were coming muffled words of comment. Also he was not unaware that the ship was nearing her end. He could detect the first pitching of her hull, the settling of the deck under his feet, even as he could hear the half-tones of the menacing voices from out of the shadows. He was aware, too, that a despairing multitude were massing on the decks above him.

Up there, he knew, they were preparing to meet the end in a hundred different fashions. Up there would be those who smiled and those who cried, those who joked or moaned, who prayed or blasphemed, those who were going with pity in their hearts and consumed with bitterness others; forgiving whoever it was that had brought it on, or wishing, the others, that they had the negligent ones to coldly and calmly wring their necks before they went themselves.

Cadogan, having found his coat, laid it on a bitt near by while he should launch his little raft. He balanced it on the rail, inserted a hook under one of his lashings at each end, folded his blankets on top, and, a boat-falls in each hand, paid out carefully, slowly. He could not have lowered a human body more tenderly. Easily, gently, he felt it settle on the bosom of the sea. He took a turn of his falls around the bitt, and, always with one eye peeping sidewise into the shadows, reached for his coat. In the pocket of that coat was the photograph of his beloved.

"You've everything fixed nicely, have you, matie?"

Cadogan had had his eye out for him, and was expecting some such salutation; and the revolver within two feet of his head was also not unexpected. A man could not attend to everything at once.

"Everything nice, yes," responded Cadogan, now with his coat in his hand.

"I'm glad o' that, matie, because, you see, I'm needing it."

"Would you take that from a man after all the work he put in on it?" He was kneading the coat into a ball in his right hand. With his left hand he was taking in a hole or two in his belt.

"You *are* a soft un! And a swell toff, too. You'll 'ave to st'y aboard, matie. I'm needing that tidy little floatin' thing you've moored below, and I'm plannin' to take it."

"Well, why don't you take it?"

"No larkin'. I'm fightin' for my life."

"I've been fighting for more than my life, or yours, and—"

His right arm had been hanging loosely down by his side. He snapped his right wrist against his hip. The coat, in a tight ball, was jolted into the man's face, just as Cadogan's left arm shot up and caught the man's pistol wrist. His open right hand followed the coat and gripped the man's throat. He had no mind for a scuffle which would attract attention, nor did he wish the man when he dropped overboard to fall too near his raft; so, with his finger to the man's windpipe, he bore him along the passageway toward the stern of the ship. The tide was setting that way. The man was kicking out with both legs, striking out with his free hand. Cadogan held the man's arm over the rail the while he twisted the pistol wrist. The revolver dropped overboard. Cadogan took a fresh hold of him, spun around with him, and let him fly. He went where the revolver went.

Cadogan, arrived back at his raft, found a man standing by the falls and calling down to somebody below: "How is it now?"

There was no answer. The man by the falls repeated his question. Only silence from below.

Cadogan was looking for his coat, when the man grasped the falls and swiftly lowered himself over the side. Cadogan let be his coat and slid down the falls after him. His feet fetched up against the man's fingers. He pressed with all his weight. The man cursed softly, let go his hold, and fell into the sea. Cadogan dropped after him. When the man came up Cadogan gripped him by the throat and held him under water.

The dim outline of another fellow was standing erect on the end of the little raft. "Norrie, me lad," he was saying in a cold voice, "it's a tidy little floater with nice warm blankets, but it will never hold up two." Cadogan could see a long spanner, or bar, held ready on the shoulder of the man on the raft. The man in the water was now twining his legs about him, whereupon, still clinging to his man, Cadogan dived, porpoise-like, head down into the sea. When he felt his feet under he kicked once, twice, three times powerfully. Deep down he went.

He came up alone.

He clung to one of the hooks of the falls to get his breath. A cap floated up to him. Smiling grimly, he set it on his head. The man on the end of the raft poised himself above him and aimed the long spanner at the cap. Cadogan diverted the blow with his free forearm, and before the other could recover wrenched the spanner from him and dropped it into the sea.

"Oh, ho! that's how it is, is it, Norrie, me lad?" He swung one foot viciously at Cadogan's hand where it was gripped around the hook. Cadogan swooped again with his free hand, caught the man by the swinging ankle, and hauled him off the raft. He released his grip of the man's ankle, only to shift it to his throat. The man seized Cadogan's free wrist with both hands. Cadogan, hanging to the hook with one hand and gripping the man's throat with the other, continued to squeeze the man's throat. The man's legs kicked convulsively. Cadogan continued to squeeze. When the legs stopped kicking, Cadogan forced the head under water and eased up on his grip. Bubbles rose up and burst on the surface. Cadogan placed his ear close to the water to hear. When he could no longer hear the bubbles he loosed his grip.

With hands to the falls and feet against the ship's side, Cadogan climbed to the deck where he had left his coat. He found it kicked to one side and trampled upon. But the little photograph was still there—in the inside pocket.

He took off his cap, the cap of the drowned man, while he kissed the little photograph. "Coming, coming, oh, coming!" he murmured.

"Have you room for a passenger?" came in a man's voice from the dark.

Cadogan whirled. "Passenger? Passenger! I've fought and schemed and—Oh!"

It was Lavis, and, clinging to his hand, was somebody in a man's long ulster.

"It's the woman—you remember her?—who passed her baby boy into the boat so that he would be saved."

Cadogan said nothing.

"A few minutes ago I found her. She was weeping for her baby. I asked her why she should be weeping now that her baby was safe, and she answered me: 'But who will be there to give him the breast when he wakes?'"

Cadogan rested his left hand, with the fingers clinched around the cap, on the ship's rail.

"If Christ on earth were to be with us once more," went on Lavis softly, "would he not say again: 'Greater love hath no man than this'? 'Who will be there to give him the breast when he wakes?'—and she about to die. Have you room for her as a passenger on your raft?"

"It will bear only one."

Lavis waited.

Cadogan unloosed the fingers of the hand on the rail. The cap dropped into the sea.

"She shall be the one," he said presently.

In the rosy flush of a beautiful dawn a lone woman on a tiny raft drifted down to her crying baby and gave him suck.

ABOUT THE AUTHOR

 **James Brendan Bennet Connolly** (October 28, 1868 – January 20, 1957) was an American athlete and author. In 1896, he became the first modern Olympic champion.

Connolly was born to poor Irish American parents, fisherman John Connolly and Ann O'Donnell, as one of twelve children, in South Boston, Massachusetts. Growing up at a time when the parks and playground movement in Boston was slowly developing, Connolly joined other boys in the streets and vacant lots to run, jump, and play ball.

He was educated at Notre Dame Academy and then at the Mather and Lawrence grammar school, but never went to high school. Instead, Connolly worked as a clerk with an insurance company in Boston and later with the United States Army Corps of Engineers in Savannah, Georgia.

Connolly became an authority on maritime writing, after spending years on many different vessels, fishing boats, military ships all over the world. In all, he published more than 200 short stories, and 25 novels. Furthermore, he twice ran for Congress of the United States on the ticket of the Progressive Party, but never was elected.

He never returned to Harvard, but received an honorary athletic sweater in 1948.

Choose from Thousands of 1stWorldLibrary Classics By

A. M. Barnard
Ada Leverson
Adolphus William Ward
Aesop
Agatha Christie
Alexander Aaronsohn
Alexander Kielland
Alexandre Dumas
Alfred Gatty
Alfred Ollivant
Alice Duer Miller
Alice Turner Curtis
Alice Dunbar
Allen Chapman
Alleyne Ireland
Ambrose Bierce
Amelia E. Barr
Amory H. Bradford
Andrew Lang
Andrew McFarland Davis
Andy Adams
Angela Brazil
Anna Alice Chapin
Anna Sewell
Annie Besant
Annie Hamilton Donnell
Annie Payson Call
Annie Roe Carr
Annonaymous
Anton Chekhov
Archibald Lee Fletcher
Arnold Bennett
Arthur C. Benson
Arthur Conan Doyle
Arthur M. Winfield
Arthur Ransome
Arthur Schnitzler
Arthur Train
Atticus
B.H. Baden-Powell
B. M. Bower
B. C. Chatterjee
Baroness Emmuska Orczy
Baroness Orczy
Basil King
Bayard Taylor
Ben Macomber
Bertha Muzzy Bower
Bjornstjerne Bjornson

Booth Tarkington
Boyd Cable
Bram Stoker
C. Collodi
C. E. Orr
C. M. Ingleby
Carolyn Wells
Catherine Parr Traill
Charles A. Eastman
Charles Amory Beach
Charles Dickens
Charles Dudley Warner
Charles Farrar Browne
Charles Ives
Charles Kingsley
Charles Klein
Charles Hanson Towne
Charles Lathrop Pack
Charles Romyn Dake
Charles Whibley
Charles Willing Beale
Charlotte M. Braeme
Charlotte M. Yonge
Charlotte Perkins Stetson
Clair W. Hayes
Clarence Day Jr.
Clarence E. Mulford
Clemence Housman
Confucius
Coningsby Dawson
Cornelis DeWitt Wilcox
Cyril Burleigh
D. H. Lawrence
Daniel Defoe
David Garnett
Dinah Craik
Don Carlos Janes
Donald Keyhoe
Dorothy Kilner
Dougan Clark
Douglas Fairbanks
E. Nesbit
E. P. Roe
E. Phillips Oppenheim
E. S. Brooks
Earl Barnes
Edgar Rice Burroughs
Edith Van Dyne
Edith Wharton

Edward Everett Hale
Edward J. O'Biren
Edward S. Ellis
Edwin L. Arnold
Eleanor Atkins
Eleanor Hallowell Abbott
Eliot Gregory
Elizabeth Gaskell
Elizabeth McCracken
Elizabeth Von Arnim
Ellem Key
Emerson Hough
Emilie F. Carlen
Emily Bronte
Emily Dickinson
Enid Bagnold
Enilor Macartney Lane
Erasmus W. Jones
Ernie Howard Pie
Ethel May Dell
Ethel Turner
Ethel Watts Mumford
Eugene Sue
Eugenie Foa
Eugene Wood
Eustace Hale Ball
Evelyn Everett-green
Everard Cotes
F. H. Cheley
F. J. Cross
F. Marion Crawford
Fannie E. Newberry
Federick Austin Ogg
Ferdinand Ossendowski
Fergus Hume
Florence A. Kilpatrick
Fremont B. Deering
Francis Bacon
Francis Darwin
Frances Hodgson Burnett
Frances Parkinson Keyes
Frank Gee Patchin
Frank Harris
Frank Jewett Mather
Frank L. Packard
Frank V. Webster
Frederic Stewart Isham
Frederick Trevor Hill
Frederick Winslow Taylor

Friedrich Kerst	Hayden Carruth	James Branch Cabell
Friedrich Nietzsche	Helent Hunt Jackson	James DeMille
Fyodor Dostoyevsky	Helen Nicolay	James Joyce
G.A. Henty	Hendrik Conscience	James Lane Allen
G.K. Chesterton	Hendy David Thoreau	James Lane Allen
Gabrielle E. Jackson	Henri Barbusse	James Oliver Curwood
Garrett P. Serviss	Henrik Ibsen	James Oppenheim
Gaston Leroux	Henry Adams	James Otis
George A. Warren	Henry Ford	James R. Driscoll
George Ade	Henry Frost	Jane Abbott
Geroge Bernard Shaw	Henry James	Jane Austen
George Cary Eggleston	Henry Jones Ford	Jane L. Stewart
George Durston	Henry Seton Merriman	Janet Aldridge
George Ebers	Henry W Longfellow	Jens Peter Jacobsen
George Eliot	Herbert A. Giles	Jerome K. Jerome
George Gissing	Herbert Carter	Jessie Graham Flower
George MacDonald	Herbert N. Casson	John Buchan
George Meredith	Herman Hesse	John Burroughs
George Orwell	Hildegard G. Frey	John Cournos
George Sylvester Viereck	Homer	John F. Kennedy
George Tucker	Honore De Balzac	John Gay
George W. Cable	Horace B. Day	John Glasworthy
George Wharton James	Horace Walpole	John Habberton
Gertrude Atherton	Horatio Alger Jr.	John Joy Bell
Gordon Casserly	Howard Pyle	John Kendrick Bangs
Grace E. King	Howard R. Garis	John Milton
Grace Gallatin	Hugh Lofting	John Philip Sousa
Grace Greenwood	Hugh Walpole	John Taintor Foote
Grant Allen	Humphry Ward	Jonas Lauritz Idemil Lie
Guillermo A. Sherwell	Ian Maclaren	Jonathan Swift
Gulielma Zollinger	Inez Haynes Gillmore	Joseph A. Altsheler
Gustav Flaubert	Irving Bacheller	Joseph Carey
H. A. Cody	Isabel Cecilia Williams	Joseph Conrad
H. B. Irving	Isabel Hornibrook	Joseph E. Badger Jr
H. C. Bailey	Israel Abrahams	Joseph Hergesheimer
H. G. Wells	Ivan Turgenev	Joseph Jacobs
H. H. Munro	J. G.Austin	Jules Vernes
H. Irving Hancock	J. Henri Fabre	Julian Hawthrone
H. R. Naylor	J. M. Barrie	Julie A Lippmann
H. Rider Haggard	J. M. Walsh	Justin Huntly McCarthy
H. W. C. Davis	J. Macdonald Oxley	Kakuzo Okakura
Haldeman Julius	J. R. Miller	Karle Wilson Baker
Hall Caine	J. S. Fletcher	Kate Chopin
Hamilton Wright Mabie	J. S. Knowles	Kenneth Grahame
Hans Christian Andersen	J. Storer Clouston	Kenneth McGaffey
Harold Avery	J. W. Duffield	Kate Langley Bosher
Harold McGrath	Jack London	Kate Langley Bosher
Harriet Beecher Stowe	Jacob Abbott	Katherine Cecil Thurston
Harry Castlemon	James Allen	Katherine Stokes
Harry Coghill	James Andrews	L. A. Abbot
Harry Houidini	James Baldwin	L. T. Meade

L. Frank Baum
Latta Griswold
Laura Dent Crane
Laura Lee Hope
Laurence Housman
Lawrence Beasley
Leo Tolstoy
Leonid Andreyev
Lewis Carroll
Lewis Sperry Chafer
Lilian Bell
Lloyd Osbourne
Louis Hughes
Louis Joseph Vance
Louis Tracy
Louisa May Alcott
Lucy Fitch Perkins
Lucy Maud Montgomery
Luther Benson
Lydia Miller Middleton
Lyndon Orr
M. Corvus
M. H. Adams
Margaret E. Sangster
Margret Howth
Margaret Vandercook
Margaret W. Hungerford
Margret Penrose
Maria Edgeworth
Maria Thompson Daviess
Mariano Azuela
Marion Polk Angellotti
Mark Overton
Mark Twain
Mary Austin
Mary Catherine Crowley
Mary Cole
Mary Hastings Bradley
Mary Roberts Rinehart
Mary Rowlandson
M. Wollstonecraft Shelley
Maud Lindsay
Max Beerbohm
Myra Kelly
Nathaniel Hawthrone
Nicolo Machiavelli
O. F. Walton
Oscar Wilde
Owen Johnson
P.G. Wodehouse
Paul and Mabel Thorne

Paul G. Tomlinson
Paul Severing
Percy Brebner
Percy Keese Fitzhugh
Peter B. Kyne
Plato
Quincy Allen
R. Derby Holmes
R. L. Stevenson
R. S. Ball
Rabindranath Tagore
Rahul Alvares
Ralph Bonehill
Ralph Henry Barbour
Ralph Victor
Ralph Waldo Emmerson
Rene Descartes
Ray Cummings
Rex Beach
Rex E. Beach
Richard Harding Davis
Richard Jefferies
Richard Le Gallienne
Robert Barr
Robert Frost
Robert Gordon Anderson
Robert L. Drake
Robert Lansing
Robert Lynd
Robert Michael Ballantyne
Robert W. Chambers
Rosa Nouchette Carey
Rudyard Kipling
Saint Augustine
Samuel B. Allison
Samuel Hopkins Adams
Sarah Bernhardt
Sarah C. Hallowell
Selma Lagerlof
Sherwood Anderson
Sigmund Freud
Standish O'Grady
Stanley Weyman
Stella Benson
Stella M. Francis
Stephen Crane
Stewart Edward White
Stijn Streuvels
Swami Abhedananda
Swami Parmananda
T. S. Ackland

T. S. Arthur
The Princess Der Ling
Thomas A. Janvier
Thomas A Kempis
Thomas Anderton
Thomas Bailey Aldrich
Thomas Bulfinch
Thomas De Quincey
Thomas Dixon
Thomas H. Huxley
Thomas Hardy
Thomas More
Thornton W. Burgess
U. S. Grant
Upton Sinclair
Valentine Williams
Various Authors
Vaughan Kester
Victor Appleton
Victor G. Durham
Victoria Cross
Virginia Woolf
Wadsworth Camp
Walter Camp
Walter Scott
Washington Irving
Wilbur Lawton
Wilkie Collins
Willa Cather
Willard F. Baker
William Dean Howells
William le Queux
W. Makepeace Thackeray
William W. Walter
William Shakespeare
Winston Churchill
Yei Theodora Ozaki
Yogi Ramacharaka
Young E. Allison
Zane Grey